LOCAL GOVERNMENT

By

P. W. JACKSON, M.A.

Senior Lecturer in Government
Swansea College of Technology

THIRD EDITION

LONDON
BUTTERWORTHS
1976

ENGLAND: BUTTERWORTH & CO. (PUBLISHERS) LTD.
                LONDON: 88 KINGSWAY, WC2B 6AB

AUSTRALIA: BUTTERWORTHS PTY. LTD.
                SYDNEY: 586 PACIFIC HIGHWAY, CHATSWOOD, NSW
                2067
                Also at MELBOURNE, BRISBANE, ADELAIDE and PERTH

CANADA: BUTTERWORTH & CO. (CANADA) LTD.
                TORONTO: 2265 MIDLAND AVENUE, SCARBOROUGH
                M1P 4S1

NEW ZEALAND: BUTTERWORTHS OF NEW ZEALAND LTD.
                WELLINGTON: 26/28 WARING TAYLOR STREET, 1

SOUTH AFRICA: BUTTERWORTH & CO. (SOUTH AFRICA) (PTY.)
                LTD.
                DURBAN: 152/154 GALE STREET

©

Butterworth & Co. (Publishers) Ltd.

1976

ISBN—Casebound: 0 406 60453 3
Limp: 0 406 60454 1

D86.44/6/2

To Audrey and Caroline

Preface to the Third Edition

Since the second edition was published in April 1970 there have been such substantial changes in the local government system that a comprehensive revision of the text became imperative. This edition examines the many developments in the intervening years and particularly the provisions of the Local Government Act 1972 which came into effect on 1 April 1974.

The Act replaced the nineteenth century structure of local government in England and Wales with two independent operational units in the counties and districts, and a third tier of parishes in England and communities in Wales. The Act also amended the law relating to local authorities in a number of respects, and the text describes the modification of the representative element with the abolition of the office of alderman, the extension of the councillors' term of office and the introduction of allowances for members. The former requirement to make statutory appointments of officers was also modified by the Act's provision for the appointment of "proper officers", whose role was meanwhile considerably influenced by developments in internal administration, in corporate management and by the introduction of functional specialisms. All these features and their significance are examined in this edition.

In addition, the services provided by the former authorities were reallocated by the Act to the new authorities, and the sections dealing with functions have been expanded to include the major developments, such as the reorganisation of the health and water services, and all the main legislative provisions since 1970. Finally, the consultative document on devolution is examined in detail and the White Paper, which appeared while this book was in the stage of proof correction, is summarised as an appendix.

P. W. JACKSON.

February 1976

Contents

CHAPTER 1

The History of Local Government

1. Pre-Industrial Origins

The present structure of local government in England and Wales is the product of the Local Government Act 1972, but its antecedent institutions originated in Saxon days. Self-governing municipalities existed even earlier in Roman Britain, but it was not until the second half of the fifth century, when the Anglo-Saxons infiltrated into east Britain and penetrated westwards along the river valleys, that we may discern the early beginnings of our local government structure.

The major territorial division, the *scir* or shire, developed from the ethnic settlements of Saxons in the middle, east, west and south parts of the country, and of the north and south folk in East Anglia, areas which later became Middlesex, Essex, Wessex, Sussex, Norfolk and Suffolk. Surrey appears to have been the "south region" of a larger territorial area, possibly of Middlesex, while Berkshire, Hampshire, Wiltshire, Somerset and Dorset apparently represented primitive subdivisions of Wessex, which had absorbed the Celtic Devonshire and much of Cornwall by the ninth century.

By the Danish invasion of 865–878 England was divided into several independent kingdoms which were not to be united under one king until the Danelaw was reconquered by the kings of Wessex in the tenth century. By that time, however, the shire system had developed in the midlands (Mercia) from the areas of the Danish boroughs, and certainly by the eleventh century all England with the exception of Northumbria was divided into shires.

"The affairs of the kingdom", remarked King Alfred (871–901), were "various and manifold",[1] and he entrusted responsibility for routine administration in each shire to an official called the *ealdorman* who, in addition, commanded the army within his district and presided at its judicial assembly. Later in the tenth century he came to exercise control over more than one shire, and when this occurred there emerged an official known as the *shire-reeve* or sheriff who presided

---

[1] D. Whitelock, *The Beginnings of English Society*, Pelican, 1952, pp. 72–80.

over the biennial shire moot as the king's representative when the ealdorman was absent.

The shire moot was an assembly of the shire's freemen for administrative, judicial and financial purposes, and much later came to play an important part in the electoral procedure for sending county members to Parliament. After the Norman Conquest, Henry I and Henry II curtailed the growing baronial threat to monopolise the office of sheriff by appointing lesser men who were supervised by itinerant justices. Nevertheless, the sheriff continued to act as the king's agent in the shire throughout the Norman period.

Shires were themselves further subdivided for fiscal, judicial and administrative purposes into *hundreds*. Their existence is first recorded about 950 and they continued until the nineteenth century. They possessed different names in different parts of the country: in Yorkshire, Lincolnshire, Nottinghamshire, Derbyshire, Rutland and Leicestershire they were known by the Danish word *wapentake* (a flourishing of weapons); in Northumberland, Durham and Cumberland they were called *wards*; and in Cornwall some were called shires. In some parts of the country another division existed between the shire and the hundred, known as the *trithing* or *riding* in Yorkshire, the *lathe* in Kent and the *rape* in Sussex.

There were approximately 700 hundreds of varying size, originating, according to one theory, from the area occupied by a hundred families, each family being supported by a *hide* of land. The royal agent in the hundred was the *reeve*, later a bailiff, and effectual control was maintained centrally by the Exchequer and locally by the sheriff. The hundred's main importance during the Middle Ages derived from its regularly held court, where customary law was administered, and as a unit for the collection of customary dues.

"The local and national affairs in early England were not relegated to a favoured few, but were settled in the councils by the people in their several 'moots', or meetings".[2] At the shire moot, each hundred would be represented by its reeve, four "best men" and the priest; at the hundred moot each village was represented; and at the lowest level, the *tun-scipe* (a hedge encircling the homesteads), or township, there was the town moot or folkmoot where every freeman participated in settling local matters. Where a township was fortified, it was named a *burh*, later a borough.

William the Conqueror removed many local powers to central government; the folkmoot was replaced by the *vill* or village, and the shiremoot by the manor court, controlled by the lord's bailiff. When

---

[2] J. J. Clarke, *A History of Local Government*, H. Jenkins, 1955, p. 6.

there was more than one bailiff, the superior bailiff became known as the "major" bailiff or major (mayor) who presided in towns over the meetings of burgesses. Ancient boroughs were often brought under the control of the manor, becoming manorial boroughs. Problems between landlord and tenants were settled at the manorial court which had two main forms—the *court baron* for agricultural problems, transfer of holdings, rights to service, and the *court leet*, dealing originally with criminal offences. Each court appointed officers for one year's compulsory service as haywards, hedge surveyors, pinders, ale-tasters, etc. Some boroughs secured independence of their lord by purchasing from him or the king charters which confirmed earlier privileges or granted various liberties, and many boroughs gained complete self-government in this way. The most important were the municipal corporations which represented the craftsmen of the guilds, the traders and the merchants.

The one institution which remained relatively unaffected by the Normans was the parish. It had developed from obscure origins as a district assigned to a bishop or priest, and in addition to its religious purpose came to possess social and deliberative functions. At its vestry meeting the parishioners discussed matters of common concern, and each year elected from among their number officers to manage parish affairs. The main offices were those of: (a) the *churchwarden*, the custodian of the parish and trustee of its common property; (b) the *constable*, responsible for supervising beggars and the poor; (c) the *surveyor of highways*, responsible for road maintenance; and (d) the *overseer of the poor*, who administered poor relief. Their duties were exacting and unpaid, and each parishioner was obligated to serve for one year when elected.

In Wales indigenous governmental divisions had developed in pre-Norman days. Each kingdom, or *gwlad*, was divided for administrative convenience into *cantrefi*, and each *cantref* comprised about a hundred townships or hamlets. For fiscal and judicial purposes each *cantref* was divided into two or more *cymydau* or commotes. After the Norman Conquest the border lords and marcher families moved into Wales, and their castles and subordinate fortresses became administrative centres for their localities. The lowland "Englishry" and the upland "Welshry" co-existed, with the latter retaining their customs and laws while recognising the overlordship of their alien masters. Where the land was cultivable, the manorial system was established on the feudal pattern of customary services, with agricultural and other matters being decided by bond tenants at the *halmote* or manorial court. Towns grew slowly and charters were bought, but the shire division did not appear until 1284 when the

Statute of Rhyddlan divided Wales into (a) the Principality, comprising the shires of Anglesey, Caernarvon, Merioneth, Cardigan and Carmarthen; (b) the shire of Flint; and (c) the Marcher Lordships, which continued to be ruled by English lords and loyal Welsh chiefs, each with their own courts, officials and laws. The shires were Crown lands and as such formed no part of the realm.

Not until the Act of Union of 1536 were the Marcher Lordships, whose disunity and legal licence had long troubled the monarchy, reorganised into Denbighshire, Montgomeryshire, Radnorshire, Breconshire, Glamorganshire, Monmouthshire and Pembrokeshire. From 1536 onwards the pattern of local government in Wales duplicated that of England.

The Justice of the Peace

The creation of the office of Justice of the Peace marks a new and important stage in the development of local government. Although the title *custos pacis* appears in 1264 to describe men appointed by the king to maintain law and order in each county, it was in 1361 that the office of Justice of the Peace is so named in Edward II's enactment that:

> "In every county of England there shall be assigned for the keeping of the peace one Lord and with him three or four of the most worthy of the counties, together with some learned in the law, and they shall have power to take all of them that be not of good Fame . . ."

They were generally members of the landed gentry entrusted with the preservation of the peace, the punishment of offenders and the control of the parish constables. By 1388 they were assembling on the quarters days at Quarter Sessions to exercise criminal jurisdiction and to deal with administrative matters appertaining to the county.

By Tudor days they had become the governors of the counties, the administrative maids of all work, and, in Maitland's phrase, "judicial beasts of burden". Being local gentry they had an intimate knowledge of their locality, and their status within rural society ensured obedience to their will. As they were unpaid and generally efficient, they were ideal functionaries as far as the Tudors were concerned, and their duties increased as need arose until they had become the main agents of royal power within the counties. They discharged the Elizabethan political and ecclesiastical policy, administered petty justice, and saw to it that all local government functions relating to roads, bridges, the maintenance of law and order were carried out, including the enforcement of the Poor Law, the Statute of Artificers and the regulation of wages and prices.

Thus, under the strict supervision of the Privy Council, the J.Ps. became the central figures in rural England in all judicial, political, economic and administrative matters, and frequently became the member of Parliament for their counties. As the population increased so did their duties, and after the weakening of the Privy Council's control in 1688, their powers grew to dominate almost every branch of social life, civil administration and judicial affairs in the counties. As Lord Coke observed: "The whole Christian world hath not the like office, if duly executed".

The system of local administration described above continued into the nineteenth century. The growth of population, the enclosure movement, the development of industries, and the growing concentrations of population threw burdens upon a local government system which was designed for the easier pace of rural life. The manorial court, the parish vestries, and voluntary service were no longer sufficient to meet the new challenges, nor were the closed oligarchies in towns prepared to relinquish their venal powers. In certain areas local acts had created such *ad hoc* bodies as Improvement Commissioners for paving, cleaning and lighting streets, Guardians of the Poor for poor-relief and Turnpike Trusts for road improvement, but their efforts were piecemeal and un-coordinated.

2. The Nineteenth Century

During the transition years from the eighteenth to the nineteenth centuries, society was consequently in flux, and the increasingly pressing problems of poverty and of community living demanded urgent attention. Leading the reform movement was Jeremy Bentham, the founder of the utilitarian school, who breathed a new life into English law reform and subjected every aspect of institutional life in Church and State to the blunt challenge of its usefulness. His incisive analysis of the utility of governmental institutions shaped not only a new philosophy, based upon the criterion of utility and the principle of the greatest happiness of the greatest number, but helped to create a new society unencumbered by the irrationalities of the past. He advocated a universal franchise, "the ascendancy of the democracy", the vesting of control over administration and expenditure to community representatives, and secret ballots by householders grouped in electoral divisions to elect an annual Parliament which was to be free from monarchic and aristocratic influence.

In local matters, he gave his attention to the main evil of the day, pauperism. His criticism of Pitt's Poor Law Bill of 1796 contributed greatly to its abandonment and he formulated the principle that the able-bodied poor should be offered no alternative to the workhouse. His influence permeated the Poor Law Amendment Act 1834, and the Commissioners adopted his scientific approach in delineating districts and allocating an assistant commissioner to each to investigate conditions. The principle of "less eligibility" bears Bentham's imprint, as do the formation of a central controlling body over the locally-provided service, the demarcation of Poor Law areas according to criteria of convenience and natural features, the payment of officers, and the locally elected body in the Board of Guardians.

A. The Poor Law Amendment Act 1834

Meanwhile, the Whigs had forced the passing of the Reform Act 1832, which not only gave the middle class the vote but abolished about fifty rotten boroughs and removed the second member from ninety small towns. These seats would now be redistributed among the fast-growing industrialised urban areas. The Whigs then turned their attention to local matters, particularly the problem of poverty and the inadequate and debasing aspects of Speenhamland and like systems of poor-relief. In 1834 they passed the Poor Law Amendment Act, the main terms being:

1. Outdoor relief was to be abolished, except for the old and the sick.
2. Poor-relief was to be provided only inside the workhouses.
3. Conditions within the workhouses were to be "less eligible", that is, less desirable than those of the lowest-paid worker outside.
4. Parishes were to be grouped into unions, and each union was to maintain a workhouse.
5. Each workhouse was to be managed locally by a Board of Guardians, elected by the ratepayers.
6. The entire scheme was to be administered centrally from Somerset House, by the Poor-Law Commission, composed of three salaried members—the so-called "pinch-pauper triumvirate"—and a secretary, Edwin Chadwick, a disciple of Bentham.

The emphasis of the Act was upon deterring the poor from applying for relief, and the workhouse or, as it was commonly called, "the new Bastille", became reviled and feared by the poor for many succeeding generations.[3] Moreover, it resulted in a drastic reduction in the poor-rates from £27 million spent on poor-relief in 1831, to £5 million in 1851, despite a 29 per cent increase in the population, and was a main contributory cause of Chartism.

---

[3] See Crabbe's poem, *The Village,* for a horrifying description of the conditions within a workhouse, or M. Goodwin, *Nineteenth Century Opinion,* Pelican, 1951, pp. 50–56.

The act did, however, introduce three basic principles of administration in local government: (a) the principle of an *ad hoc* authority in the local Board of Guardians who were elected for the provision and control of a single service within a given area; (b) the principle of an area, the union of parishes, which was appropriate to the service to be provided; and (c) the principle of central control over a local service through the Poor Law Commission.

B. *The Municipal Corporations Act*, 1835

Having abolished corruption at parliamentary elections, the Whig government turned its attention to corruption in the government of towns, and set up a Royal Commission, composed mainly of young Whig lawyers to enquire into the defects in their administration. The majority of town corporations were ruled by self-perpetuating oligarchies of freemen whose status was defined by the charter which had constituted the particular borough. Their right to this status depended upon birth, purchase, gift or apprenticeship to a freeman, and generally they possessed exclusive rights of trading within the borough, of voting at elections and standing for election to the borough council. Charged with the administration of corporate property, the freemen could interpret their functions to include feasting and entertaining, payment of disproportionately large salaries to officials with few duties, and the promotion of self-interest. That they misused corporate property, legally, was indisputable, but as far as the Whigs were concerned, their main besetting sin was the fact that such corporations were controlled by Tories and Anglicans. As Professor Smellie has written:[4]

> "They were snug oases of privilege whose religious discrimination against dissenters, manipulation of markets, tolls and harbours for their more comfortable provision, and indifference to the provision of such urban necessities as competent police, firemen, or clean water and lighted streets, exasperated their under-privileged middle-class neighbours".

The result of the Royal Commission's quickly-drafted and condemnatory report was the passing, after compromises with vested interests in the House of Lords, of the Municipal Corporations Act 1835, which applied to 178 chartered boroughs but omitted London. Its provisions were:

1. Corporate property was to be put under the control of elected councils, who could also, if they wished, take over the duties of the

---

[4] K. B. Smellie, *A History of Local Government*, Allen & Unwin, 1968, p. 30.

Improvement Commissioners and statutory authorities which managed streets, paving, drains and lighting.

2. All ratepayers who had resided in an incorporated town for three years were to receive the vote.

3. One quarter of the council was to consist of aldermen elected by the council (a House of Lords compromise).

4. The accounts of the town clerk were to be audited once a year.

5. Council meetings were to be open to the public.

6. The administration of justice was separated from municipal government by the provision that borough magistrates would in future be appointed by the Crown, as in the counties, and not as formerly, by the borough corporations.

7. Urban communities which were unchartered could adopt the constitution of a municipal corporation.

8. No new areas were created, the council governing either the old borough area or the area of the parliamentary borough.

9. Councils were authorised to appoint paid officials—at least, a Town Clerk and a Treasurer.

10. No new powers, apart from the permissive powers in paragraph 1 above, were conferred. The main difficulty here was the vast population range of boroughs from small and ancient market towns to populous industrial centres, which complicated the framing of provisions about the powers which could be vested in each of them. They were all, however, compelled to appoint Watch Committees to exercise control over the police, to make bye-laws and to control the collection of rates. If they already possessed the statutory power to light part of their area, this power was extended to cover the whole area.

11. Licences might be granted for the sale of drink. To extend such powers the Corporation had to resort to Parliamentary legislation either by general legislation or by local Acts.

The 1835 Act was of fundamental importance to the development of town government. It eradicated existing abuses and prevented their perpetuation in the emergent and fast-expanding communities of industrial England and Wales. Although the franchise appeared to be more democratic than that of 1832, it was, in fact, narrower, and it was still a public vote; but the way was now clear for many of the formerly excluded residents, particularly among the new middle-class industrialists and merchants, to participate in the administration of their towns, and to ensure a high degree of responsible self-government. Finally, in contrast with the strong central control imposed by the 1834 Poor Law Amendment Act, it is noteworthy that this Act imposed little central control upon the corporations, apart from Treasury approval being required for the floating of local loans and to the alienation of any of the corporate real estate.

A similar lack of centralised control was evident in the Highways Act of the same year, which provided that the vestry of a parish maintaining highways should elect, for one year's duration, one or more persons to fulfil the office of surveyor, or should appoint a salaried surveyor. A well-populated parish could nominate, through its vestry, a highway board; a more sparsely populated parish might apply to the J.Ps., for the formation of a highway district from its combination with a neighbouring parish or parishes, and served by a paid surveyor. The significance of this act lies mainly in its provision for the creation of an *ad hoc* body by the vestries and J.Ps., not its election. It was, moreover, devoid of direction from a central authority. The extension of this model in the proliferation of boards for health, burial, schools and school attendance was to complicate even further local administration later in the century, when a state of chaotic diversity prevailed. Redlich and Hirst cite an earlier writer who described the confused system of 1885 as "a chaos of areas, a chaos of franchises, a chaos of authorities and a chaos of rates".[5]

C. Public Health Legislation

The rapid increase in the population, and its concentration in industrial townships, where houses were quickly erected for the lower orders of society, without such basic amenities as adequate and clean water supplies, refuse disposal arrangements, main drainage or any form of sanitation, had a deleterious effect upon the health of the populace. Filth accumulated in the streets and in the narrow alleyways between the overcrowded dwellings; drinking-water from polluted wells or contaminated rivers was used for cooking and drinking purposes. Contemporary descriptions of the period conjure up an odoriferous nightmare and it is little wonder that disease flourished. Mortality, especially amongst children, was high, and the disposal of the dead created major problems for the living; dirt and disease were everywhere apparent, but the precise nature of the connection was not known until the microbe was discovered. Meanwhile, no machinery existed to alleviate the horrific conditions which promoted ill-health and which in turn helped to increase pauperism.

The extent of the problem had been made apparent to the Poor Law Commissioners when they investigated the causes of destitution, and from their data Edwin Chadwick was able to prepare a memorandum in 1838 which showed that if sickness were prevented, poverty would be reduced and the poor rates would consequently fall. Chadwick established the correlation between ill-health, poverty and

---

[5] J. Redlich and F. W. Hirst, *History of Local Government* (Ed. B. Keith-Lucas), Macmillan, 1958, p. 199.

the foetid sanitary conditions, and wrote about his conclusions in the three-volumed *Report on the Sanitary Conditions of the Labouring Population of Great Britain* in 1842. A Royal Commission was nominated and it reported in 1844 and 1845, confirming Chadwick's conclusions. Legislation was delayed by Corn Laws agitation, but fear of epidemics particularly typhus and cholera, and the visitation of the latter scourge in 1845, claiming 55,000 lives, stimulated the passing of the Public Health Act 1848.

The Act created a strong central authority in the General Board of Health, which had the power to set up boards of health for local health districts, either on petition of one-tenth of the local ratepayers or where the death rate exceeded 23 per 1,000, regardless of whether the inhabitants petitioned for a board. Where a municipal borough adopted the Act, the town council became the local sanitary authority under the control and inspection of the General Board of Health. Outside the boroughs, the urban parts of the unions, established for poor relief under the 1834 Act, were made separate boards of health and became urban sanitary districts. Both districts performed a number of duties which included sewerage, drainage, water-supply, street management, supervision and maintenance of cemeteries and the regulation of offensive trades.

In all, 670 local boards of health were established, but the provision was inadequate to mitigate the health problems of communal living and the powers granted were far too slender. The austere zeal of Chadwick and the coercive central control of the General Board of Health attracted so much criticism that it was reconstituted in 1854 and lingered on until 1858 when its powers were finally transferred to the Privy Council. A series of epidemics between 1858 and 1871 prompted further research into the causation of disease, and the Royal Sanitary Commission of 1868, reporting in 1871, proposed the consolidation of the existing "fragmentary and confused sanitary legislation". It added that "the administration of sanitary law should be made uniform, universal, and imperative throughout the Kingdom", and also that "all powers requisite for the health of towns and country should in every place be possessed by one responsible local authority, kept in action, and assisted by a superior authority".

The Government accepted the Royal Commission's report immediately and the Local Government Act 1871, was passed. It created the Local Government Board, to which the Privy Council transferred its public health functions as did the Home Office; also transferred were the functions of the Poor Law Board and those of the Registrar-General's office. A further Act of 1872 transferred the Home Office's functions under the Highway Acts and Turnpike

Acts to the Local Government Board, and local sanitary authorities were established throughout England and Wales, outside London.

Finally, all the laws relating to public health were consolidated by the important Public Health Act 1875, which divided England and Wales, outside London, into urban and rural sanitary districts, the former being the districts of boroughs, of improvement commissioners, and of local *ad hoc* boards, and the latter being the poor law unions minus those parts which were within the urban districts. The local boards of the urban sanitary authorities were to be elected, whilst the rural authorities were to be governed by the poor-law guardians. Exercising supervisory control over the entire system was the Local Government Board.

The structure which thus emerged from the 1875 Act presaged the future pattern of local government, embodying the twin principles of central control of local authorities through a government department and of local responsibility for the administration of services through elected representatives. The assumption of additional responsibilities e.g., by the 1875 Act urban sanitary authorities also became highway authorities for their areas, and by the Elementary Education Act of 1870 boroughs and conurbations of parishes became school districts, anticipated the emergence of omnibus authorities and foreshadowed a dwindling reliance on *ad hoc* bodies for the running of local services. Moreover, the Reform Act of 1867, which had extended the franchise to the urban workman in municipal as well as parliamentary elections, had infused a new and radical vigour into the municipal administration of the big towns and had predisposed their councils to welcome responsibility for additional community services.

D. *Reform of County Government*

In the counties numerous attempts had been made since Joseph Hume's County Board Bill in 1836, to substitute elected representatives for the bench of nominated magistrates, "who levy and direct the expenditure of rates", yet, "are independent of those who pay them". The J.Ps.' powers appeared unassailable and their functions increased during the first half of the nineteenth century, particularly in the rural areas. Their judicial powers in Petty Sessions had been widely extended and by legislation of 1835 and 1839 they had added functions relating to highways and the police. Moreover, they wielded great influence at county elections where, up to 1884, there was a more favourable representation, proportionate to population, than in the boroughs.

Hume wanted to transfer their administrative functions to a new authority, the County Board, elected by the county ratepayers, but the Bill got no further than the first reading on two occasions. In 1849, with county rates rising steadily, Hume introduced a moderate County Rates and Expenditure Bill, which proposed County Boards comprising an equal partnership of J.Ps. and representatives nominated by county Boards of Guardians. This was dropped, and in 1850 a second County Rates and Expenditure Bill was introduced by Milner Gibson, which recommended County Boards made up half of J.Ps. and half of directly elected representatives of the ratepayers. The Select Committee to which it was referred reported against it, and it too was unsuccessful. A like fate befell similar bills in 1851, 1852 and 1860. Three further attempts were made in 1868 and in that year a Select Committee of Inquiry was appointed.

It reported in July, and in February 1869 the Queen's speech included a reference that "a measure will be introduced for applying the principle of representation to the control of the county rate by the establishment of financial boards for the counties". The bill proposed to add members elected by the Board of Guardians to the County Bench for administrative matters. It was finally introduced in May, and withdrawn two months later.

Thus thirty-three years of effort and campaigning to give the counties representative government came to an abortive conclusion. Happily, county government was not in the same corrupt state as the boroughs had been, and the J.Ps. on the County Bench provided a generally efficient standard of administration which was acceptable to the landed gentry and merchants from whose numbers they were appointed and whose interests they safeguarded.

However, with the increasing unionisation of agricultural employees and the spirit of radicalism in the counties, legislation to extend the franchise to agricultural workers could not be postponed indefinitely, and was finally achieved by the Reform Act 1884.

E. *The Local Government Act* 1888

The Conservative Government of 1886 depended upon the support of Joseph Chamberlain's Liberal Unionists, and it was under their influence that the Local Government Bill was introduced in 1888. Previously Sir Charles Dilke, the president of the Local Government Board from 1882 to 1885, had drawn up a bill which had envisaged elected councillors, without aldermen, for the counties, a reform of the unions and the districts, the dissolution of school boards and the transfer of their functions to the borough and district councils, and the exclusion of boroughs with a population of 100,000 or more from control by the county.

Such a radical and wide-ranging measure would undoubtedly have stimulated much political controversy, and little further was heard of it until it was presented in a much-modified form by the Conservatives in 1888. According to Redlich and Hirst (p. 197) the Bill

"was much more than a party manoeuvre. It was a measure conceived in a statesmanlike spirit to get rid of anomalies, and to supply wants which could not be supplied by the existing organisation. In truth, the substance of 'administrative law' had so grown in bulk and variety during the past two decades, that it could not satisfactorily be dealt with by the old machinery".

The main features of the Act were:

1. The administrative powers and duties of the J.Ps. were to be transferred to sixty-two administrative county councils. With certain exceptions[6] the counties were co-extensive with the geographical counties or shires and were based on the areas to which the commissions of the various county justices in Quarter Sessions applied.

2. Each county was to have a council composed of representatives directly elected by the ratepayers, and the county was to be divided into electoral districts of equal size.

3. All towns and boroughs with a population of more than 50,000 (i.e. fifty-seven towns), together with Burton-on-Trent, Canterbury, Chester and Worcester, were excluded from the administrative county structure and granted the status of county boroughs. Their burgesses were to take no part in county council elections. Boroughs which failed to obtain county borough status became subordinated to the counties and were designated non-county boroughs.

4. The major problem of London government was to be resolved by the creation of an administrative county for the metropolitan area, excluding the City and Corporation of London.

The 1888 Act was a major reform which established the dual system of local government in the autonomous county borough and the administrative county; bodies which formed the twin bases of local government in England and Wales to 1974. The diminution in the role of the J.P. was lamented by the landed and manufacturing classes in the counties, but lauded by others who saw the J.Ps. as

---

[6] The need to take account of ancient franchises and liberties produced administrative counties whose boundaries did not coincide with geographical county or shire boundaries, e.g. Lincolnshire was trisected into the administrative counties of Holland, Kesteven and Lindsey, as was Yorkshire into East, North and West Ridings; and Suffolk, Sussex, Cambridgeshire, Northamptonshire and, in 1890, Hampshire, were all divided.

embodiments of a regressive oligarchic control, and regretted that their judicial functions had not also been removed.

The Act did nothing, however, to simplify the structure of government in the districts, although the original bill had included proposals relating to district councils. These proposals had been excluded before the committee stage, partly because they appeared to be premature. The subordinate authorities needed to be reformed and integrated into the democratic structure which was coalescing.

The Liberal party hoped that the extension of the franchise to the agricultural workers would rebound to its advantage within the counties and particularly in the parishes which had long been the focus of their attention. Since Goschen's Bill of 1871 had highlighted the parish unit as the basis of a reconstituted local government system, the Liberals had campaigned to reform rural and parochial government. Their resolutions to extend representative government to the rural divisions to some extent re-echoed the earlier nostalgia of Toulmin Smith who, on the basis of a mistaken interpretation of history, advocated a return to village democracy as exemplified in the Greek city states. Throughout the 1880's Gladstone reaffirmed the belief of the National Liberal Federation that the inhabitants of rural divisions should receive the benefits of local government, and in 1889 he censured the government for not establishing district councils, adding that the government should "go still nearer to the door of the masses of the people".

F. *The Local Government Act* 1894

The pressure (for the establishment of elected councils in parishes and rural districts) continued unabated during the next four years, until, in March, 1893, the President of the Local Government Board in Gladstone's fourth administration introduced "the last of the great constructive measures which built up a democratic system of local government in England".[7] After much opposition, particularly from the Lords, the bill was enacted in March, 1894. The main provisions were:

1. Local self-government was introduced into rural parishes by providing for parish councils, elected by all the rate-paying inhabitants, in the larger parishes, and establishing parish meetings of all rate-paying inhabitants in the smaller parishes.

2. The urban and rural sanitary districts established by the Public Health Acts of 1848–75 were reconstituted as urban and rural district councils, elected by the same popular suffrage as the parish councils.

---

[7] Redlich and Hirst, *op cit.*, p. 216.

3. Boards of Guardians were reconstituted, and guardians were elected as above. In rural parishes, there was to be no special election of Guardians, and each rural district councillor would represent his parish on the Board of Guardians.

Thus within the span of sixty-two years from the first Reform Act, every part of England and Wales was administered at the local level by an elected council, and the pattern of organisation completed by the Local Government Act of 1894 remained unchanged until it was restructured by the London Government Act 1963 and the Local Government Act 1972.

Each type of local authority was collectively represented by voluntary associations which were formed soon after the 1888 and 1894 legislation. The County Councils Association represented all counties; the Association of Municipal Corporations, formed in 1873, represented member boroughs; the Urban District Councils Association, formed in 1890 as the Local Boards Association, looked after the interests of urban districts; and the Rural District Councils Association, founded in 1895, represented the R.D.C's. Not until 1947 was the National Association of Parish Councils formed.

3. Twentieth Century Developments

One of the problems which had remained unsolved by the end of the nineteenth century was the continued existence of the Poor Law Guardians. The absorption of the work of this *ad hoc* body by the existing local authorities had been contemplated during the last quarter of the nineteenth century, but little was done about the Poor Law until Balfour's appointment in 1905 of a Royal Commission on the Poor Law and the Relief of Distress through Unemployment.

The Poor Law was still that of the 1601 Act as amended by the principles and machinery of 1834. Studies such as those of General Booth, Charles Booth and B. Seebohn Rowntree showed the chronic state of poverty of the working class in the 1890's. The Commisson found that during 1906–7 nearly two million people, excluding casuals and inmates of lunatic asylums, were in receipt of poor relief. The Poor Law was not administered uniformly, with outdoor relief in the form of money or in kind still being given, and mixed workhouses had barely changed since 1834. In 1909 the commissioners produced a majority report and a minority report.

The former, signed by fifteen members, advocated the abolition of mixed workhouses and proposed that the children, the aged and the infirm should be housed in separate institutions, and that the Poor Law should be radically reformed. The Minority Report,

signed by four members who included Beatrice Webb and George
Lansbury, went much further. It showed that since 1834 such services
as public education, public health regulations, workmen's compensation, unemployment legislation and old age pensions had developed
to prevent poverty, not cure it, and they consequently proposed the
repeal of the 1834 Act and the abolition of Poor Relief and the Boards
of Guardians, with their punitive attitude towards poverty. The
powers and duties of Destitution Authorities were to be transferred
to county and county borough councils, and children, the infirm,
the aged and the mentally defective were to be cared for by *ad hoc*
committees of these councils.

No action was taken by the government, however, to carry out any
of the proposals, and the Poor Law and its Guardians continued to
carry out their functions. The number of Labour or Socialist Guardians had, however, increased after the early 1890's, particularly in
the poor areas of London, and there followed a period of activity
particularly under the leadership of Lansbury and Crooks on the
Poplar board, when relief was provided freely, much to the chagrin of
the ratepayers and the Local Government Board. Eventually, after
the imprisonment of the Poplar mayor and twenty-nine council
members, for refusal to pay the London County Council precept on
the pretext of the high cost of the poor relief, the cost was spread to the
richer London boroughs by the Local Authorities (Financial Provisions) Act 1921. This Act gave the Poplar Guardians the money
they wanted and they continued to distribute it freely, undeterred by
threats from the Ministry of Health.

Briefly, in 1923, and again from 1924, the Minister of Health was
Neville Chamberlain. His antipathy to "Poplarism", where surcharges
had amounted to £86,600, together with evidence of corruption and
nepotism in other authorities, and the financial difficulties of some
Boards during the General Strike, with some allegedly financing the
strike out of rates, ultimately led to Chamberlain's resolve to reorganise the Poor Law and abolish the Guardians. This was eventually
achieved with the Local Government Act 1929, which abolished the
Boards of Guardians and transferred their functions to the county
and county borough councils.

The same Act also reorganised local government finance. Some
measure of rating reform had been achieved four years earlier by the
Rating and Valuation Act 1925, which abolished the overseers and
transferred their powers to the local authorities. In addition, the
variety of rates, the poor rate, the district rate, etc., were replaced
by a single consolidated General Rate. Chamberlain had wanted to
rationalise the structure of the grants-in-aid by substituting block

grants for health services and needy areas for most of the assigned revenues and some of the percentage grants.

However, Winston Churchill as Chancellor wished to integrate these ideas with his own to remit the major part of the rates paid by industrial hereditaments, and to reimburse local authorities with a bigger block grant. The arrangement which was finally written into the bill was for the relief of industrial hereditaments of three-quarters of their rates, and agricultural lands and buildings were wholly derated. Additionally, the majority of assigned revenues and the percentage grants for public health were abolished. To compensate for these and to help equalise the burden of local expenditure an annual exchequer grant was to be made, computed for each local authority for a five-year period and paid out on the basis of need.

Other provisions of the Act included the transfer of many minor roads from county districts to county councils, and the latter were also required to undertake ten-yearly reviews of county district boundaries, and submit their reorganisation plans to the Minister. As a result of the reviews undertaken between 1929 and 1938, urban districts were reduced in number by 255, and rural districts by 169.

The main achievement of Chamberlain's successor, Arthur Greenwood, was the codification of the law relating to local government. He appointed the Chelmsford Committee in 1930 and from it emerged three major consolidating acts—the Local Government Act 1933, the Public Health Act 1936, and the Food and Drugs Act 1938—which effectively clarified the intricacies and inconsistencies of a mass of prior legislation. Thus by 1939 there existed

"both the beginnings of a consistent code of local government law and a uniform hierarchy of local authorities constituted in accordance with uniform principles. . . . At last, it was thought, local government had been rationalised, and a logically consistent picture of its principles could be drawn".[8]

Certain changes had been taking place in the scope of local authority functions. In 1929 responsibility for hospitals was transferred from the minor to the major authorities; in 1930 the licensing of passenger road services was removed from local authorities to Traffic Commissioners; and in 1936 the trunk roads in counties became the responsibility of the Traffic Commissioners. The 1939–45 war accelerated the changes and imposed new demands. The im-

---

[8] W. O. Hart, *Introduction to the Law of Local Government and Administration* (9th Edn.), Butterworths, p. 33.

mediate need was for national defence and local authorities were required to build air-raid shelters, organise warden and reserve services, appoint an Air-Raid Precautions Controller, arrange for the evacuation of children from target areas and their billetting in the regions. Such extra duties had to be provided in addition to the usual range of services, and provided, moreover, with a depleted staff. The tendency towards centralisation of control was intensified and may be seen, for example, in the merging of local fire brigades into a National Fire Service which was to remain until 1947. At the same time, the threat of imminent invasion and the capture of London necessitated the decentralisation of certain ministries concerned with civil defence and other wartime services into twelve regions, each with its own regional headquarters.

Between 1934 and 1948 various enactments transferred functions from the minor to the major authorities, and from local government to central departments and *ad hoc* bodies. The Education Act 1944, placed the responsibility for public education upon the counties and county boroughs. The National Health Service Act 1946, transferred all local authority hospitals and nursing homes to the control of Regional Hospital Boards and Hospital Management Committees, while county districts lost responsibility for their health and welfare services to the counties. By the Police Act 1946, county districts lost their police function to the counties. The Trunk Roads Act 1946, removed responsibility for certain highways in specified districts to the Minister of Transport. Under the Fire Services Act 1947, county district fire brigades were taken over by the counties, as were their town and country planning functions by the Town and Country Planning Act 1947. The Transport Act 1947, transferred canal and harbour undertakings to the British Transport Commission, and under the River Boards Act 1948, responsibility for the prevention of river pollution was transferred to the River Boards. Valuation for rating became an Inland Revenue function by the Local Government Act 1948.

Meantime, two of the main municipal undertakings were nationalised by the Electricity Act 1947, and the Gas Act 1948, both industries passing out of the control of municipal and private enterprise to the control of area boards. The Transport Act 1947, threatened local authorities with the loss of municipal passenger road transport services.

The gains by local authorities during this period were the powers to provide and administer civic restaurants, under the Civic Restaurants Act 1947, to provide and support entertainments and the arts, under the Local Government Act 1948, and certain extended powers were given to the major authorities by the Town and Country Planning Act 1947, and the Children Act 1948.

Thus within four years there was a considerable recasting of local authority functions, and an overall loss of power and responsibility by local government. Meanwhile, the control exercised by the central departments continued to increase and the functions remaining to local authorities became more complex and specialised. One result was a questioning of the adequacy of local government as it was constituted to cope with the demands being made upon it and whether its structure should be reorganised. The twenty years following the 1945 White Paper, *Local Government in England and Wales during the Period of Reconstruction* (Cmd. 6579) were largely absorbed by attempts to effect changes which were desirable "in the interests of effective and convenient local government", and the next chapter considers the various attempts made to achieve this purpose. At the same time, however, much consideration has been given to the supersession of the traditional structure by some form of regionalism.

Regionalism

Regionalism has a variety of meanings, but broadly it may be associated with either (a) administrative decentralisation or deconcentration of central government departments and public utilities to regional outstations for the better provision and regulation of services, or (b) the restructuring of local government into far larger territorial units than exist at present. The former is a bureaucratic structure implying no direct accountability to an electorate, while the second meaning entails the creation of an intermediate tier of elected bodies between central departments and existing local authorities and the possible diminution in status and powers of the latter.

The concept of regionalism is not new. In 1655 Cromwell attempted to consolidate his position by dividing England and Wales into eleven military districts under Majors-General who sternly supervised the J.Ps. in the performance of their local duties and performed the functions of tax collectors, policemen and custodians of public morality. Apart from that brief constitutional imposition upon the local government system, the cause of regionalism awaited an advocate until 1902 when H. G. Wells predicted the development of urban regions. In 1905 a Fabian study *Municipalization by Provinces* by W. Sanders proposed a revived heptarchy of seven or eight provinces administered by boards elected by local authorities. In 1921 G. D. H. Cole in *The Future of Local Government* proposed the division of England into nine regions, each having a directly elected council. These and similar pioneering schemes "were plans for reorganising and simultaneously strengthening the apparatus of *elected* authorities".[9]

During the 1914–18 war food supplies and labour deployment were controlled from regional offices of government departments, and during the post-war years regional offices were set up to deal with housing shortages and the administration of social services. The Royal Commission on the Distribution of the Industrial Population (the Barlow Commission) had recommended in 1940 that local government should be structured on a regional pattern. Although the report was not adopted the threat of invasion had resulted in a contingency plan which entailed the division of Britain into twelve autonomous areas, each under a Regional Commissioner with wide powers of co-ordination and control. The arrangement was not popular with local authorities who feared the reserve powers of the Commissioners to act as the executive government in each region, and it was quickly abandoned after the war.

The process of decentralising government departments continued after the war in an unsystematic fashion, but gradually "there tended to be a growing recognition of the contribution which the decentralization of departments and inter-departmental co-operation in the regions could make to efficient administration".[10] Despite the Treasury's delineation of nine standard regions in 1946 the regional boundaries established by government departments did not always coincide because of the different functions and requirements of each department. The nationalised gas, electricity, coal and transport undertakings also established regional structures, as did the hospital service.

Under the Conservatives in the 1950s the process of regionalisation slowed down and many regional offices, including, remarkably, those of the Ministry of Housing and Local Government and the Ministries of Power and Supply were closed down, but other departments maintained and expanded their regional outstations. During the 1960s there was a renewed emphasis on regional planning, stimulated by governmental concern over regional imbalances caused by the pressure of population in the South and the Midlands, by the decline of traditional industries in the North, in Scotland and in Wales, and the under-utilisation of the resources of these areas. The employment problems of the North-east were studied in 1963 by Lord Hailsham and a White Paper designated the area as a

---

[9] A. H. Hanson and M. Walles, *Governing Britain*, Fontana 1970, p. 214.
[10] *Royal Commission on the Constitution 1969–1973*, Vol. 1 Report (Cmnd. 5460), H.M.S.O. 1973, p. 63.

"growth zone". Further studies followed in the South-east, the West Midlands, the North-west and in Mid Wales, and the need to promote their economic development led in 1964 to the division of the country into six (later eight) planning regions. Each planning region was to be served by (a) an executive *Planning Board* comprising representatives of the main economic and social departments (i.e. all civil servants) and a chairman appointed by the Secretary of State for Economic Affairs (George Brown), and (b) an advisory *Planning Council* with a small membership representing industrial management and employees, local authorities, universities and commerce. The councils were to have no executive powers nor were they to replace the local authorities, but were to analyse their region's problems and give advice. Both Planning Boards and Councils would collaborate with the local authorities who would be responsible for implementing regional plans. *The Times* (11 December, 1964) commented that the proposals revealed

> "a clear spreading of the Whitehall machinery into the regions. The Department of Economic Affairs is about to spawn provincial tentacles. . . . This will make for better decisions in the light of local conditions and will make co-ordination with the national plans all the easier . . . The snags may arise when these new links with Whitehall have to be fitted alongside the existing relations of local authorities with individual ministries in London. The machinery for carrying out changes in land use, for example, will presumably remain unaffected, although overall strategy will now be worked out by the new boards".

Mr. Brown emphasised that the regional bodies "will not affect the existing powers of local authorities", but many councils were perturbed about the long-term effect of the regional bodies upon their functions, particularly town and country planning. They suspected further limitation of their powers and feared that the regional bodies would form an intrinsic new tier, intruding upon and crossing their direct line of communication with Whitehall. The *Municipal Journal* (18 December, 1964) referred to "the feeling that there is a threat to eliminate democratic local government", and the *Local Government Chronicle* (23 January, 1965) commenting on the "wide misgiving" stated that "a Birmingham alderman said that the people of Birmingham were not going to be 'shoved around'. The principal objection of many Local Authorities seemed to be that they would prefer to be obstructed by a Minister than by a regional economic board".

Some local authorities responded to the perceived threat by

combining for joint action, e.g. in the North local authorities combined for industrial development, airport provision, tourism, sport and art; in the West Country a number of local authorities commissioned an economic survey of their combined areas; in the North-east the London Standing Conference on Regional Planning brought the planning authorities of the area together; and in South-east Lancashire and North-east Cheshire a Transportation Study involved sixty-two local authorities.[11] Nevertheless, local authorities remained suspicious, and justifiably so if the following statement accredited to the chairman of the North-west Regional Council represented a typical attitude:

> "At the moment we are no more than caretakers conducting psychological warfare. If, as a result, local authorities begin to think on a regional basis all could be well. If the authorities do not co-operate we will have to be given executive powers. This is the rock on which we shall split."[12]

The establishment of economic planning machinery at a regional level and the economies of scale achieved by regionalised public utilities stimulated the advocacy of elected regional authorities, "as the region provides the most viable administrative sub-division for the provision of an increasing variety of services".[13] Directly elected regional councils, larger than the existing counties and with commensurately greater powers devolved by central government, could pose a further challenge to established local authorities. A notable contribution to the cause of regional decentralisation was that of John P. Mackintosh who proposed eleven regions, with nine regional councils in England and two regional assemblies for Wales and Scotland.[14] Each would have "considerable power in terms of population and resources", would discharge extensive functions and would engage staff comparable in quality with the Civil Service. The regional councils would be directly elected for three years and organised on a parliamentary pattern with a prime minister and a cabinet, the latter consisting of about eight ministers responsible for departments not committees. Second-tier authorities would be decided by the regional governments and would vary from region to region in accordance with need, opinion and tradition. Such a scheme, it was suggested, would make a degree of devolution of central powers possible, permit regional variations

[11] *District Bank Review*, March, 1966.
[12] *Sunday Times*, 6 February, 1966.
[13] Hanson & Walles, *ibid.*, p. 224.
[14] J. P. Mackintosh, *The Devolution of Power*, Chatto & Windus, 1968.

of policy and local control, and meet "the legitimate aspirations of the Welsh and Scots for a degree of self-government".

A less radical and a more locally based approach was that of the *city region*, which is an administrative unit based on a large town and its hinterland. According to Derek Senior,[15] England and Wales could be divided into thirty city regions which he classified as (a) *mature*—six based on London, Birmingham, Manchester, Liverpool, Leeds and Newcastle upon Tyne, where the centre of each was readily accessible to a population of over two million people; (b) *emergent*—six based on the centres of Nottingham, Sheffield, Preston, Southampton, Cardiff and Bristol, all with ample dependent populations of over 1 million each, but whose centres are either not so readily accessible from some parts of their hinterlands or for various reasons are less fully equipped; (c) *embryonic*—twelve based on centres at Swansea, Brighton, Hull, Leicester, Norwich, Stoke, Oxford, Exeter, Cambridge, Coventry, Middlesbrough and Gloucester, with hinterland populations between one-third and four-fifths of a million; and (d) *potential*—proposed expansions near Ashford, Newbury, Northampton, Ipswich, Peterborough and Bournemouth which by the end of the century might be effective counter-magnets to London with populations of half a million each. The city region was to Derek Senior "a social entity much more relevant to the concerns of local government than any other . . .", and as a member of the Royal Commission on Local Government in England (1969) he was the sole signatory of a Memorandum of Dissent which advocated thirty-five directly elected regional authorities. The Royal Commission decided that "the city region was not an idea which could be applied uniformly all over England", but its proposals did include regional groupings of unitary and metropolitan areas into eight provinces with indirectly elected councils responsible for the determination of "the provincial strategy and planning framework within which the main authorities must operate".

When, on 1 April, 1974, local government was reorganised there were no provincial or regional tiers in the new structure, but on the same day local government did lose important services to the newly created regional health authorities and regional water boards. The local authority associations condemned this loss of functions at a time when the whole purpose of the radical surgery it was undergoing was designed to strengthen not weaken local government. Moreover, the inadequacy of local authority repre-

---

[15] D. Senior, "The City Region as an Administrative Unit", *Political Quarterly*, Vol. 36, No. 1.

sentation on the regional health authorities, which is discussed more fully later, gave additional cause for concern.

In the meantime, the *Royal Commission on the Constitution*, set up by Harold Wilson's government in 1969 as a response to the insistent and growing voice of nationalism in Scotland and Wales, had spent four years examining relations between central, local and regional governments and determining whether any changes were desirable. Under the chairmanship of Lord Kilbrandon (since March 1972) the Royal Commission produced its Report and a Memorandum of Dissent in October 1973, and both proposed the devolution of some powers and functions from central government to Scotland, Wales and the English regions. The Report stated that nearly all the significant complaints made against the working of central government sprang either from its centralisation in London or from developments in the operation of government which had tended to run counter to the principles of democracy. The Commission had examined and rejected the case for the transfer of complete sovereignty to an independent Scotland and Wales, mainly because the necessary political will for separation did not exist among the Scottish and Welsh people. Members also concluded that there was little demand for federalism in Scotland and Wales, and practically none in England. However, it was felt that the devolution of central government functions to Scotland and Wales and the English regions would preserve the essential political and economic unity of the United Kingdom and retain the legal and effective sovereignty of Parliament, and also do much to reduce discontent with the governmental system.

The members differed in the forms of devolution, but they agreed in recommending that the executive functions of government should, where practicable, be devolved direct to the newly created local authorities which, in the exercise of those functions should be subjected to a minimum of control. Functions retained by central government should where practicable be exercised in the regions, with the various departments and agencies of government so far as possible, operating in the same regions and from the same regional centres.

The Prime Minister (Edward Heath) commented upon the complex and interrelated issues of major political, constitutional and practical importance examined by the Report, and felt that there should be the widest public discussion before any decisions could be taken on matters which fundamentally affected the way the country was governed. A consultative document *Devolution within the United Kingdom* was issued in August, 1974, with the intention of carrying the discussion a stage further. It set out clearly the seven main schemes of devolution proposed in the Majority Report and the Memorandum of Dissent. Separatism and federalism were both rejected. Three of the schemes (A, B, and C below) involved major constitutional change, while the remaining four schemes envisaged the creation of bodies which were primarily advisory and consultative, and therefore did not raise major constitutional issues.

Scheme A: Legislative Devolution for Scotland and Wales. This was recommended for Scotland by eight of the thirteen members of the Commission and for Wales by six members. Responsibility for legislating on specific services would be transferred from Westminster to directly elected Scottish and Welsh legislatures, each having about 100 members elected for four years by the single transferable vote (S.T.V.). The sovereignty of Parliament would be preserved, but it would not legislate on transferred matters without the agreement of Scottish or Welsh governments. Each government would have its own ministers, cabinet system and civil servants, and a large measure of financial independence, especially over expenditure, but would be subject to such restraints as were necessary for the economic interests of the U.K. as a whole.

Legislative power would be transferred for local government, town and country planning, new towns, housing, building control, water supply and sewerage, ancient monuments and historic buildings, roads, road passenger transport, harbours, environmental services, education, youth and community services, sports and recreation, arts and culture, social work services, health, miscellaneous regulatory functions, agriculture, fisheries and food, forestry, crown estates and tourism. Additionally, the Scottish assembly would obtain legislative power for police, fire services, criminal policy and administration, prisons, administration of justice, legal matters, highlands and islands development, and sea transport.

Both countries would continue to send representatives to the House of Commons, but in proportion to population thus reducing the number of Scottish M.P.s from 71 to about 57 and Welsh M.P.s from 36 to about 31. The offices of Secretary of State for Scotland and for Wales would disappear, but each country would be represented by a minister in the Cabinet.

Scheme B: Elected Assemblies for Scotland, Wales and the English Regions. This scheme of intermediate level governments was the main proposal of the *Memorandum of Dissent* signed by Lord Crowther-Hunt and Professor Peacock. They sought to achieve a substantial increase of devolution to Scotland, Wales and about five English regions, or to Scotland and Wales alone. Parliament would remain responsible for the framework of legislation and major policy, but the assemblies, each comprising about 100 members directly elected by the S.T.V. system for four years, would be responsible for adjusting U.K. policies to the needs of their areas and for putting them into effect.

The governments of the assemblies would be run on a local government pattern with a functional committee structure and not a cabinet, and would assume control of the Scottish and Welsh Offices and the regional and local offices of central government departments. The civil servants employed in these offices would be "hived off" from central government although the Secretaries of State would remain in the Cabinet and be joined by a Minister for the English Regions. Each intermediate government would take over the functions of the *ad hoc* authorities (e.g. health and water) and assume some supervisory responsibilities for the industrial and commercial authorities (e.g. gas and electricity boards) in their areas.

They would not be limited to the specific duties conferred by Parliament, but would have a general residual competence to act for the welfare of their populations. Each assembly would make "ordinances" to implement and adapt U.K. policies and legislation and to give effect to their residual power. They would have some independent revenue-raising powers and sufficient financial independence of central government to allow some freedom to carry out their duties. Each government would have its own civil service and ombudsman.

The functions of local authorities would remain as at present, but they would deal with the appropriate intermediate level government instead of with central government, and local authorities would have direct representation in the government for their area. M.P.s, being relieved of much detail, would have more time for sharing in central government policy-making and in influencing U.K. ministers in Brussels. For these purposes M.P.s would need to be organised into functional committees matching each central government department. It was also visualised that the composition of the House of Lords might be altered to include members of the intermediate level governments.

Scheme C: Executive Devolution for Scotland, Wales and Eight English Regions. Recommended by two signatories of the Majority Report who wanted a substantial measure of devolution but in a more restricted and less radical form than that outlined in Scheme B.

The U.K. Parliament and Government would be responsible for the framework of legislation and major policy in all matters, but whenever possible would transfer the responsibility for devising and executing specific policies and for general administration to directly elected assemblies in Scotland, Wales and eight English regions. Each assembly would comprise about 100 members elected by S.T.V. for four years. Executive authority would be vested not in the members but in the assemblies themselves, which would delegate much of their authority to functional committees.

The objective would be to promote maximum regional partipation and variation consistent with the general policy aims of the U.K. Government. Like Scheme B it could be considered for application to Scotland and Wales only, but unlike Scheme B the assemblies would have no independent revenue-raising powers, no residual competence, no wide ordinance-making power, and would not necessarily take over *all* the existing executive functions of the Scottish or Welsh Offices, nor all the outposts of Government Departments, nor effect a general take-over of non-industrial and non-commercial *ad hoc* bodies. Moreover, the assemblies' relationship with local authorities might also be different from that envisaged in Scheme B, and three possible relationships are described: local authorities would be completely subordinate to the regional governments and the distribution of functions would be decided between them and their local authorities; local and regional authorities could be autonomous in functions allocated from the centre and could work in parallel, with local authorities accountable to the U.K. government; or the relationship could depend on what Paliament considered appropriate in each separate field of legislation.

Scheme D : Welsh Advisory Council. Recommended by three members who aimed to retain the Secretary of State and the Welsh Office but to replace the existing nominated Welsh Council by a directly elected Welsh Advisory Council of about sixty members elected by the S.T.V. It would have no legislative, executive or administrative powers, but would scrutinise, debate and make representations to the Secretary of State about Government policies and activities in Wales, including the activities of nationalised industries and other *ad hoc* bodies. It would not supervise the activities of local authorities. Every matter concerning Wales and its economy would come within its remit, and it would operate through standing committees and be financed from the U.K. Exchequer. It would have the right to nominate some members of *ad hoc* bodies in Wales. The Secretary of State and other Welsh Ministers would be invited to attend the Council to explain policy, answer criticism and receive advice. Officials of the Welsh Office would be invited to report to the Council and to answer questions on their work. Welsh M.P.s might attend and speak but not vote at the Council's plenary sessions.

Scheme E: A Scottish Council with Advisory and Legislative Functions. One signatory of the Majority Report recommended the establishment of a Scottish Council with the same advisory functions as the Welsh Advisory Council but having also some powers in relation to Scottish legislation. The Council would take the Second Reading, Committee and Report stages of Scottish Bills referred by the House of Commons. If a Scottish Bill were not recalled by the Leader of the House, the Scottish Council would give it a Third Reading and submit it for Royal Assent without any reference back to the House of Commons or passing it through the House of Lords.

Scheme F: Regional Co-ordinating and Advisory Councils for the English Regions. Recommended by eight members of the Commission who felt that it would not be right to give any legislative or executive powers of central Government to the regions, and that it would be illogical after local government reorganisation for the regions to take over powers from local government. However, they believed that there was scope for more effective co-operation between local authorities and a need for more open discussion and democratic influence on regional matters which are decided by central Government or by *ad hoc* bodies. To meet this need and to give advice to central Government they recommended eight English regions (those already established for economic planning purposes), each with an advisory council of about sixty members, four-fifths of whom would be elected from the members of local authorities in the regional area. One-fifth would be nominated by central Government to secure representation from industry, commerce, trades unions, education and other interests. The Councils would have no legislative, executive or administrative powers but would take over the functions of the existing regional economic planning councils, advise on Government spending in the regions, advise on Government policies including the operation of the nationalised industries and *ad hoc* bodies, and have a co-ordinating function in local government in respect of helping to formulate broad economic and land use strategy. The structure plans of local authorities would have to fit into this general strategy and would be submitted for Ministerial approval through the Regional Council. The Council would by agreement promote and co-ordinate action by local government, but would have no power of direction over local authorities nor would it administer services or undertake works.

Scheme G: Co-ordinating Committees of Local Authorities. Recommended by one member, the scheme is based on the view that the best way of devolving power is to concentrate on strengthening the power of the new large local authorities. The only need at regional level would be to co-ordinate local authorities' planning activities. In place of the present voluntary co-operation between authorities there would be a formal system of regional committees, each consisting of indirectly elected representatives of local authorities and no nominated members. Local authorities would be required to submit their plans to the regional committee and obtain its comments before submitting them for Ministerial approval. The present economic planning councils would be abolished, and the scheme might be combined with regional committees of the House of Commons which might vet regional plans and Government expenditure in the regions.

The Government sought comments on a number of specific matters which were raised by the major schemes (A, B, and C) of devolution and posed several questions which would have to be discussed and answered before any scheme could become a practical proposition. The main problems related to the possible effects of the three major schemes on the powers and functions of local authorities:

(i) How acceptable was the recommendation that local authorities would mainly be limited to dealing with the regional governments and would cease to deal with Parliament and the central departments?

(ii) Which of the three possible types of relationship between regional assemblies and local government outlined in Scheme C was preferable?

(iii) What problems would be posed for local authorities under Scheme A where Scottish and Welsh governments would have very considerable legislative power over local authorities, particularly in respect of grants and the powers of local authorities ("it would be theoretically possible for them to re-cast completely the structure and powers of local government")? Similar problems might arise under Schemes B and C, depending on the powers devolved by central government.

(iv) Would the regional governments under Schemes B and C seek to compensate for their lack of legislative power by exerting greater control over the activities of local authorities or by pressing to take over their functions?

The remaining schemes were of a different order and involved the creation of assemblies which were advisory and consultative, and possessed no specified powers in respect of local authorities. Schemes F and G assumed the devolution of as many functions as possible to local authorities, but the document questioned whether the eight regional authorities would strengthen local government and improve its relations with central government or whether they would set up an additional barrier between local and central government. The view of the Association of Metropolitan Authorities was unequivocal. It supported Scheme G in preference to the others as it was "based on the view that in England the best way of devolving power from central government is to concentrate on strengthening the power of the new larger local authorities".[16]

Such an opinion reflects the deep-seated but natural antipathy of local authorities to any threat to their status or powers. In the next chapter the attempts made since 1945 to reform the structure of local government are described. Here too it will be apparent that with every proposal to reorganise, the one persistent fear was that change involving larger and fewer authorities would sweep away many councils and their members, so weakening the allegedly democratic nature of local government. The real problems associated with change are largely human and emotional, and it may be unrealistic to expect vested interests to agree willingly to their own demise without some defensive resistance and a strongly emotive appeal to loyalty and tradition. It would also appear, however, that the only alternative to change was the perpetuation of the failings revealed by successive analyses since 1945 and the consequential atrophy of local government as an effective representative institution.

The Department of the Environment

The Conservative Government's White Paper *The Reorganisation of Central Government* (Cmnd. 4506, 1970) proposed a number of improvements in the methods and machinery for policy formulation and administration, and one emphasis of the review was upon the grouping of functions into unified departments. The Department of the Environment was one of the new "giant" departments to be created, and in November 1970 it took over the functions previously carried out by the three separate Ministries of Housing and Local Government, Transport, and Public Buildings and Works. Its responsibilities include: reorganisation and finance

---

[16] See Appendix 7 for subsequent developments.

of local government; housing policy and finance; control of environmental pollution; highway strategy and road programme; policy for the port industry; regional development (in co-operation with the Department of Trade and Industry); correlation of urban and transport planning; investment policies for the nationalised transport industries; responsibility for the construction industry; and conservation and amenity, particularly of the countryside.

In Wales the Welsh Office deals with all the services affecting the physical development of the country, including housing and slum clearance, new towns, water supplies, sewerage, roads (including motorways), town and country planning, general local government matters, health and welfare services, child care, and primary and secondary education. Under its general supervision, most of these services are administered by local authorities, local health authorities and other statutory bodies.

The Department of the Environment is headed by the Secretary of State for the Environment in whom is vested all the Department's statutory powers. He is assisted by a team of three ministers (for housing and construction, for transport, and for planning and local government), two Ministers of State and three Parliamentary Under Secretaries. Together with their senior civil servants, these ministers take major policy decisions, but each minister also takes responsibility under the Secretary of State for specific areas of policy. The Lord Privy Seal is the Department of Environment's spokesman in the House of Lords. The Secretary of State for Wales supervises the implementation in Wales of the national policy of the Department of the Environment and the Departments of Education and Science, Trade and Industry, and Employment.

CHAPTER 2

Structural Reorganisation

1. The Units of Local Government 1894 to 1974

The Local Government Acts of 1888 and 1894 established an unitary form of organisation in the county boroughs and a more complex tiered structure in the administrative counties and their county districts and parishes. Subsequent years witnessed piecemeal changes in the numbers of authorities but not in the basic framework whose inherent faults became increasingly apparent after the second world war.

County boroughs increased in number from sixty-one in 1888 to eighty-two by 1923, and many of the original county boroughs had been enlarged. The population requirement of 50,000 for county borough status was raised to 75,000 by the Local Government (County Boroughs and Adjustments) Act 1926 and later raised to 100,000 by the Local Government (Boundary Commission) Act 1945 and the Local Government Act 1958. Towns with smaller populations were not precluded from applying for county borough status as population was only one of the criteria, the prime requirement for promotion being the local authority's fitness to discharge the functions of a county borough. Other factors taken into account were resources, administrative record, and the likely effect of promotion upon the "parent" county whose predictable reaction was to resist the loss of prosperous towns who desired autonomy and financial independence. After the creation of Doncaster C.B. in 1926 there were no further applications until the boroughs of Ealing, Ilford and Luton introduced bills between 1949–53 for the promotion of county borough status. Their county councils objected, and no bill reached the Statute Book. During the 1954–5 parliamentary session Ilford, Luton and Poole attempted to gain county borough status but withdrew their bills when the Minister announced that proposals for reorganisation were being considered. Not until 1964 did any authorities achieve county borough status, when Luton and Solihull were successful; but in 1965 Croydon, East Ham and West Ham lost their county borough status in the reorganisation of London. Lastly, on 1 April, 1968, the two new county boroughs of Teeside and Torbay were created. Thus by 31 March, 1974, there were eighty-three county boroughs in England and Wales, thirty-four of which had population figures below 100,000.

The number of *administrative counties* remained unchanged until the abolition of the counties of London and Middlesex by the London Government Act 1963. On 1 April, 1965, two new administrative counties were created in Cambridgeshire and Isle of Ely (from the separate administrative counties of Cambridge and the Isle of Ely) and in Huntingdon and Peterborough (from the separate administrative counties of Huntingdonshire and the Soke of Peterborough). By 31 March, 1974, there were fifty-eight administrative counties, forty-five in England and thirteen in Wales (including Monmouthsire).

The Local Government Act 1933 listed 273 *non-county boroughs* or municipal boroughs. By 31 March, 1974, there were 259. They had the same constitution as county boroughs but their functions resembled more closely those of an urban district. Varying widely in population, resources and antiquity, they were generally smaller than county boroughs whose independence the more substantial boroughs envied from their position of subordination to the county council's control. Most owed their origin either to charters granted by the Crown or to special Acts of Parliament, but by the Local Government Act 1958 boroughs could also be created by ministerial order.

By the provisions of the same act the possibility also existed for the creation of a new type of borough in the *rural borough*. This would be an ancient non-county borough which was small and unable to provide the services demanded by law. It would merge with an adjacent rural district but continue to preserve its traditional and ancient privileges although its powers would be those of a parish council. Its corporation comprised a mayor, councillors, but no aldermen. By 1968 seven rural boroughs had been created.

Urban and rural districts were created by the Local Government Act 1894 from the urban and rural sanitary authorities. The Local Government Act 1933 made provisions for a county council to review the circumstances of its county districts and to consider the need for effecting changes by the alteration or definition of their boundaries, their division, the transfer of parts, the conversion of rural into urban districts, or vice versa, or the formation of new urban or rural districts or parishes. Such changes would be effected by ministerial order.

On 1 April, 1967, the three urban district councils of Ellesmere,

Wem and Whitchurch were abolished on incorporation into the rural district of North Shropshire. On 1 April, 1968, a number of amalgamations reduced the number of urban districts to 522 and rural districts to 469 (including the Isles of Scilly).

Parishes were resurrected as local government units by the Local Government Act 1894, when every rural parish was required to have a parish meeting at which every local government elector could participate. By the Local Government Act 1933, rural parishes with a population of 300 or more were required to have a parish council consisting of a chairman and between five and twenty-one councillors, meeting at least four times a year. If the population were between 200 and 300 the county council was required by order to create a parish council if the parish meeting asked for one. If the population numbered fewer than 200 there was no requirement for the county council to create a parish council but could do so at the request of the parish meeting. By 1974 there were about 7,500 parish councils and meetings in England and Wales.

Every rural parish was required to have a parish meeting which all the local government electors in the parish could attend. If there were a council for the parish, the parish meeting had to meet at least once a year between 1 March and 1 April. If there were no parish council the parish meeting was the local authority for the parish but with restricted powers, and it had to assemble at least twice a year.

A parish council was incorporated but parish meetings were not. When there was no parish council, property was to be held by the chairman of the parish meeting and the representative of the parish on the R.D.C. and together they formed a body corporate known as "the Representative Body". Urban parishes, i.e. civil parishes within the boundaries of boroughs or urban districts, had no local government significance. Their functions, apart from those of an ecclesiastical or charitable nature, had been transferred to the borough or urban district councils by the Local Government Act 1933.

Finally, mention must be made of the units of local government in the Greater London area. Under the provisions of the London Government Act 1963, the Greater London Council and thirty-two London Boroughs came into being on 1 April, 1965, while the City of London Corporation retained its unique status and added to its powers.

The pre-1974 structure of local government is customarily illustrated by the following diagram which conveniently summarises the foregoing description:

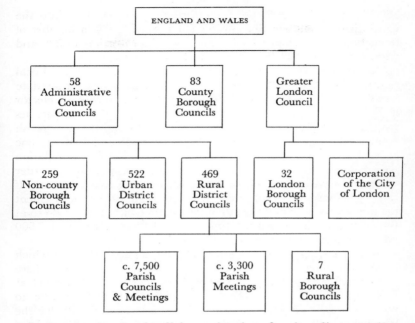

Unfortunately, the simplicity and order of such a diagram gives little indication of the weaknesses in the structure. Criticisms were directed at: the existence in all categories of too many small local authorities with inadequate resources, population and areas to provide and support adequate services; the difficulties of accommodating a number of services, each requiring different conditions for optimum efficiency and economy, in areas which were rigidly defined; the dual system of single-tier government in the county boroughs and the two or three tiers in the counties which was irrational, uneconomic, administratively wasteful and aggravated by mutual rivalry and suspicion; and the sometimes tense relationships which existed between counties and county districts. Moreover, the diagram gives no indication of the vast disparities in population, size and rateable value of local authorities of the same and different types, nor of the incompatibility between size and status of many local authorities. The following data from *The Municipal Year Book 1973*, illustrate these points:

(a) *Population at 30 June 1971:*

Councils	Largest	Smallest
Counties	Lancashire 2,513,400	Radnorshire 18,270

Councils	Largest	Smallest
County Boroughs	Birmingham 1,013,420	Canterbury 35,530
Non-county Boroughs	Poole 106,610	Montgomery 980
Urban Districts	Basildon 129,900	Llanwrtyd Wells 450
Rural Districts	Meriden 102,670	Painscastle 1,430

(b) *Area in acres:*

Councils	Largest	Smallest
Counties	Devon 1,612,310	Isle of Wight 94,146
County Boroughs	Birmingham 51,598	Bootle 3,725
Non-county Boroughs	Rhondda 23,885	Cowbridge 84
Urban Districts	Lakes 49,905	Narberth 122
Rural Districts	North Westmorland 288,688	Isles of Scilly 4,041

(c) *Rateable Value at 1 April 1972:*

Councils	Largest	Smallest
Counties	Lancashire £93,924,462	Radnorshire £617,657
County Boroughs	Birmingham £55,192,379	Merthyr Tydfil £1,498,438
Non-county Boroughs	Slough £8,309,889	Montgomery £18,359
Urban Districts	Thurrock £9,072,137	Llanwrtyd Wells £13,409
Rural Districts	Eton £5,191,726	Painscastle £27,980

2. Reorganisation of Local Government Structure

Many of the criticisms stemmed from the age of the structure. Since the structure was crystallised by the Local Government Acts of 1888 and 1894, Britain has experienced a complex of internal changes which have transformed its social, economic and political life.

The population of England and Wales increased by nearly 20 million between 1891 and 1971 and became overwhelmingly urbanised. Agriculture as a main source of employment declined seriously after 1880 and accelerated the movement of population from the country to the towns. Rural depopulation and migration to towns coupled with the peripheral growth of neighbouring towns into continuous built-up areas resulted in an urban population of about 80 per cent in Britain, and made nonsense of the dichotomy between town and country which was perpetuated in the dual system. Thus Victorian local government boundaries had become irrelevant, and had helped to exacerbate relationships between rural and urban authorities, the former consistently opposing the extension of the latter or the creation of county boroughs, and the resultant conflict lessening the likelihood of willing inter-authority co-operation when the need arose.

Moreover, during this period, there had been a radical extension in the range and quality of the services provided by local authorities. Following the Education Act of 1902, a spate of social legislation had required local authorities to provide a wide array of personal and

environmental services, far beyond the limited protective and public
health functions of the late nineteenth century, and had greatly
widened the functional role of local government units. An unprecedented scientific, technical and communications revolution, the
evolution of the concept of a Welfare State, and the need for the
provision of national standards, have formed the background to
these changes, providing the tools and a philosophy for local government's assumption of increased responsibility for the welfare of the
population.

Yet the dynamic aspect of these changes did not affect the basic
structure of local government which remained broadly unchanged
since the 1888 and 1894 legislation, and the Minister's indictment of
pre-1963 London Government as "ossified and anachronistic" might
equally have been applied to the local government structure outside
the metropolis. Moreover, there was no significant attempt to adapt
areas to the requirements of the services which had been allocated to
them, resulting in varying standards of service from authorities
whose resources were too slender to fulfil their responsibilities.

3. Local Government Boundary Commission

The 1939–45 war brought an end to the piecemeal reorganisation
of county districts, and many claims for county borough status and
the extension of county borough boundaries were held in abeyance.
The Coalition Government and the Local Authority Associations,
however, continued discussions and in January, 1945, a White Paper
was published entitled, *Local Government in England and Wales during
the Period of Reconstruction* (Cmd. 6579). It was, according to Professor
Robson "mainly an escapist document . . . in many ways a highly
misleading document", and its introductory statement indicates that
the government was not convinced of the need for a root and branch
reform of local government. The government had considered reform
proposals put forward by the Associations and "other authoritative
sources" and decided there was "no general desire to disrupt the
existing structure", but that there was "need and scope for improvements" particularly in the amendment of the machinery for
the adjustment of status, boundaries and areas. The White Paper did,
however, create the Local Government Boundary Commission, not
in the powerful form suggested by N.A.L.G.O. and the Labour Party,
but with equivalent functions to those of the county councils and the
Minister of Health in the case of county district reviews.

The Local Government (Boundary Commission) Act 1945,
granted statutory powers to the Commission to review the boundaries,

and, in certain cases, the status of local authorities. The Commission's highly experienced members[1] described their purpose briefly in their first report:

> "Our task is to make, so far as is practicable, all local government authorities, both individually and collectively, effective and convenient units. This is the language of our governing principle."[2]

Their task was immense, unprecedented and "the procedure is frankly experimental", but they began by reviewing the boundaries and status of the counties and county boroughs. There were 144 of these in England and Wales, and 117 (thirty-seven counties out of sixty-one and eighty county boroughs out of 83) had asked or indicated their intention to ask, for some boundary alteration which in the counties involved relatively small adjustments. Additionally, proposals were received from forty-four local authorities for the creation, either individually or in amalgamation, of thirty-three new county boroughs. The extent and significance of these creations would have had a radical effect upon the counties. As the Report said (at p. 11):

> "The proposals in the case of England would, if adopted in full, increase the area of the county boroughs by at least 2,160,000 acres (266 per cent), and would reduce the population and rateable value of the administrative counties as a whole 26 and $25\frac{1}{2}$ per cent respectively, and, as an extreme example, those of Lancashire by at least 63 per cent in each case."

The counties would never have tolerated such losses which would undoubtedly have destroyed county government, but the county boroughs and those keen on achieving county borough status had nothing to lose from pressing home their respective claims. The many suggestions received by the Commission were classified under three heads:

    (a) Limited extension of county boroughs, in accordance with past policy

    (b) Large extensions of county boroughs, resulting in some areas in the creation of a solid block of county boroughs.

    (c) The creation of new county areas within which all existing county boroughs would relinquish their county borough status.

---

[1] Sir Malcolm Trustram Eve (Chairman), Sir Evelyn John Maude (Deputy Chairman), Sir George Hammond Etherton (resigned January 1947 through ill-health), William Holmes, Sir James Frederick Rees, and Fred Webster (appointed January 1947).

[2] *Report of the Local Government Boundary Commission for the year* 1946, H.C.82, 1946–47, H.M.S.O., p. 3.

It was the Commission's Report for 1947[3] which caused the greatest stir, however, and some 34,000 copies were sold. Having completed two years' work, the Commissioners diagnosed the weaknesses of local government and made specific proposals for remedying them. Their introductory section began:

".. . we may be asked why the Commission after two years of existence have made no single order altering the status or boundaries of any local authority. The answer is to be found in our Report as a whole . . .

"It would have been possible for us to have made some Orders . . . which would, in our view, have resulted . . . in 'effective and convenient units of local government administration' . . . But we have definitely reached the conclusion that in many areas—and these cover the bulk of the population—our present powers and instructions do not permit the formation of local government units as effective and convenient as in our opinion they should be. Thus the alternatives before us were to make Orders which would in many cases have resulted in second best arrangements or, taking the opportunity presented to us by our statutory duty to make an Annual Report, to set out our views. We have chosen the latter course, . . .

"We should add that much of our Report is devoted to the subject of functions of local authorities. Our experience amply confirms the statement made recently in Parliament by the Minister of Health. . . . 'Everyone who knows about local government feels that it is nonsense to talk about functions and boundaries separately. They have to be taken together . . .' We have no jurisdiction over functions."

Having underlined the fault in their terms of reference, the Report outlined the main defects in the system which impeded effective local government and gave rise to frustration:

1. The disparity in size and resources between individual counties, individual county boroughs and county districts, owing partly to historical causes but mainly to structural changes failing to keep pace with population and function changes.

2. The concentrations of population "living in neighbouring towns, which are closely knit as economic and industrial units but have little or no connection or cohesion as local government units", particularly in the five conurbations of the Black Country, Manchester and District, Merseyside, Tyneside and the West Riding, and in smaller degree in Tees-side, the Potteries and the areas in and near Brighton and Bournemouth.

---

[3] *Report of the Local Government Boundary Commission for the year* 1947, H.C.86, 1947–48 H.M.S.O.

3. Increased central control of local government "which, if carried much further, would cut at the root of local government".

4. Haphazard allocation of functions to authorities "without much reference to local government as a balanced organism".

5. Conflicts over boundaries between counties and county boroughs which have been a "constant feature" since 1888 "should cease". To do so: "We have sought a remedy which removes the causes of the battle rather than one which disables either combatant".

The major recommendations were:

(i) There would be three main types of local government units: counties (new counties), county boroughs (new county boroughs) and county districts.

(ii) The whole of England and Wales including the existing county boroughs would be divided into new counties. The bulk would be the existing counties, some being combined and some divided and arranged on a two-tier system; the remainder of the new counties would be large cities and towns, with suitable boundary changes and administration, as now, on a one-tier system. The former would have populations between 200,000 and 1,000,000 and the latter between 200,000 and 500,000.

(iii) The new county boroughs would consist broadly of the middle size towns—boroughs with populations between 60,000 and 200,000 and would include the cities of Liverpool and Manchester which would form the centres of two new counties. They would all be part of the administrative county and would look to the county for certain services but would control a number of important autonomous functions.

(iv) County districts would include all non-county boroughs except those forming new county boroughs and the distinction between urban and rural districts would be abolished. All would have similar autonomous functions.

(v) Delegation of functions by county councils would be effected by "county schemes" taking into account the nature of the function to be delegated and the circumstances of the county and of each second tier authority.

In comparison with the 1947 Report's sixty-seven pages of detailed analysis and recommendations, the 1948 Report consists of eight pages, four of which review the first two Reports. It noted that neither Report had been discussed in the House of Commons, and as a result they had written to the Minister of Health, Mr. Aneurin Bevan, asking for "some idea of the Government's intentions in the matter of local government legislation" and whether their proposals were to be put before Parliament. Four months later, on 29 March, 1949, the reply included a copy of an answer to a Parliamentary question which stated that the Government had "decided that it will not be practicable to introduce comprehensive legislation on local government reconstruction in the near future". The Commissioners nevertheless reiterated in the concluding sentence to the 1948 Report their central belief that "neither we nor our successors can everywhere create effective and convenient units of local government without some amendment of local government legislation".

Very shortly afterwards, in the same year the Boundary Commission was abolished by the Local Government Boundary Commission (Dissolution) Act and the previous procedure for effecting boundary changes was reinstated with minor amendments.

It may well have been "impracticable to adopt the far-reaching changes in local authority areas, status and functions"[4] prescribed by the Commission, but it was also "a promising experiment which might have produced good results",[5] and its complete dissolution a regrettable decision in the light of the virtual standstill in structural reform over the next decade.

Discussions on reform continued at joint conferences between the four Local Authority Associations and the Government, with the Association of Municipal Corporations withdrawing in May, 1952, to prepare a separate statement. The National Association of Parish Councils subsequently joined in the discussions with the remaining three associations and in 1954 they jointly submitted a memorandum outlining their recommendations. The Association of Municipal Corporations submitted a separate memorandum which, not surprisingly, "showed a considerable divergence of opinion". The Joint Report of the four associations stated that "the existing framework of local government has proved to be not only satisfactory but also so flexible as to be capable of modification and evolution without the necessity of any alteration of structure". Its proposals were therefore confined to a preservation of the status quo, with the two-tier system in the conurbations (which were to be defined by the Minister) and administrative counties, and parish councils should be retained as a third tier in rural districts. One-tier government should continue elsewhere, but the nineteen county boroughs with populations under 75,000 should lose status and non-county boroughs outside conurbations were not to be permitted to apply for county borough status unless they had a population of 100,000 or more. This would have made only Luton Municipal Borough and the Rhondda Urban District eligible. The Minister was asked to conduct a general review

---

[4] *Local Government in Britain*, C.O.I. Reference Pamphlet No. 1. 1963, p. 24.
[5] W. A. Robson, *Local Government in Crisis*, Allen & Unwin, 1966, p. 91.

of the boundaries of administrative counties and be authorised to change them by division, amalgamation, or extension if this were necessary to produce effective governmental units. The counties would undertake a similar review of the county districts. Finally, there was some disagreement between the associations on the distribution of services.

The memorandum of the Association of Municipal Corporations "favoured the one-tier system in all-purpose authorities and recommended its extension as far as circumstances allowed" (Cmd. 9831 p. 5). The Association was strongly critical of the proposals of the four associations, rejecting the suggestion that any county boroughs should lose status and moreover advocated 50,000 as a population minimum for county borough status.

At the end of 1954 the new Minister, Mr. Duncan Sandys, met the five associations and his attitude was that,

> ". . . it would not be fruitful to embark on any extensive reform unless there existed some broad measure of agreement among the local authorities themselves. Moreover he made it clear that he did not consider that the existing system of local administration had broken down, and that he would not be prepared to contemplate eliminating either the two-tier system in the counties or the one-tier system in the big towns" (Cmd. 9831 p. 5).

A fresh attempt to find a basis of agreement was thus made and a number of meetings followed culminating in an agreement by the associations' representatives "that this structure works well and that it should be maintained" but that certain matters needed attention. These were: (a) the constitution of all local authorities so as to be effective and convenient local government units; (b) claims by county boroughs to extend their boundaries and by non-county boroughs and urban districts to become county boroughs; (c) the resultant effect upon counties of extensions and promotions claimed; (d) the wish of county districts to exercise "as of right" or by delegation some of the functions discharged by county councils; (e) the need to improve the organisation of local government in the conurbations; (f) the desirability after the necessary changes were made, to avoid further changes for a substantial period.

The policy proposals which catered for these issues and which were referred to the respective associations, stipulated that promotion to county borough status outside conurbations should be considered on the basis of ability to discharge the county borough's functions effectively and conveniently, the effect of the promotion on the county, and a minimum population, whether as a single or an amalgamated authority, of 100,000 unless it could "show exceedingly good reason to justify promotion". Inability by an existing county borough to discharge its functions effectively and conveniently could result in withdrawal of that status. The division, amalgamation, alteration and extension of counties might also be considered as part of any reorganisation. In conurbations the pattern of local government was to be looked at as a whole, with the aim of ensuring, throughout the conurbation, individually and collectively effective and convenient units of local government. The creation, or the boundary extension, of a county borough within a conurbation "should be looked at equally with the need for securing a proper organisation of local government on a two-tier basis in the parts of the conurbation outside county boroughs". Subject to this, applications for promotion to county borough status within conurbations should be treated in the same way as elsewhere *but* the minimum population should be 125,000. Middlesex should be preserved as a two-tier urban county. County councils should review county districts and make recommendations to the Minister for dividing, extending, altering or amalgamating their areas, having regard to such factors as community of interest, economic, and industrial characteristics, financial resources and population, but no non-county borough should lose status without the consent of the Minister and then only after he had held an enquiry to ascertain objections. The policy proposals concluded with a section concerning the extent of delegation of functions within counties, the allocation of responsibility for functions, and the preparation of a "county delegation scheme"; it also noted that the role of parish councils in focussing local opinion should if possible be strengthened.

The implementation of this policy was to be based on the creation of a Local Government Commission which would undertake reviews and, after consultation with all the local authorities concerned, make recommendations regarding, (a) promotion to county borough status; (b) extension of county borough boundaries; (c) withdrawal of county borough status; (d) division, amalgamation, alteration and extension of counties and of areas in conurbations. A separate Commission with similar terms of reference was proposed for Wales. Their reports would be presented to the Minister and their recommendations, subject to the Minister's amendments, would be embodied in orders which Parliament would approve or reject but not amend. After Parliament had made its decision no further changes should be made in the areas, or status of counties or county boroughs for fifteen years unless there were exceptional circumstances.

The Government accepted virtually all the recommendations and in July 1956 issued a White Paper, *Areas and Status of Local Authorities in England and Wales* (Cmd. 9831). It accepted the "far-reaching alterations" which had occurred since 1888 and 1894 but went on to state that "it does not necessarily follow that radical changes in organisation are needed". The structure had withstood the tests of the previous half century and "despite certain weaknesses, had on the whole shown itself capable of adaptation to changing conditions. . . . There is, therefore, no convincing case for radically reshaping the existing form of local government in England and Wales. What is needed is to overhaul it and make such improvements as are necessary to bring it up to date".

4. The Local Government Act 1958

This Act embodied the substance of three white papers, one being that mentioned above. Part II of the Act related to reviews of local government areas in England and Wales and proposed:

1. The establishment of two Local Government Commissions, one for England and one for Wales, to review the organisation of local government in:

(a) five "special review areas" (i.e. Tyneside, West Yorkshire, South East Lancashire, Merseyside and the West Midlands) and

(b) the remainder of England (excluding the metropolitan area) and Wales which were to be divided into "general review areas". The Commissions were to make proposals for changes which were desirable in the interests of effective and convenient local government.

2. The Commissions were bodies corporate with a common seal and each would comprise a chairman, a deputy chairman, and not more than five other members appointed by the Queen.

3. The changes which the Commissions might put forward in their proposals were to be produced by any one, or combination of, the following means:

(a) the alteration of the area of an administrative county or county borough (including the abolition of any county district in the course of the extension of a county borough);

(b) the constitution of a new administrative county by the amalgamation of two or more areas, whether counties or county boroughs, or by the aggregation of parts of such areas or the separation of a part of such an area;

(c) the constitution of a new county borough by the amalgamation of two or more boroughs (whether county or non-county), the conversion of a non-county borough or urban district into a county borough, or the division of an existing county borough into parts and the constitution of all or any of the parts of a county borough.

(d) the abolition of an administrative county or county borough and the distribution of its area among other areas, being counties or county boroughs;

(e) the conversion of a county borough into a non-county borough and its inclusion in an administrative county;

(f) the inclusion of the Isles of Scilly, as one or more county districts, in an administrative county.

4. In the special review areas, the Commission for England might, in addition to the changes in (a) to (f) above, make proposals for:

(a) the alteration of the area of a county district;

(b) the constitution of a new non-county borough by the amalgamation of a non-county borough with one or more other county district;

(c) the constitution of a new urban or rural district by the amalgamation of areas being urban or rural districts or by the aggregation of parts of county districts or the separation of a part of a county district;

(d) the abolition of an urban district or rural district.

(e) the conversion of a rural district into an urban district or of an urban district into a rural district.

Thus in the general review areas the Commissions were concerned mainly with administrative counties and county boroughs, whereas in the special review areas the Commission for England might also deal with county districts and put forward proposals, in certain cases, for the redistribution of functions between county and county district councils. In addition, in special review areas, a wholly new type of local authority was proposed, namely the "continuous county", i.e. a county within which there are no county boroughs.

5. The review procedure would take the following form:

(a) the intention to review an area had to be publicly advertised at least two months beforehand. The Commission would invite written observations from all the local authorities in the area and all public authorities and bodies of persons who appeared to be concerned.

(b) The Commission would investigate the circumstances of local government in the area holding consultations with local authorities and the forementioned bodies.

(c) the Commission would then prepare draft proposals if changes were deemed desirable, and these were to be made available for public inspection.

(d) Representations about the draft proposals might then be made by local authorities and other bodies and these would be discussed at Statutory Conferences called by the Commission.

(e) Following the Statutory Conferences, the Commission would submit their final proposals to the Minister of Housing and Local Government in the form of a Report.

(f) The Minister would publicise the Commission's Report and local authorities and other interested bodies would have a right of objection. If this right were exercised, the Minister would normally hold a public inquiry and he would be under a statutory duty to do so where a local authority objected to being downgraded or abolished.

(g) Having heard any objections, the Minister would embody his decisions in an Order which would be laid before Parliament with the Commission's Report for the approval of both Houses.

6. In each review area county councils must review the circumstances of the county districts and make such proposals for effecting changes which were desirable in the interests of effective and convenient local government. This duty was to be carried out as soon as the reviews by the Commission "have been carried to the point at which it is practicable" for the county. As with the Commission in the special review areas, the county councils might recommend the creation, amalgamation, alteration and abolition of county districts, parish councils and (excepting abolition) of non-county boroughs. In addition, they might recommend the conversion of rural into urban districts, or vice versa, and the inclusion of a borough in a rural district. In this last instance, if the borough wished it, a new type of authority, a rural borough, would be created. The amalgamation of a borough and an urban district would create a new borough.

In carrying out their reviews, the county councils had to consult county district representatives who would have the right of objection to the Minister. In such an instance, provision was made for the holding of a local inquiry. The Minister would give effect to district review proposals through orders tabled in Parliament and subject to annulment in pursuance of a resolution of either House. Each county review would have a separate order, and each review would be followed by a period of at least ten years when no claim for change might be presented.[6]

5. The Local Government Commissions for England and Wales

Both Commissions produced detailed analyses of what they considered to be the organisational defects of their review areas and proposed remedies. Nine reports were issued by the Commission for England and one report by the Commission for Wales and these are briefly summarised below in the order in which they were published.

A. *West Midlands Special Review Area*

The principal recommendation was the creation of five enlarged

---

[6] Circular 35/62, issued on 2 October, 1962, gave further advice to county councils on carrying out the county reviews.

county boroughs in the Black Country based on the existing boroughs of Dudley, Smethwick (now Warley), West Bromwich, Walsall, and Wolverhampton. Despite a court action brought against the Ministry by certain authorities threatened with extinction, the Order was subsequently approved and the five county boroughs became operative on 1 April, 1966. Proposals in the *West Midlands General Review Area* to reduce Burton-on-Trent and Worcester to the status of non-county boroughs were not proceeded with, but Solihull gained county borough status in 1964 and approval was granted for boundary extensions to Coventry and Stoke-on-Trent.

B. East Midlands General Review Area

The draft proposals recommended (a) the abolition of Rutland as a county and its merger with Leicestershire; (b) the creation of a large new administrative county by merging Cambridgeshire, Huntingdonshire, the Soke of Peterborough, and the Isle of Ely; and (c) the granting of county borough status to Luton. The first proposal inaugurated a four-year fight by the small county against "the cloven hoof of Whitehall" to preserve its independence and status; the second proposal was also strongly opposed by the counties affected; but the third proposal was approved in 1964. Rutland finally retained its independent status, while the four counties were formed into the two new administrative counties of Huntingdon and Peterborough and of Cambridgeshire (incorporating the Isle of Ely) in 1965.

C. Wales

The report of the Local Government Commission for Wales was presented in May 1961 and recommended that the thirteen administrative counties of Wales (including Monmouthshire) be reduced by amalgamation to five. The final proposals which followed in December 1962 were: (a) the administrative counties should be reduced from thirteen to seven (Mid Wales, Anglesey, Gwynedd, Flint and Denbigh, West Wales, Glamorgan, and Gwent); (b) the county boroughs of Cardiff, Newport and Swansea should receive certain boundary changes, largely in their favour; (c) the county borough of Merthyr Tydfil should be reduced to non-county borough status and absorbed into Glamorgan; and (d) Rhondda and Wrexham non-county boroughs should not receive county borough status.

In February 1964 the Minister stated that the Government had decided not to implement these proposals because they would not "provide a fully satisfactory basis for an effective local government structure". He proposed that the pattern which reform should take should be reconsidered and that a White Paper would set out suggestions for discussion. This ultimately appeared in July, 1967 (Cmnd. 3340) and proposed a structure based on five counties (later six: Gwynedd, Clwyd, Powys, Dyfed, Glamorgan and Gwent), three county boroughs (as above, with Merthyr Tydfil losing its status), thirty-six (later thirty-five) new districts in place of the existing 164 county districts, and "common councils" at parish level. Legislation to implement the proposals was expected but the debate on the Queen's Speech in October 1969 indicated that there would have to be a new approach in the light of the Redcliffe-Maud proposals for England. The proposal to establish a Welsh Council of nominated members with advisory and promotional duties was, however, proceeded with and it first met in May 1968.

D. *South Western General Review Area*

The final report in 1963 recommended (a) the amalgamation of Torquay, Paignton and Brixham as a county borough to be called Torbay; (b) extensions to the boundaries of Bath, Bristol, Gloucester and Plymouth; (c) county borough status for Cheltenham; and (d) the transfer of Lyme Regis from Dorset to Devon. Ministerial approval was given to the creation of the new county borough of Torbay and it came into being in 1968. The boundary extensions in (b) were also approved, with modifications in respect of Bath, but the minister rejected proposals (c) and (d).

E. *Tyneside Special Review Area*

The Commission proposed that a continuous county, the Tyneside County Council be created consisting of four boroughs, with a population of 900,000 and replacing seventeen existing local authorities. The four boroughs were to be based on the existing county boroughs at Newcastle upon Tyne, Tynemouth, South Shields and Gateshead. The Minister, however, opposed the proposed two-tier structure and recommended that Tyneside should be reorganised as a single all-purpose borough. The reorganisation of the area was still under consideration when the work of the Commission was discontinued in 1965.

F. *North Eastern General Review Area*

The main recommendation was for the creation of a single county borough for the whole of Tees-side, replacing twelve existing local authorities. The Minister accepted the proposal with certain modifications and the new Tees-side C.B. came into being on 1 April, 1968.

Ministerial approval was also given to the extension of Sunderland and to the proposed merger of the Hartlepools into a county borough (came into effect 1 April, 1967).

G. *West Yorkshire Special Review Area*

The final report recommended the creation of a new county borough based on Dewsbury with a population of about 165,000, and the reduction in status of Wakefield county borough whose population (about 60,000) was insufficient for the effective provision of services. No decision had been taken on these proposals, however, when the Commission was disbanded.

H. *York and North Midlands General Review Area*

The main recommendations were aimed at (a) considerably increasing the size and populations of Derby, Doncaster, Hull, Nottingham, Rotherham and Sheffield, and limited boundary extensions for York; (b) the reduction of Barnsley C.B. to non-county borough status; and (c) the transfer of Harrogate and Ripon from the West Riding to the North Riding, and of Scarborough from the North Riding to the East Riding. Proposals (b) and (c) were rejected by the Minister, and certain of the proposals under (a) were accepted with modification.

I. *Lincolnshire and East Anglia General Review Area*

The Commission's proposal to reduce Great Yarmouth C.B. to non-county borough status was rejected by the Minister, as was the proposal to amalgamate the two administrative counties of Holland and Kesteven into a single county. While agreeing to some extension in Lindsey of the city boundaries of Lincoln C.B., the Minister rejected proposals to transfer substantial areas from Kesteven to Lincoln. Certain of the boundary extensions proposed for Grimsby and Norwich were approved, but the amalgamation of Grimsby and Cleethorpes was rejected.

J. *North Western General Review Area*

The draft proposals recommended boundary extensions to Blackburn, Blackpool, Burnley, Carlisle, Chester, Preston, St. Helens, Southport, Warrington, and Wigan, and that Barrow-in-Furness should lose its county borough status. The review of the area was not proceeded with, however, owing to the dissolution of the Commission.

K. *Merseyside Special Review Area*

The main proposal was for a joint planning board to cover Liverpool, Birkenhead, Wallasey, Bootle and an outer area, with representatives from Lancashire and Cheshire county councils and the four Merseyside county boroughs. The board was intended to co-ordinate development and deal with all major planning decisions. The proposals were not proceeded with.

L. *South East Lancashire Special Review Area*

The creation of a new county of 500 square miles and a population of 2½ million was proposed. There was to be a second tier of nine most purpose boroughs which would replace more than sixty existing local authorities. The proposals, if they had been proceeded with, would have entailed a loss by Lancashire and Cheshire of half their existing population.

M. *County Reviews*

Shropshire, Cornwall and Worcestershire undertook internal reviews and submitted reorganisation reports. The Shropshire plan included the merger of Britain's oldest borough, Bishop's Castle, whose charter dated from 1203, with an adjacent rural district to form a rural borough. In July 1966, the Ministry's circular 35/66 announced that county councils were to be relieved of their duty to carry out reviews.

The fifth and last stage was to have comprised the counties of Essex, Hertford and Kent, and the counties falling roughly within a triangle bounded by and including East Sussex, Buckinghamshire and Dorset. However, in December, 1965, the Local Government Commission suspended its operations on its own initiative, and in a letter sent with the Minister's knowledge, told local authorities affected by its reviews in southern and north-western England not to spend more time preparing evidence.

Since the summer of 1965 the Minister had expressed his feelings on a number of occasions about the limited terms of reference and inadequate tools of the Commission. At the annual conference of the Association of Municipal Corporations in September, 1965, he declared that he had seriously considered winding up the Commission, whose boundary review procedures, leading to long delays, had frequently been criticised by local government administrators. The results, however, had proved worthwhile and he had decided that it should continue. He said that the Commission's terms of reference prevented it from producing the reorganisation that local government desperately needed, and the best it could achieve was a patchwork; and when it did a good job of patching in one or two areas, the improvement showed up the threadbare fabric in other areas. He had considered establishing a new commission with clear terms of reference and instructions, but had come to the conclusion that any government would hardly be reckless enough to do so without first agreeing on the principles of reorganisation and analysing the main problems. These he saw as the relation of size and function in modern circumstances and the relation of local democracy and efficiency.

> "There are no accepted principles of reorganisation, no established doctrine according to which a commission could proceed to reshape the areas and the functions of local government so as to enable it to regain the public confidence that has been lost."

The government believed that only a committee which was sufficiently powerful and impartial to command the respect of the parties concerned in the conflict could produce such an analysis. Mr. Crossman stated that he was to discuss with the Local Authority Associations the precise form that the committee should take for he was anxious to get it working quickly as any results from its findings could take up to five years.[7]

In December Mr. Crossman rejected the commission's plan for two-tier government on Tyneside and a few days later the Commission after seven years of intensive and detailed work, voluntarily suspended its activities because of doubts about its future in the context of the Minister's expressed wish for something more radical.

On 10 February, 1966 the Prime Minister announced the appointment of Royal Commissions to undertake a comprehensive review of local government in England and Scotland respectively.[8] Wales was excluded because proposals for the reorganisation of its local government were in an advanced state of preparation and a White Paper was to be produced in due course. Mr. Crossman's statement followed and announced the discontinuation of the review of the Local Government Commission,[9] which had "produced some valuable results within the limits open to it . . . but its terms of reference did not enable it to propose the changes either in structure or in boundaries which fully meet present-day needs". He added that most of

---

[7] *The Times*, 23 September, 1965.
[8] Commons Vol. 724, cols. 638–654.
[9] *Local Government (Termination of Reviews) Act* 1967.

the work which it had completed would be "carried through", and where decisions had been made on its proposals the necessary orders would be presented before Parliament. "Other proposals on which decisions have not yet been taken will be considered on their merits. . . ." He went on to say that the Royal Commission could "do its work in not more than two years. . . . Then the legislation will immediately follow, I hope".

6. Royal Commission on Local Government in England, 1966–69

The terms of reference of the Royal Commission were announced in May, 1966:

> "To consider the structure of local government in England, outside Greater London, in relation to its existing functions; and to make recommendations for authorities and boundaries, and for functions and their division, having regard to the size and character of areas in which these can be most effectively exercised and the need to sustain a viable system of local democracy."

The Royal Commission, under the chairmanship of Lord Redcliffe-Maud, extended an open invitation to anyone who wished to submit evidence on any matter within its terms of reference, and during its three years' existence evidence was taken from 2,156 witnesses. A variety of proposals was made.[10] Some favoured a regional system of elected councils, based roughly on the areas of the Economic Planning Boards and Councils, e.g. the Liberal Party suggested twelve regional authorities, each with a wide range of legislative and executive functions, while N.A.L.G.O. saw regional authorities as first-tier units with executive authority for a wide range of services and a strong second tier handling local matters. Another body of opinion recommended the establishment of a new two-tier structure based on the major authorities, these being variously described as "city regions"[11] or "continuous counties" or "provinces", and

---

[10] I. Gowan and L. Gibson, "A survey of some of the written evidence to the Royal Commission on Local Government in England", *Public Administration*, Spring, 1968; and Chapter 10 of the first edition of this book.

[11] See D. Senior, "The City Region as an Administrative Unit", *Political Quarterly*, Vol. 36, No. 1, where he suggests that England and Wales could be conveniently divided into thirty city region units. The city region was later defined by the M.H. & L.G. as "a conurbation or one or more cities or big towns surrounded by a number of lesser towns and villages set in rural areas, the whole tied together by an intricate and closely meshed system of relationships and communications, and providing a wide range of employment and services".

varying in size between the present counties and the economic planning regions. Some saw the top tier limited to a few functions and emphasized the services to be provided at the local level (e.g. the Association of Municipal Corporations and the Corporation of Secretaries); whereas other bodies (the Institute of Municipal Treasurers and Accountants, the Communist Party, the Confederation of British Industry and several Government Departments) saw the top tier with great operational and executive powers and little emphasis given to the second tier authorities. A third group of proposals centred on a two-tier structure comprising the existing counties with some mergers and the absorption of county boroughs and larger authorities at the local level. These views were largely those of the County Councils Association and the Rural District Councils Association. Another set of proposals suggested a single-tier system of all-purpose authorities only, based on the city region or the continuous county (evidence of the Royal Institute of British Architects, Institute of Local Government Administrators and "The Guardian"). Lastly, a few local authorities recommended the perpetuation of the *status quo*.

After assessing the voluminous evidence and detailed research findings the Commission concluded that: "We are unanimous in our conviction that local government in England needs a new structure and a new map". The Commission stated that English local government was "in a sense a random growth" which had "not been planned systematically in the light of what it has to do and the social and geographical conditions of each place". After commenting upon the "vast changes" with which local government had to deal, the four basic faults in the existing structure, which demanded "drastic change", were outlined: (a) the existing areas failed to fit the pattern of life and work in modern England; (b) the fragmentation implied by the dual system divided town from country, made the planning of development and transportation impossible, and stimulated hostility; (c) services were split between several authorities and so complicated the work of meeting personal needs; and (d) many authorities were too small in size and revenue, and consequently in qualified manpower and technical skill, to fulfil what was required of them. In addition, there were "serious failings in local government's relationships with the public and with national government".

The solution hinged on the "one fundamental question" of "size . . . or range of size, in terms of population and of area", for the "democratic and efficient provision of particular services and for local self-government as a whole". Each of the main services was therefore examined, and it was "decided that the answers to that question must be found by seeking to apply to each part of the country the following general principles":

1. The areas of local authorities "must be so defined" that citizens and councillors "have a sense of common purpose".
2. "The areas must be based upon the interdependence of town and country."
3. In each part of the country all "environmental" services—planning, transportation, and major development—must be run by one authority.
4. Similarly, all "personal" services such as education, personal social services, health and housing should be in the hands of one authority.
5. Both "environmental" and "personal" services should be controlled by a single authority in each area.
6. Authorities must be bigger than most county boroughs and all county districts.
7. The population of each authority should be a minimum of around 250,000.
8. For the personal services a population of 1 million should be the maximum.
9. Where the area required for planning and other environmental services contained too large a population for personal services, responsibilities should be divided between two tiers and related services kept together.
10. Where practicable, the new pattern should stem from the existing one.

In considering the structure which would do most justice to these principles, the idea of the city region which had been advocated by the Ministry of Housing and Local Government and others was examined. It appeared feasible in the great urban concentrations and where a big town was the natural centre for a wide area, but it could not be applied uniformly because "in some parts . . . it did not seem to us to fit reality". Various alternatives were therefore examined, but there was now a growing conviction of the need for (i) "local councils" at the grass roots level "to promote and watch over the particular interests of communities", but not to provide services, and (ii) "provincial councils" to "handle the broader planning issues, work out provincial economic strategy in collaboration with central government and be able to act on behalf of the whole province".

Between the local and provincial councils, the operational authorities with responsibility for the provision of services would have to be areas which: (i) could properly be treated as units for carrying out the "environmental" services; (ii) have populations broadly within the range of 250,000 to not much more than 1 million, the size which would be appropriate for the efficient performance of the "personal"

services; and (iii) could be looked after effectively and democratically by one council. Where there existed areas which met these
three conditions, "the argument in favour of one authority for each
of them would be decisive"; but elsewhere, where the planning
problems of areas with large urban concentrations had to be dealt
with, the single authority would be unwieldy and remote and there
would be need for the division of responsibility between two tiers.

The structure which best gave effect to these considerations was
as follows:

1. England (excluding London) should be divided into sixty-one
   new local government areas, each covering town and country.
2. In fifty-eight of them a single (unitary) authority should be
   responsible for all services.
3. In the remaining three—the metropolitan areas around Birmingham (West Midlands), Liverpool (Merseyside) and
   Manchester ("Selnec"[12])—responsibility for services should
   be divided between:
   (i) the three metropolitan authorities, whose key functions
       would be planning, transportation and major develop-
       ment; and
   (ii) a second tier of twenty metropolitan authorities[13], whose
        key functions would be education, the personal social
        services, health and housing.
4. The sixty-one new areas, together with Greater London,
   should be grouped in eight provinces, each with a provincial
   council. Its key functions would be to settle the provincial
   strategy and planning framework within which the main
   authorities would operate.
5. Provincial councils would be indirectly elected by the authorities for the unitary and metropolitan areas (including the
   Greater London authorities), but would also include a maximum of 25% and a minimum of 20% co-opted members. The
   provincial councils would replace the regional economic
   planning councils.
6. Within the 58 unitary authorities, and wherever they were
   wanted by the inhabitants within the three metropolitan
   areas, local councils should be elected for the area of each
   existing county borough, borough, urban district and parish
   council. The local council would serve as a link between the

---

[12] The designation "Selnec" is an acronym derived from South-East Lancashire
and North-East and Central Cheshire, the area covered.
[13] Seven in the Birmingham area, four in the Liverpool area and nine in the
Manchester area.

public and the main authority, and its most important function, and only duty, should be to make known the views of the local community on any matter affecting it.

In the opinion of the Royal Commission, the main gains resulting from the proposed changes would be: (i) greatly improved service to the public, both in providing a better environment and in taking care of the needs of individual people and families; (ii) more effective use of scarce resources of money and skilled manpower; (iii) increased ability of local governors to meet the challenges of technological and social change; (iv) more likelihood that people would recognise the relevance of local government to their own and to their neighbour's well-being; and (v) the revitalising of local self-government throughout the country, so that in England as a whole the people would have a greater sense of participation in their own government.

One member of the Commission, Mr. Derek Senior, produced a memorandum of dissent in which he proposed a two-level system comprising (a) thirty-five directly elected regional authorities responsible for the planning-transportation-development complex of functions, for capital investment programming, and for police, fire and education; and (b) 148 directly elected district authorities responsible for the health service, the personal social services, housing management, consumer protection and all other functions involving personal contact with the citizen. In four areas regional and district responsibilities would be exercised by the same authority.

These two levels would be complemented, for other purposes, by (i) directly elected common councils at grass roots level, representing existing parishes and towns or parts of towns small enough to have a real feeling of community and to act as a sounding board for opinion; and (ii) five appointed provincial councils with members predominantly nominated by the regional authorities within their areas and responsible for long term strategic planning but having no executive powers.

Mr. Senior also proposed the removal of advanced higher education and parks from local government control, but the acquisition by local government of all branches of the health service, all roads other than national motorways, the management through executives of all ports and airports outside the London Metropolitan Region, and the discharge of all the functions of river authorities.

On 11 June, 1969 the Prime Minister said that the Government

accepted in principle the main recommendations of the Royal
Commission and aimed to reach decisions on the main structural
reforms as soon as possible. In doing so the separate proposals for the
reorganisation of local government in Wales and in Scotland would
have to be taken into account. The 1967 White Paper on Wales had
proposed county amalgamations and, more significantly, had retained the county boroughs. The Report of the Royal Commission
on Scotland (Cmnd. 4150), published in September 1969, proposed
a two-tier system of seven regional and thirty-seven district authorities and non-statutory community councils if required, but rejected
the all-purpose unitary authority and a single all-Scotland authority.
Meantime, in July 1969, the Northern Ireland Government had
produced its proposals for reshaping Ulster's local government
system and had favoured a unitary structure of seventeen area
councils based on the interdependence of town and country.

There had thus crystallised four distinctively different local
government structures for the four parts of the kingdom. Whereas
Scotland and Northern Ireland are likely to retain their separate
systems, the Secretary of State for Wales was required "to make a
further urgent review of the structure in Glamorgan and Monmouthshire" (which contained all the Welsh county boroughs) to work
out a pattern which would "avoid the continual division between
county borc ighs and administrative counties". In October 1969
the Prime Minister annc unced the appointment of a Secretary of
State for Local Government and Regional Planning, with responsibilities for housing, local government, regional planning, land use,
transport and the environment generally; this "overlord" would
take "personal charge of the consultations with the principal local
authority organisations about the future of local government"
and a White Paper would be produced "giving the Government's
conclusions about the main principles in Maud and the main structural change that will form the basis of legislation".[14] The White
Paper *Reform of Local Government in England* (Cmnd. 4276) was published in February 1970 and proposed a structure based on the
retention of fifty-one of the fifty-eight unitary areas recommended by
the Royal Commission, the remaining seven areas being grouped
into two new metropolitan areas; the creation of five metropolitan
areas comprising the three recommended by the Royal Commission
(viz. Merseyside, Selnec and the West Midlands) plus the two new
areas in West Yorkshire and South Hampshire; the deferment of
the proposal for eight provincial councils until the Constitution on

---

[14] *Parliamentary Debates*, Vol. 790, No. 1., 28 October, 1969.

the Commission had reported and the continuation of the regional planning councils; and the adoption of the recommendation for local councils throughout unitary areas and where people wanted them in the metropolitan areas. Further recommendations included: the abolition of the office of alderman, improvements in allowances for councillors and discussions about the size of councils, the timing of elections, and the possible extension of the term of service to four years; liberalizing the law disqualifying local government employees from membership of their employing councils; fewer committees and the delegation of more detail to officers; a review of non-financial controls and a reduction in statutory control; a Green Paper on revenue, with rates remaining the principal local tax; and the appointment of ten or more "local commissioners for administration".

A Bill to introduce the new system was to be brought before Parliament in the 1971–72 session but the General Election of June 1970 intervened and brought an end to the Labour government and its plans. The Conservative manifesto for the election had committed the new government to "a sensible measure of local government reform which will involve genuine devolution of power from the central government and will provide for the existence of a two-tier structure".

7. The Local Government Act 1972

On 16 February 1971 the Secretary of State for the Environment presented to Parliament the White Paper *Local Government in England : Government Proposals for Reorganisation* (Cmnd. 4584) which implemented the pledge in the Conservative election manifesto to "provide for the existence of a two-tier structure". It rejected the unitary concept proposed by the Royal Commission and based the reorganised system on two forms of operational authorities which were referred to as counties and districts.

Forty-four new counties were proposed outside Greater London which would bind together " . . . all of the urban and rural areas within their boundaries". Their populations would range from $\frac{1}{4}$ million to 1 million and "where possible, existing county boundaries will be retained in order to keep the maximum existing loyalties and to minimise the administrative problems". The metropolitan concept was retained in six of the counties, viz. Merseyside, South East Lancashire and North East Cheshire (Selnec), the West Midlands, West Yorkshire, South Yorkshire and the Tyne and Wear area. These six metropolitan counties were to be treated as entities for such major functions as land-use, planning and transportation, but their councils would not administer (as would other county councils) education, personal social services or libraries.

Within the counties the Government proposed a rationalisation of the existing boroughs and districts "so as to provide districts with the resources to carry out efficiently the very considerable responsibilities that will continue to be placed on them". The bigger cities and towns would retain their identities but elsewhere "it would be right to re-unite smaller towns with the rural communities associated with them. Where there is no clear centre to act as a focal point for a new unit, it may still be desirable to form a new district by the amalgamation of rural areas", but the Government must be assured "that the special interests of rural areas are not overshadowed". Even with rationalisation the district boundaries would vary in size but it was expected that they would have populations ranging from 40,000 to 100,000. The districts in the metropolitan areas "will be substantial units in terms of population and resources", and as the Government felt that "services should be administered as locally as possible, it would be right for the district councils here to be responsible for education and the local authority personal social services".

A Local Government Boundary Commission would be established to make recommendations regarding the final pattern of the new districts in the counties outside the metropolitan areas. No decision on any machinery needed for the provinces could be taken before the Commission on the Constitution had reported.

The Government noted the need for authorities at the parish level and wished "to give every encouragement to the existing rural parishes outside the metropolitan counties", but their retention or establishment in urban areas raised different problems.

The White Paper also considered: local authority finance, which would be the subject of a Green Paper; the legislation since 1888 which contained "over a thousand statutory controls by central Government over local government", which the Government intended to reduce; the improvement of allowances to councillors, their term of office, the timing of elections, single member constituencies and the future of aldermen; the disqualification of council employees from council membership; the establishment of a Staff Commission for safeguarding staff interests during reorganisation; and improved arrangements for investigating citizens' complaints.

A Consultative Document *The Reform of Local Government in Wales* was published by the Welsh Office at the same time. This broadly accepted the previous Government's proposals for North, West and Mid-Wales but rejected the proposal that Glamorgan and Monmouthshire should be divided into three unitary areas. It was proposed that Wales should be reorganised into seven new counties and thirty-six districts, most of the counties having populations between 200,000 and 430,000, though East Glamorgan would be over 900,000. Most of the districts would have populations between 40,000 and 100,000. Community councils would be erected at the level of rural parishes and, if residents wished, in urban areas.

The Local Government Act 1972 gave effect, with modifications, to the proposals contained in the White Paper and the Consultative Document. It superseded the Local Government Act 1933 as the principal act in local government and incorporated, with some changes, the provisions of the London Government Act 1963 relating to the constitution of Greater London authorities. The major structural provisions introduced by the act to take effect on 1 April, 1974, were as follows:

1. England, excluding Greater London and the Isles of Scilly, and Wales, now formally including Monmouthshire and Newport C.B., were divided into local government areas known as counties and districts.

    2. In England there were to be forty-five counties:

    (a) Six were to be metropolitan counties covering the major urban conurbations of Greater Manchester, Merseyside, Tyne and Wear, South Yorkshire, West Yorkshire and West Midlands.

    (b) Thirty-nine were to be non-metropolitan counties, the majority of which retained the same names and approximately the same areas as in the previous structure (See Appendix 1).

3. In the six metropolitan counties a second tier of thirty-six metropolitan districts was specified. Provision was also made for non-metropolitan districts to be defined by order or orders made by the Secretary of State on the advice of a Local Government Boundary Commission for England which was to be established, and 296 were so defined and named in orders in 1972 and 1973. The districts replaced the many county boroughs, non-county boroughs, urban and rural districts.

4. In England the parish was retained as a third tier. Every parish was to have a parish meeting comprising local government electors to discuss parish affairs and to exercise any functions conferred by law upon such meetings. Rural parishes having a council before 1 April, 1974, were to continue in existence, and additionally there was to be a separate parish council for each

COUNTY STRUCTURE

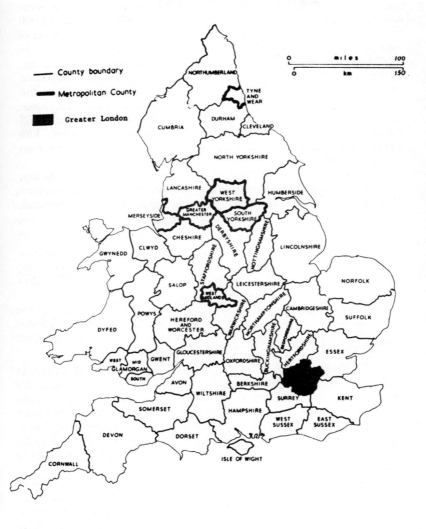

parish which was a rural borough or co-extensive with a rural district, for former boroughs and urban districts designated by the Secretary of State to have "successor" parish councils, and for those divided parishes which were bisected by new county or metropolitan district boundaries.

5. Where no council existed the district council (which replaced the former county council as the authority concerned with order making) was required to establish a parish council

    (a) if the population included 200 or more local government electors, or

    (b) if the population included between 150 and 200 local government electors and the parish meeting had asked for one.

Where the population was below 150 the district council could create a parish council if the parish meeting asked for one. A parish meeting could also ask the district council to group it with another or other parishes to be administered by one parish council, but all the parish meetings involved must agree. The district council was empowered to dissolve the council of a parish which

STRUCTURE OF LOCAL GOVERNMENT FROM 1 APRIL, 1974

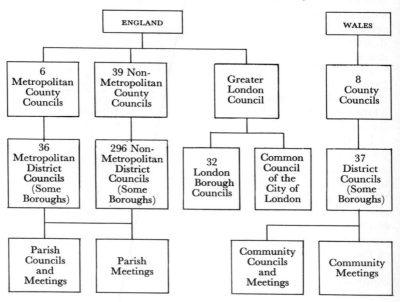

had a separate council and fewer than 150 electors if the parish meeting made such a request.

6. In Wales eight new counties replaced the former thirteen. Except for West, Mid and South Glamorgan, the remainder have names which reflect the historic or traditional associations of their areas: Clwyd, Dyfed, Gwent, Gwynedd and Powys.

7. Within the eight Welsh counties thirty-seven districts were specified. Names were to be given to them by order of the Secretary of State for Wales.

8. There would be no parish councils or meetings in Wales, but every district would consist of one or more communities which would comprise the area of former boroughs, urban districts and rural parishes, and would generally bear the names of the authorities they succeeded. As soon as practicable after 1 April, 1974, a special community review would be conducted by a Local Government Boundary Commission for Wales to propose changes which appeared necessary in the pattern of communities and to decide whether each new community should have a council. Until the review was completed there would be community councils for those rural parishes where there were parish councils.

9. The Secretary of State for Wales was obliged to create other community councils from boroughs or urban districts who applied to him before 1973 or, without application, he could establish a community council for the area of an existing borough or urban district. A community council could also be established by a district council.

10. Community councils would not be established in the "excepted boroughs" of Cardiff, Merthyr Tydfil, Newport, Port Talbot, Rhondda and Swansea because their populations were such a large proportion of the districts with which they would be included, the whole of it in the case of Rhondda.

11. Community meetings comprising local government electors for a community might be convened to discuss community affairs and to examine the very few functions which might be conferred upon them. They were not obliged to meet, and the functions which in England would be performed by parish meetings would almost invariably be exercised in Wales by community or district councils. A community meeting of a community having a separate community council might ask the district council for the dissolution of the community council. A community meeting might also ask the district council to group it with a neighbouring community or communities so long as all the communities agreed; a group of communities or a community meeting might ask the district council

for an order dissolving the group or separating one or more communities from the group.

12. All new district councils would be able to petition the Queen for a Royal Charter of incorporation conferring borough status on the district and enabling their chairman and vice-chairman to have the title of mayor and deputy mayor as from 1 April, 1974. It would also be possible for a district to petition for the grant of any special distinction (such as "Royal Borough", "City", or "Lord Mayor") enjoyed by its predecessor or predecessors.

13. Separate Local Government Boundary Commissions were to be established on a permanent basis for England and for Wales. Their purpose was to review local government boundaries and local electoral arrangements. Both Commissions would be advisory and would report to the appropriate Secertary of State, who could give effect by order to their recommendations. The English Commission, whose chairman would be Sir Edmund Compton, the former Parliamentary Commissioner for Administration, would begin work immediately and its first task would be to make recommendations on the pattern of new districts within the non-metropolitan counties. The Welsh Commission would begin work only after the reorganisation in 1974 and its first task would be to draw up a pattern of communities for Wales and to recommend whether each community should or should not have a community council. Both Commissions were required to take account of the wishes of local inhabitants in making their proposals.

14. These structural changes were to come into effect on 1 April, 1974, when all local government areas existing before that date, excepting Greater London and the Isles of Scilly, and the council of every such area ceased to exist. Additionally, the municipal corporation of every borough outside Greater London and the corporation of every rural borough ceased to exist.

A superficial glance at the county map and the continued use of such familiar names as county, district, borough and parish might suggest a marginal restructuring based broadly upon the former administrative units. The retention of historic names tends, however, to "mask a fundamental change of circumstance" and to suggest "a false air of continuity".[15] The dual system has disappeared with the abolition of the county boroughs, and although the county is retained only five of the forty-five new English counties are identical with the former administrative counties. In Wales

---

[15] W. O. Hart and J. F. Garner, *Hart's Introduction to the Law of Local Government and Administration*, Ninth Edition, Butterworths, 1973, p. 54.

the change is even more radical with the replacement of the former thirteen counties by eight new counties which are completely different in name and area, while the absorbtion into Wales of the administrative county of Monmouth and Newport county borough has created a new boundary between England and Wales. The recognition of the special problems of the major conurbations by the creation of metropolitan counties is yet another major innovative feature of the Act.

The biggest change from the White Paper's proposals was the creation of the new county of Humberside, comprising approximately the former East Riding of Yorkshire, the industrial south bank of the Humber, and northern Lincolnshire as far as and including Grimsby. Other new counties were Avon, created from North East Somerset (despite an active "Save Somerset" campaign) and South Gloucestershire, and including Bristol and Bath; Cumbria, comprising Cumberland, Westmorland, and the Furness district of Lancashire; and the merger of Herefordshire and Worcestershire into what was to have been called Malvernshire but which became, in deference to local opinion, the county of Hereford and Worcester. For the same reason the name of the new county of Teeside, as proposed in the Bill, was changed to Cleveland, and the new metropolitan county of Tyneside was renamed as Tyne and Wear.

At the second tier, 369 new districts replaced the 83 county boroughs, 259 municipal boroughs, 522 urban districts and 469 rural districts. In all 1,333 authorities were reduced to less than a quarter of that number. The population figures of the districts show considerable variation:

	Metropolitan		*Non-Metropolitan*		
			England		*Wales*
Largest Birmingham	1,087,660		Bristol	421,880	Cardiff 285,760
Smallest South Tyneside	172,990		Teeside	24,060	Radnor 18,670

One-third (121) of the non-metropolitan districts have populations below 75,000, which is the minimum of the preferred population range.

At the third tier the difference between the English and Welsh structures is marked. In England rural parishes were not affected by the reorganisation and their parish meetings and councils continued to exist from 1 April, 1974. So too did the councils of former boroughs and urban districts as "successor" parish councils which were created by the Secretary of State on the advice of the Local Government Boundary Commission. Each is a clearly distinguishable community with a population of fewer than 20,000 and less than 20 per cent of the new district population. Their councils have the same powers as existing parish councils and they have the right to adopt town status and have a town mayor. The successor parishes of Ely, Ripon and Wells have been granted city status. In Wales all the former parishes were abolished on 1 April, 1974, to be replaced by a system of communities which, unlike the English parishes, cover the whole country. All the communities have community meetings and some also have community councils.

A measure of corporate unity was given to the new authorities by the formation of local authority associations which superseded those created after the Local Government Acts of 1888 and 1894. The Association of County Councils was formed in July, 1973, and all the non-metropolitan counties are members of the Association. The Association of Metropolitan Authorities consists of the metropolitan county and metropolitan district councils, the Greater London Council (including the I.L.E.A.), the London Borough councils and the Corporation of the City of London. The Association of District Councils comprises the non-metropolitan district councils in England and the district councils in Wales.

Their objectives are to protect and further the interests of their member authorities as they may be affected by legislation or proposed legislation, to provide a forum for discussing matters of common concern and a means for formulating joint views, and to provide appropriate central services.

In addition, there are the London Boroughs Association, formed in 1964 to advise and assist its constituent authorities, and the National Association of Local Councils which is a federation of county associations formed in 1947 to promote the interests of local councils, and now of parish and community councils, and to foster the co-operation of these councils with other local authorities.

Initial reactions to the reorganisation proposals varied considerably. When the White Paper was published in February 1971 *The Economist* (20 February) referred to its contents as a "lame duck reform" which "in certain key respects" was "a disaster of political prejudice" surpassing "the wildest dreams of the conservative clubs of Worcestershire and Wilmslow". The proposals were compared unfavourably with the "bold reform scheme" of the Redcliffe-Maud Report, but those for Wales and Scotland were praised as "more thorough and convincing jobs". However, in the context of the reduction in the numbers of authorities it was forecast that "there will be much more efficiency and, on the whole, better and more varied services". The *Daily Telegraph* was delighted with "this workmanlike and thoroughly Tory piece of reform", but *The Guardian* headed its leader "No cheers for two tiers". *The Times* was marginally in favour, though with several reservations, seeing the main weaknesses in the division of functions between the tiers and the narrow confines of the metropolitan boundaries which "betrays too simple a belief in the green belt as a governing principle of town and country planning, and does less than justice to the acute social problems of the conurbations". The *Daily Mail* thought that some county councils would be too remote and impersonal, and the *Daily Express* deplored the sweeping away of traditional bonds with the community. Reaction in the provincial press reflected local fears of loss of status or autonomy (*Nottingham Evening Post* and *Birmingham Post*) or satisfaction with proposed territorial gains (*Liverpool Echo*), while the *Western Mail* and *The Scotsman* concentrated on the national and political implications of the proposals and the lack of more independence from Whitehall.

The abolition of the county borough was particularly regretted. Baroness Sharp, former Permanent Secretary at the Ministry of Housing and Local Government, castigated the "indefensible political gerrymandering" and referred to the county borough as potentially the strongest and most creative organisation in local government. Professor Stewart, Associate Director of the Institute of Local Government Studies, regarded the demise of the county borough as "a decisive step backwards in the management of urban problems" (*Municipal Review*, August, 1972).

Others questioned the synonymous usage of "reorganisation" and "reform" and the assumption that the former necessarily entailed the latter.[16] R. A. W. Rhodes of INLOGOV cogently argued that local government had been reorganised but had certainly not been reformed, that its capacity to carry out its functions effectively had been weakened and that reorganisation had been effected "without considering the basic question of what is the desirable distribution of functions between central and local government". Local government had lost functions to other governmental units and the need to co-ordinate four organisations, the two tiers and the health and water authorities, would greatly weaken comprehensive planning. Membership of the E.E.C. would also create "pressures for a regional tier of government". Local

---

[16] Note the observation of Gaius Petronius in *Satyricon*: "We tend to meet any new situation by reorganising, and a wonderful method it can be for creating the illusion of progress while producing confusion, inefficiency and demoralization."

government now needed to be "reformed so that it is in a position to meet the challenges of the 1970s".[17]

Equally critical was G. W. Jones of the London School of Economics who stated that the new authorities were still too small and too numerous, and that the metropolitan districts appeared to be too small to tackle the major problems of urban life. The new areas did "not fit the facts of social geography", while the tiers fragmented local government and made it difficult for the citizen to understand. There was a failure also in the confused allocation of functions and this could only produce tension and conflict, and "frustrate corporate planning—or planning of any sort". He claimed that central control was not diminished, that the new structure marked the end of urban government, that popular representation was reduced, that greater demands would be made on staff and members, and that expenditure would increase. It was "an inadequate Act" which would not enable "a strong local governmental system to tackle and defeat the social problems of the future".[18]

The validity of these opinions will be corroborated or disproved only when the new system has had sufficient time to settle down to deal with the manifold and complex tasks which confront it. To redress the weight of criticism the opinions of Lord Redcliffe-Maud, who chaired the Royal Commission whose proposals for reorganisation so nearly became the basis of a new system, are significant. He was in no doubt that the reorganisation proposals did amount to reform: "I am prepared to prophesy that the students and historians of the future will most emphatically refer to this Bill as local government reform. I believe quite seriously that you must go back to the great Statute of Queen Elizabeth I in 1601 to find any measure as comprehensive and important. . . . But I believe that the 1972 Act . . . will rank as the first major systematic and comprehensive measure which Parliament has placed on the Statute Book in the field of local democracy in this country." Some months earlier he had asked rhetorically if the results of reorganisation were going to be "worth all the turmoil" and he stated: "I believe it will be worth while, because I think there is a good chance of our children and grandchildren living to bless us for this great and drastic change in local government."[19]

---

[17] R. A. W. Rhodes, "Local Government Reform: Three Questions", *Social and Economic Administration*, Spring 1974.

[18] G. W. Jones, "The Local Government Act 1972 and the Redcliffe-Maud Commission," *The Political Quarterly*, April–June 1973.

[19] H.L. Deb., Vol. 335, cols. 2040–1, 19 October, 1972, and Vol. 334, col. 61, 31 July, 1972.

CHAPTER 3

Local Government in Greater London

1. The City and its Environs to the Nineteenth Century

Throughout its long history the City of London has displayed a singular ability to withstand external threats to its independence and an unwavering tenacity in preserving its unique governmental system. As early as A.D. 61 it was already "a town of the highest repute and a busy emporium for trade and traders" and it developed to become the centre of provincial government under the Romans.

Its fortunes declined after the Roman departure in A.D. 410 and little is known of its fate during the subsequent centuries when the teutonic invaders established their communities throughout the present home counties. As the emergent kingdoms of the Saxons crystallised into being, London was gradually resurrected and its commercial life and community organisation developed together. Its growing prosperity attracted the plundering Danes in A.D. 839 and again after 1010, but the City survived and continued to maintain its autonomy and privileges. Deriving its power from trade and finance, its leaders excluded even the monarch, and it is significant that the restored Saxon dynasty in the person of Edward the Confessor established his governmental seat not in the City but beyond its walls at Westminster.

From William the Conqueror the City received a charter ratifying the rights and privileges of its citizens, and in 1132 a further charter recognised its full county status and granted unrestricted freedom in the choice of a Sheriff.

By this time the City's ward structure was almost fully formed, with twenty wards in existence in 1130. By the beginning of the thirteenth century there were twenty-four wards; in 1394 Farringdon was divided into two wards and in 1550 Bridge Without was created, bringing the complement to twenty-six. The last named ward no longer exists, but an alderman still represents it. Each ward had its wardmote comprising one hereditary alderman, who generally gave the ward his name, and common councilmen whose numbers varied according to the size of the ward. They performed such public services as existed and had wide powers in preserving the peace and for imposing sanctions.

In 1141 the citizenry confederated into a single community and London's first mayor was appointed in 1192 to supersede the Sheriff of London and Middlesex who had formerly governed the City.

Territorially, the City has barely changed since the Norman Conquest, with its boundaries enclosing an area of 677 acres. Its governmental machinery originated during the years chronicled above and its present constitution reflects the outward semblance of a far distant age.

The City of London possesses no charter of incorporation but is a corporation by prescriptive right, and functions through three institutions which themselves originated in the ancient assemblies of the Folkmoot, the Husting and the Wardmote:

A. *The Court of Common Hall*

This was developed from the Congregation of all freemen who elected the main municipal officers. By the thirteenth century the assembly had become too large for Guildhall, and attendance came to depend upon a personal summons issued by the Mayor and Aldermen.

In the fourteenth century prominent citizens in the wards were also summoned, but by the mid-fifteenth century only Common Councilmen and "other powerful and discreet citizens" were called upon to attend.

In 1467 the masters and wardens of the guilds were invited, and eight years later the liverymen of the companies replaced the Ward notabilities. This privilege was confirmed by statute in 1725 requiring electors to be freemen and liverymen of at least one year's standing.

A Common Hall is summoned by precept from the Lord Mayor to the masters and wardens of the Livery Companies, and on 29 September the assembly nominates two Aldermen who have served as Sheriffs to be presented to the Court of Aldermen who elect one Lord Mayor, two Sheriffs, a Chamberlain, Bridgemasters, Aleconners, and Auditors of the Chamberlain's and Bridgemasters' Accounts are elected on 24 June by the Court of Common Hall.

B. *The Court of Aldermen*

This is generally believed to have developed from the weekly meetings of the pre-Conquest Court of Hustings where each Alderman, representing his Ward, discussed matters of common concern and determined municipal policy for the federal City.

The Court provided centralised and unified civic administration, and became responsible for the organisation and control of essential public services until the seventeenth century. They possessed great powers and exercised judicial and administrative functions.

Nowadays the Aldermen are elected by the Ward voters, unlike those in any other local authority, and hold office for life. The Court meets about fifteen times a year and is presided over by the Lord Mayor. Their functions are still extensive and include *inter alia*, the final choice between the two candidates presented by the Liverymen for the office of Lord Mayor; the adjudication of disputed elections of Common Councilmen and on alleged election irregularities; the approval of the terms of the livery companies' charters of incorporation; the granting of consent to the wearing of livery; and the administration of justice in their capacity as J.Ps.

C. *The Court of Common Council*

It was customary for important decisions at the Folkmoot or the Court of Hustings to be put before the citizens, or commonalty, for assent, and it is from such direct democracy that the Court of Common Council originated. Ward representatives later came to be consulted by the Mayor and Aldermen and in the thirteenth century the concept of representation was extended by summoning representatives to discuss matters affecting the City.

Further developments between 1319 and 1384 led to the establishment of a permanent Common Council, chosen by the citizens of the wards "to treat the arduous affairs affecting the Commonalty". The court persisted and grew in power over the following centuries as an elected, though strictly limited, representative council when regressive oligarchic control characterised the management of local affairs throughout the remainder of the kingdom.

During the seventeenth century it superseded the Court of Aldermen as the main governing body, and absorbed its major executive and administrative functions.

To-day it consists of the Lord Mayor, twenty-five other aldermen and 159 Common Councilmen. Working through more than thirty Committees, the court undertakes (i) all the ordinary functions of a London Borough (q.v.) financed by rates, and (ii) a number of special activities financed by revenue from the City's Cash and Bridge House Estates—such activities include the running of the Corporation's four City Schools, Open Spaces outside the City like Epping Forest, and four City Bridges, etc.

These municipal institutions and the men who served them guided the fortunes of the mediaeval city to an unparalleled eminence in power and prosperity. In their dual role as leaders of great merchant companies and as mayors or aldermen, they governed London with the same shrewdness which had built their trading empires.

Outside the city the Saxon communities provided the nuclei of many of Greater London's towns and villages. These were firmly established by the eighth century, as were the shire outlines of Essex, Middlesex, Kent and Surrey.

London was excluded from the Domesday Survey of 1086 but the parishes on the periphery were well documented. The drift of population from country to town had already begun, but the city's jurisdiction extended no further north than the bars which had been set up on the roadways outside the city walls by the thirteenth century or earlier. South of the Thames, Southwark had developed as a strategic bridgehead settlement in Roman and Anglo-Saxon days, becoming a busy concentration of prosperous workshops during the early mediaeval period as Chaucer's pilgrims gathering at *The Tabard* would have seen.

Communities of such substance were few, however, and the growth of the city's suburbs into the afforested hinterland was gradual. The local services which existed were based upon the same customary communal activities which typified the rest of the country.

By the late sixteenth century the population of London and its environs had grown to approximately 300,000; and the expansion of commercial activity stimulated the growth of many towns such as Uxbridge, and London expanded rapidly westwards and down-river to Stepney, Deptford and Woolwich. To the *Liberties* adjoining the city walls were attracted the poor migrants from the shires and Europe, and overcrowded slums developed.

The opportunity occasioned by the Great Fire of 1666 for the systematic rebuilding of the City was not taken, and the suburbs spread outwards as land speculation and building increased. The population had grown to 674,350 by 1700, and although many of the outlying communities were still rural in character and continuing to supply London with their produce, by the end of the seventeenth century the signs of a coming industrialism could be seen in embryo in the dockyard towns of Deptford and Woolwich.

The coaching era stimulated further extension into the outskirts during the eighteenth century, and in some directions an almost continuous development stretched from the city to a distance of five or six miles. Many of the outlying towns such as Twickenham, Richmond and "Royal" Kensington were themselves growing to meet the spreading London perimeter. The movement was mainly westwards towards the City of Westminster whose jurisdiction began at the Strand. Unlike the City of London, whose 12,000 ratepaying householders democratically elected their aldermen and common councillors, the City of Westminster was not self-governing but was controlled by twelve burgesses appointed for life by the High Steward. Their control was tenuous, however, and their powers were gradually being absorbed by the J.Ps. and the parish vestries in the area. The titled, the wealthy middle class, the civil servants and the professional men came to reside in the fashionable "Squares" around Covent Garden, Piccadilly, St. James's, and the rich merchants, closely followed by the upper middle class, established their country houses anywhere within a twenty mile radius of the City of London.

2. The Nineteenth Century

The land to the south of the river was opened to the speculative builders after the construction of Westminster Bridge in 1750, Vauxhall Bridge in 1816, Waterloo Bridge in 1817, Southwark Bridge in 1819, Hammersmith Bridge in 1827 and the new London Bridge in 1831. To the east in Bethnal Green an estate was built for the locally employed weavers, and in the eastern and northern suburbs rows of working-class cottages became more common. By 1835 the built-up area of the metropolis, Cobbett's "Great Wen", had extended to approximately twenty-two square miles, with a population of over one million people. They were ill-served by about 172 vestries and a confusion of *ad hoc* bodies, the latter comprising seven boards of commissioners of sewers, nearly one hundred paving, lighting and cleansing boards, a number of boards of guardians set up by the 1832 Poor Law Reform Act, several commissioners of highways and bridges, and numerous turnpike trusts, commissioners of police and of woods and forests, grand juries, inquest juries, leet and annoyance juries, the Middlesex bench of magistrates and the salaried police magistrates.[1]

The suggestion that the City of London should follow the practice of the newly created boroughs (under the 1835 Municipal Corporations Reform Act) and assimilate the surrounding suburbs, was rejected by the City Corporation who saw no reason to relinquish its exclusive status for the dubious privilege of becoming responsible for the problems of such a vast and heterogeneous conurbation. To have done so would have entailed a radical alteration in the character of City government and this suggestion was steadfastly and successfully rejected, as were so many future attempts to change the City.

In 1854 a Royal Commission reported on the problems of control posed by the multiplicity of distinct communities which made up the

---

[1] W. A. Robson, *The Government and Misgovernment of London*, Allen & Unwin 1948, p. 21.

vast urban sprawl of Geater London and by the unco-ordinated activity of 300 or so different *ad hoc* bodies which "carried out what parody of local government there was".[2] Such problems, the Commission felt, would not be solved by bringing the entire area of 75,000 acres with a population which by now had grown to 2,800,000 people living in 260,000 houses under the aegis of an extended City Corporation. They recommended the establishment of a body with responsibility for certain services over the entire area, and to this end the Metropolitan Board of Works was created by the Metropolis Local Management Act of 1855.

The Metropolitan Board of Works comprised forty-five members and a paid chairman, the members being indirectly elected for three years by the vestries of the larger parishes and by the district boards which represented combinations of the smaller parishes. The Board was given responsibility for drainage, paving, cleansing, lighting and improvement in the area of the former Metropolitan Commissioners of Sewers (1848). This area comprised approximately 117 square miles with its central areas in Holborn, Westminster, Kensington, the Thames-side parishes and parts of the East End and south-east districts being fully built over, but over a half of the entire area was undeveloped land. The Board had no control over the City of London.

The Board's main task was to build a sewer system to stop sewage entering the Thames, and within a decade a main drainage system had been constructed to outfalls outside the town. The Board also took over control of the river embankment, many of its bridges and the prevention of Thames floods; it undertook metropolitan street construction and improvements[3]; and it ran the fire engine establishment of the London fire insurance companies from 1866, and in 1867 the Society for the Protection of Life from Fire; by Acts of 1874 and 1875 it was given power to regulate offensive trades and explosives in the metropolis; it was the authority under the 1875 Artisans and Labourers Dwelling Act, and under other legislation controlled the height and frontage line of buildings; and for building control purposes the Board divided London into sixty-seven districts.

Despite the extensive improvements accomplished, the Metropolitan Board of Works had a number of defects. It was indirectly elected; there was no central government control; and, in particular, it lacked executive authority over the vestries and district boards who were frequently neglectful in executing their responsibilities for street paving, cleansing, watering and lighting. Additionally, there

---

[2] K. B. Smellie, *A History of Local Government*, Allen & Unwin, 1949, p. 180.
[3] Roads from Blackfriars Bridge to Westminster Bridge, from Lambeth to Vauxhall, Southwark Street (1864) and Holborn Viaduct (1869).

co-existed other major *ad hoc* bodies in the Metropolitan Asylums Board (1867), the London School Board (1870) and the Port of London Sanitary Authority (1872). The result was a lack of standardisation and coordination of services with irresponsibility and neglect characterising much of the work of the minor authorities.

Meanwhile, major population changes had been further stimulated by railway developments after 1836. Terminals were built at London Bridge, for the Greenwich line, in 1836; at Euston in 1838 and at Cannon Street in 1866. The Victoria and Hungerford Bridges, completed in 1862 and 1864 respectively, brought passengers from the South to Victoria and Charing Cross; the Liverpool Street and Holborn Viaduct of 1874, and the Blackwall Tunnel of 1897, linking Poplar with Greenwich also helped to promote Victorian London's growth. It was now easy for the town-worker, whatever his economic status, to flee the overcrowded centre and set up his family in one of the many contrasting architectural assortments of Victorian surburbia which suited his pocket. The commuters who swarmed into London added to the centre's traffic congestion for they needed conveyance from the railway terminals to their work. After years of violent opposition Charles Pearson's "sewer railway", the underground system, was eventually begun in 1860 by the North Metropolitan Railway Company, and the line from Paddington to Farringdon Street was opened in 1863. Railways extended to the suburbs and with direct access to the commercial centre business premises were established in the environs, and communities quickly grew around the source of employment. Row upon row of terraced houses, supplemented by the conversion of many of the elegant residences of former years into tenements, accommodated working-class families, and within a few decades rural serenity gave way to densely populated towns.

Many of the work-hungry immigrants to Greater London brought poverty with them and, if unemployed for any length of time, they would gravitate to nauseous tenements and insanitary overcrowded slums, creating social problems which the parish vestries were incapable of remedying. Population growth rates were unprecedented; West Ham grew from 2,500 in 1801 to 267,000 in 1901, a century when 130 factories were established there; even the comparatively sedate Hammersmith grew from 25,000 to over 150,000 in the second half of the century alone; Willesden, on the Metropolitan line, grew from 750 in 1851 to 16,000 in 1871 and 115,000 in 1901; and Walthamstow, after the laying of the Chingford line in 1870–73 increased from 11,000 in 1871 to 97,000 in 1901.

Population increases on this scale coupled with the obvious inadequacies of local government to cope with the manifold problems necessitated radical remedial action. The Local Government Act, of 1888 attempted to resolve the situation with the creation of a new authority to replace the Metropolitan Board of Works.[4] The area of the Metropolitan Board of Works became the Administrative County of London and the Board's powers were slightly increased and vested in the new London County Council made up of 124 councillors[5] and twenty aldermen. The main new powers were the right to oppose bills in Parliament, to appoint medical officers and to contribute to the maintenance or enlargement of highways. A number of *ad hoc* bodies such as the Metropolitan Asylums Board, the London School Board, the Boards of Guardians, Burial Boards, the Thames and Lee Conservancy Boards, and the Metropolitan and City Police Forces remained, as did the vestries and district boards. The City was included in the London County Council for administrative purposes, but for "non-administrative" purposes (i.e., functions performed by quarters sessions, J.Ps. coroners, sheriffs, etc.) it remained a separate body.

The reluctance of the legislators to extend the powers of the London County Council beyond those noted, or to limit the number or powers of the multiplicity of authorities which had contributed to the abuses and disunity of the previous administration was largely motivated by the fear that such a large council in the capital was becoming dominated by radical interests. This same fear is alleged to have influenced Balfour's London Government Act of 1899 which divided the county of London into twenty-eight metropolitan boroughs on the basis of the old vestry outlines. This act gave the metropolitan boroughs the same powers as county boroughs in promoting and opposing bills, and, according to Professor Smellie:

> "everything was done to make them a political and administrative counterweight to the possible prestige of a reforming London County Council".[6]

The two-tier pattern of government completed by the 1899 Act remained in existence for over sixty years. The principal powers of the London County Council were: housing, which service was operated in conjunction with the metropolitan boroughs, town and country

---

[4] The Board had become progressively corrupt and a series of scandals involving improper transactions culminated in an investigation by a Royal Commission in 1888.

[5] Two councillors for each of London's sixty Parliamentary divisions plus four members elected by City electors.

[6] K. B. Smellie, *op. cit.*, p. 183. See also W.A. Robson, *op. cit.*, pp. 84–99 for account of hostility against London County Council.

planning, education, welfare services, parks and open spaces, entertainment, finance[7], care of children, health services, fire service, civil defence, main drainage, municipal trading, bridges, youth service and bye-laws. The metropolitan boroughs, each with its mayor, aldermen[8], and councillors, were responsible for housing, public health, libraries, rating, bye-laws, entertainments, finance, roads and highways, parks and open spaces, baths and washhouses, and recreational facilities.

Several *ad hoc* bodies administered services both within and outside the London County Council area, and foremost amongst these were the Metropolitan Police Force, whose jurisdiction covered most of London with the exclusion of the City, the Metropolitan Water Board, the London Transport Executive operating over a radius of twenty five miles from the City, and the Port of London Authority.

Suburban London, however, soon grew beyond the 1888 boundary, spilling into the adjoining local authorities, and an impression of this outward growth is given by the following table of census returns.

POPULATION OF INNER AND OUTER LONDON FOR SELECTED
YEARS, 1851–1961

Census Year	Inner London		Outer London	
	Popl. '000's	Per cent popl. change	Popl. '000's	Per cent popl. change
1851	2,363	—	322	—
1881	3,830	+62	940	+192
1901	4,536	+18	2,050	+118
1951	3,348	−26	5,000	+144
1961	3,195	−5	4,977	−0·46

For convenience, Inner London is equated with the London County Council area, and Outer London with the Registrar General's conurbation (720 square miles), but excluding Inner London. The table shows clearly how the former has decreased from its peak in 1901 and the latter continually increased. Similarly at the centre, the

---

[7] L.C.C. derived its income from precepts upon the metropolitan boroughs and the City Corporation, grants-in-aid, rents, charges and payments and trading undertakings.

[8] Aldermen numbered one-sixth of the councillors on the metropolitan boroughs and on the L.C.C.

City of London, which had experienced steady depopulation from the seventeenth century, declined from 120,000 in 1801 to 26,000 in 1901, and by 1966 had a night population of 4,580.

This overflow of population outwards from the centre has been accelerated during the present century by a number of factors: slum clearance and rehousing policies; redevelopment and the replacement of living areas by office accommodation, particularly in the commercially prestigious central area; the advent of the low-priced family car and the ubiquity of omnibus and underground railway services have increased individual mobility; the rash of speculative building between 1918 and 1939 which doubled the built-up area of London;[9] ribbon development along new arterial and by-pass roadways; air raids during the Second World War and consequent population dispersal; shortage of attractive building sites; natural population increase; the employment growth; the continual attraction of London for immigrants from the provinces and beyond. All these factors and others have combined to increase and redistribute the population, from the City and the metropolitan boroughs of inner London to the ever-expanding communities in the outer zone, and in the process engulfing all Middlesex and parts of Essex, Kent, Surrey and Hertfordshire.

3. The Reorganisation of London Government

During the inter-war years a number of inquiries and a Royal Commission (the Ullswater Commission) into local government in Greater London proved abortive. Meanwhile the problems of this vast amorphous area, of approximately 720 square miles and a population of over eight million, multiplied. Within this urban agglomeration over ninety local authorities carried out their separate functions, with varying resources and degrees of efficiency, and no single overall authority existed to co-ordinate services and be responsible for the problems of the area as a whole, particularly in the sectors of housing, roads and town and country planning.

Concern for these problems led, in the post-war years, to the 1945 Reading Committee's examination of the number, size and boundaries of the metropolitan boroughs and the distribution of functions between them and the London County Council. The Committee was finally dissolved because it could not separate the problems of the London County Council from those of Greater London as a whole. In 1946 the Clement Davies Committee came to the conclusion that a

---

[9] J. T. Coppock and H. C. Price, *Greater London*, Faber & Faber, 1962, p. 29.

review of the London region should be undertaken by a local government commission, but no action followed. Finally, in opening the debate on the three White Papers of 1957, referred to on page 38, *ante*, the Minister of Housing and Local Government indicated his intention to set up a Royal Commission to examine the problems of Greater London.

In November, 1957 the Royal Commission on Greater London was established with six members under the chairmanship of Sir Edwin Herbert (now Lord Tangley). Their unanimous report was issued in October, 1960 and in its 400 pages the inadequacies of the existing structure were analysed and recommendations for their resolution detailed.

The Royal Commission noted that:

> "The machinery is untidy and full of anomalies. There is overlapping, duplication, and in some cases, gaps. . . . The fact that local government in London does manage to hang together and avoid a breakdown says much for the British knack of making the most cumbrous machinery somehow work. . . . We are convinced that the choice before local government in Greater London is . . . to abdicate in favour of central government, or to reform so as to be equipped to deal with present-day problems. A surrender to central government . . . would be the death-knell of local government in the review area. Local government means local self-government."

The reforms which the Royal Commission advocated entailed a major structural reorganisation and included:

1. The abolition of London and Middlesex county councils.
2. The creation of a Council for Greater London which would include the London County Council area, nearly all Middlesex county council, the county boroughs of Croydon, East Ham and West Ham, and the metropolitan areas of Essex, Kent, Surrey and Hertfordshire.
3. The amalgamation of the ninety-five local authorities in the area to fifty-two, to be termed Greater London Boroughs.
4. The retention by the City of London of its powers and functions, the Court of Common Council to possess the same powers as a Greater London Borough.

In addition, detailed suggestions were made relating to the constitution of the new authorities and to the allocation and administration of functions.

The Report was studied by the Conservative Government for more than a year and the opinions of over a hundred interested local authorities were heard before a White Paper was issued in November, 1961. It stated that the Government generally accepted the Commission's main recommendations but added that the boroughs should be larger and therefore fewer, and that the educational arrangements were not satisfactory. The White Paper concluded with a declaration of the Government's intention to examine the details further with local authorities before legislative proposals could be presented to Parliament, and added that "the change-over should be made at the earliest practicable date". Some days later the Minister of Housing and Local Government sent a circular to all interested local authorities detailing the Government's proposals for a Greater London of thirty-four boroughs each with a population of 180,000 to 360,000.

Opposition to the Government's plans came mainly from the following sources:

A. *The London County Council*

With a Labour majority for nearly thirty years, the London County Council had "resolutely refused to discuss" with the Herbert Commission, "any of the wider issues of the government of London as a whole," and stuck firmly to the proposition that "'London' and the Administrative County of London are synonymous terms and that the London County Council is the government of London".

The opposition had not abated by March, 1962 when at the end of an eighteen-hour debate at County Hall, the second longest in the council's history, the London County Council adopted a resolution by its General Purposes Committee which said that the Government's proposals would offer few, if any, practical advantages to offset the disorganisation and disruption of existing services which would be entailed, and requested the Prime Minister (Harold Macmillan) to receive a deputation as a matter of urgency.

The Prime Minister received the deputation in April but despite the appeal made to reconsider the proposals, he felt that no fundamental changes to the plan were necessary. This was followed in July by a further resolution by the London County Council to refuse to co-operate with the Government in implementing the reorganisation.

B. *Certain Affected Authorities*

Middlesex county council was also unwilling to agree to its own demise, stating in February, 1962 that "there was no justification for destroying the fabric of local government in Middlesex and indeed in Greater London", and requesting the Government to "think again so as to . . . avoid the enormous disruption which could well have a paralysing effect on the public for many years to come". Similarly, Surrey County Council urged the Government not to proceed with its proposals, "the drastic nature of which cannot be justified."

C. *The Parliamentary Labour Party*

The Party announced its opposition to the plan shortly before a two-day debate in February, 1962 on a Government motion "taking note" of the White Paper proposals. One of the plan's bitterest antagonists was Lord Morrison of Lambeth, who as Herbert Morrison had been for many years leader of the council's Labour group and Chairman of the London County Council. During the debate on the White Paper he said:

> "Hitler tried to destroy London and failed. Now the Conservative Party, for Party political reasons, is trying to destroy the municipality of the Capital City. It is my belief and hope that they will no more succeed than did Hitler".[10]

Another former chairman of the London County Council, Lord Latham, later said of the Bill that it was

> "the most insidious ever introduced in the history of local government . . . conceived in malice, born in iniquity, and will function in confusion . . . may the wrath of the people descend upon those who have done this wicked thing . . ."

The Government's final pattern for Greater London was drawn up by an independent panel composed of the Town Clerks of Plymouth, Cheltenham, Oxford and South Shields. They investigated objections and suggestions by the local authorities involved and their recommendations were accepted by the Government without modification.

The London Government Bill was published on 22 November, 1962, and during its passage through Parliament some 1,000 amendments were suggested in the House of Commons, it occupied four days in a Committee of the Whole House and twenty-one sittings in Standing Committee. Additionally, the House of Lords considered 785 proposed amendments. The Bill was strongly opposed at all stages by the Opposition in both Houses, and was before Parliament for eight months before the "guillotine" was applied, and it received the Royal Assent on 31 July, 1963.

The main provisions of the London Government Act 1963 were:

1. The creation of thirty-two new administrative areas to be known

---

[10] Lords, Vol. 238, col. 189, 14 March, 1962.

as London Boroughs which were to be the primary units of local government.

2. The area comprising the London Boroughs, the City and the Temples was to constitute an administrative unit to be known as Greater London.

3. The administrative counties of London and Middlesex, the eighty-five metropolitan boroughs, county and municipal boroughs, and urban districts within the Greater London area would cease to exist on the creation of the Greater London Council.

4. The independent position and status of the City of London would remain unchanged, the Common Council having the powers of a London Borough Council.

5. The first elections for Greater London councillors were to be held in April, 1964 and for the London Boroughs in May, 1964. The new councils were to continue side by side with the old authorities and would take over their full functions on 1 April, 1965.

6. The establishment of the Inner London Education Authority, a special, i.e., virtually autonomous, committee of the Greater London Council, to provide the full range of educational services, including the youth employment service, for Inner London. In each of the twenty outer London Boroughs education and youth employment would be borough services. There was to have been a review of the I.L.E.A. system before 1970, but this provision has been repealed (s. 2 of Local Government (Termination of Reviews) Act 1967) and the I.L.E.A. will continue in being.

7. As the administrative counties of Essex, Hertfordshire, Kent and Surrey were to be reduced in size and would consequently lose population and rateable value to Greater London, these counties would be able to obtain transitional financial assistance from the G.L.C. if the effects of the reorganisation caused the county rate to rise by 6d. in 1965–66.

8. A Staff Commission would be established to safeguard the interests of local government employees affected by the reorganisation.

(a) *The Greater London Council.* This originally consisted of the "Dais" (Chairman, Vice-Chairman and Deputy Chairman), 100 councillors and sixteen aldermen. The first election was held on 9 April, 1964, with each of the thirty-two London Boroughs being an electoral area and returning two, three or four councillors, according to the size of the electorate. For this election the Cities of London and Westminster were joined to form one electoral area.

At the election 44·2% of the Greater London electorate of 5,466,756 voted, and the resulting political composition of the Greater London Council was: sixty-four Labour councillors and eleven Labour aldermen, and thirty-six Conservative councillors and five Conservative aldermen. Councillors hold office for three years and retire together; aldermen number one-sixth of the council and are elected by the councillors from among their number or from persons qualified to be councillors, and eight retire every third year. In April, 1973, the elections were held in ninety-two single-member constituencies, corresponding to the parliamentary constituencies in the capital, thus reducing the membership of the G.L.C. from 100 to 92. The office of alderman will cease to exist in the G.L.C. in 1976; there were fifteen aldermen in 1975.

(b) *The London Borough Councils.* By the end of January, 1964, final approval had been given to the names of the thirty-two London Boroughs which were to form Greater London (see map). Details of the amalgamations which produced the new boroughs, their population and rateable values are as follows:

Inner London Boroughs

1. WESTMINSTER (Paddington, St. Marylebone, Westminster)	270,140	£108 million
2. CAMDEN (Hampstead, Holborn, St. Pancras)	246,000	£35,250,000
3. ISLINGTON (Finsbury, Islington)	259,600	£19,450,000
4. HACKNEY (Hackney, Shoreditch, Stoke Newington)	254,300	£14,409,000
5. TOWER HAMLETS (Bethnal Green, Poplar, Stepney)	204,000	£14,582,000
6. GREENWICH (Greenwich, Woolwich—south of Thames)	230,100	£12,440,000
7. LEWISHAM (Deptford, Lewisham)	291,670	£11,620,000
8. SOUTHWARK (Bermondsey, Camberwell, Southwark)	310,600	£17,866,000
9. LAMBETH (Lambeth, Wandsworth—eastern part)	340,800	£19 million
10. WANDSWORTH (Battersea, Wandsworth—western part)	335,000	£15,384,000
11. HAMMERSMITH (Fulham, Hammersmith)	217,400	£13,993,000
12. KENSINGTON AND CHELSEA (Kensington and Chelsea)	220,600	£24,990,000

Outer London Boroughs

13. WALTHAM FOREST (Chingford, Leyton, Walthamstow)	248,500	£11,555,000
14. REDBRIDGE (Ilford, Wanstead, Woodford, Chigwell—southern part, Dagenham—northern part)	248,600	£12,365,000

15. HAVERING (Hornchurch, Romford)	249,300	£11,492,000
16. BARKING (Barking—eastern part, Dagenham—southern part)	178,900	£9,858,500
17. NEWHAM (Barking—western part, East Ham, West Ham, Woolwich— north of the Thames)	264,000	£14,500,000
18. BEXLEY (Bexley, Crayford, Erith, Chislehurst and Sidcup—northern part)	212,900	£10,083,000
19. BROMLEY (Beckenham, Bromley, Chislehurst and Sidcup—southern part, Orpington, Penge)	294,300	£15,187,000
20. CROYDON (Coulsdon and Purley, Croydon)	328,300	£17,909,000
21. SUTTON (Beddington and Wallington, Carshalton, Sutton and Cheam)	167,400	£9,185,000
22. MERTON (Merton and Morden, Mitcham, Wimbledon)	189,000	£10,834,000
23. KINGSTON UPON THAMES (Kingston upon Thames, Malden and Coombe, Surbiton)	186,300	£9,459,000
24. RICHMOND UPON THAMES (Barnes, Richmond, Twickenham)	182,000	£10 million
25. HOUNSLOW (Brentford and Chiswick, Feltham, Heston and Isleworth)	209,100	£15,013,000
26. HILLINGDON (Hayes and Harlington, Ruislip-Northwood, Uxbridge and Yiewsley, West Drayton)	232,000	£15,428,000
27. EALING (Acton, Ealing, Southall)	303,800	£17,125,000
28. BRENT (Wembley, Willesden)	296,600	£19,678,000
29. HARROW (Harrow)	209,500	£10,974,000
30. BARNET (Barnet, East Barnet, Finchley, Friern Barnet, Hendon)	316,400	£21,600,000
31. HARINGEY (Hornsey, Tottenham, Wood Green)	258,400	£13,222,000
32. ENFIELD (Edmonton, Enfield, Southgate)	271,600	£17,240,000

Twenty-three of these Boroughs had a council membership of seventy, while the remainder varied from sixty-five (Barnet, Bexley

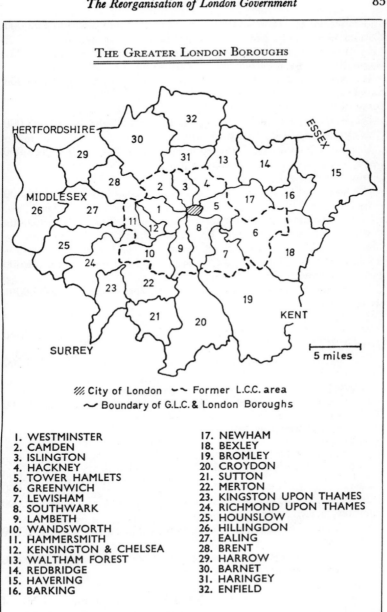

THE GREATER LONDON BOROUGHS

HERTFORDSHIRE

ESSEX

MIDDLESEX

KENT

SURREY

5 miles

///// City of London   ‿‿ Former L.C.C. area
‿ Boundary of G.L.C. & London Boroughs

1. WESTMINSTER
2. CAMDEN
3. ISLINGTON
4. HACKNEY
5. TOWER HAMLETS
6. GREENWICH
7. LEWISHAM
8. SOUTHWARK
9. LAMBETH
10. WANDSWORTH
11. HAMMERSMITH
12. KENSINGTON & CHELSEA
13. WALTHAM FOREST
14. REDBRIDGE
15. HAVERING
16. BARKING

17. NEWHAM
18. BEXLEY
19. BROMLEY
20. CROYDON
21. SUTTON
22. MERTON
23. KINGSTON UPON THAMES
24. RICHMOND UPON THAMES
25. HOUNSLOW
26. HILLINGDON
27. EALING
28. BRENT
29. HARROW
30. BARNET
31. HARINGEY
32. ENFIELD

and Harrow) to fifty-six (Waltham Forest). Each London Borough Council consists of a Mayor, Deputy Mayor, Aldermen and Councillors, the Aldermen numbering one-sixth of the councillors. All councillors retire together every three years.

By the Local Government Act 1972 the Secretary of State may by order provide for G.L.C. elections to take place in the same years as the elections for county councillors, and for London Borough elections to take place in the same years as for district councillors. Provision is also made in the act for the abolition of aldermen from the G.L.C. in 1976 and from the London Boroughs in 1977, and for the limit of sixty on the number of elected councillors in the London Boroughs to be removed.

(*c*) *Powers and Duties*. As these boroughs were intended to be the primary units of local government their responsibilities were greater than those of the former metropolitan boroughs. The Greater London Council, for its part, was to be made responsible for the "greater strategic tasks" which required planning over the area as a whole. The Common Council of the City of London received the powers of a London Borough Council. Services for which the London Borough Councils and the Greater London Council were separately responsible were:

London Borough Councils

Personal Health Services.
Maternity and Child Welfare, Mental Health, etc.
Welfare Services—care of aged, handicapped, blind and homeless
The Children's Service
Libraries
Cemeteries and crematoria
Registration of local land charges
Allotments
Registration of births, marriages and deaths
Swimming baths and washhouses
Inspection of premises for health and overcrowding

Refuse collection
Control of vermin, pests and infectious diseases
Disease of animals
Sanitation
Noise and smoke abatement
Weights and measures
Food and drugs
Street Markets and slaughterhouses
Street cleansing
Administration of Shop Acts
Licensing of various establishments, e.g. employment agencies
Information services about the Borough
Elections and registration of electors

Greater London Council

London Fire Brigade
London Ambulance Service

Places for public entertainment,

Greater London Council—continued

Refuse disposal (London Borough Councils may do this until 1967)

Land drainage—in the London excluded area

Thames flood prevention

Smallholdings

Licensing—Motor vehicle and driving licences, Petroleum storage licences,

Iveagh Bequest, Kenwood

Geffrye Museum, Hackney

Horniman Museum, Lewisham

Marble Hill House, Twickenham

Crystal Palace

Tracks for betting

Supplies Services—purchase and supply of goods and equipment for the G.L.C., the I.L.E.A., the London Borough Councils, if required, and other public bodies

Royal Festival Hall, etc. on South Bank

Scientific Services for the I.L.E.A., the London Borough Councils, if required, and other public bodies

Research and intelligence organisation for Greater London

Services for which responsibility was to be shared comprised:

Planning: The Greater London Council was the overall planning authority and was required to produce the strategic Greater London Development Plan. It would deal with or give directions on planning applications which were of major importance in the planning of Greater London. The London Borough Councils were the local planning authorities and were required to produce Borough Development Plans within the framework of the strategic Greater London Development Plan. They would receive all planning applications and deal with all those which were not reserved for Greater London Council decision.[11]

Roads: The Greater London Council was responsible for the construction, improvement, maintenance and lighting of main roads (other than trunk roads) in Greater London and for all Thames bridges, other than the four City bridges. It would delegate some of its road functions to the Borough Councils who would be responsible for the construction, improvement, maintenance and lighting of roads other than main and trunk roads.

Traffic: The Greater London Council was the overall traffic authority for roads in Greater London and would authorise traffic

---

[11] The Greater London Development Plan, published in March 1969, gave priority to the improvement of housing, roads and communications, and aimed at pegging the population of Greater London at 7·3 million in order to maintain an adequate labour force.

management schemes, traffic control, speed limits, pedestrian crossings on main roads, traffic signs, and street parking schemes. It could also provide off-street car parks. The London Borough Councils could provide on- and off-street car parking. They would provide and maintain traffic signs and signals, road markings, pedestrian crossings, subways and metered parking places. The Transport (London) Act, 1969, provided for the complete reorganisation of public transport in Greater London, the G.L.C. becoming the overall planning authority for London's internal transport facilities—buses, underground, **highways, traffic and parking** arrangements.

Housing: For the time being the Greater London Council had all the housing powers of the London County Council and its stock of houses (about 220,000). The Greater London Council was required to survey the housing needs of Greater London, help to provide houses and employment for Londoners both in London and in the new and expanding towns, maintain a housing exchange bureau, and could make loans for house purchase. The London Borough Councils had full housing powers within their Boroughs, including the provision of new houses, improvement schemes, slum clearance and loans for housing purchase. They took over some 338,000 houses from their predecessors.

Parks: The Greater London Council took over all the parks and varied activities provided by the London County Council; but some of them might later be transferred to the Borough Councils. The Greater London Council had power to provide new parks and open spaces that were of more than local significance. It also took over Green Belt land formerly vested in the London County Council and the Middlesex County Council. The London Borough Councils have power to provide parks and open spaces within their Boroughs and they took over all parks and open spaces provided by their predecessors.

Sewerage and Sewage Disposal: The Greater London Council took over all main sewers and sewage disposal works in the Greater London Council sewerage area including the control of discharges of trade effluents to sewers. In general the London Borough Councils were responsible for sewers other than main sewers, and had control over drains.

Civil Defence: The Greater London Council was responsible for the auxiliary Fire Service and the ambulance and first-aid sections of the Civil Defence Corps and would co-ordinate transport for the dispersal in an emergency of children and their mothers, and young persons. The London Borough Councils each provide a Civil Defence division including headquarters, rescue, welfare (dispersal and care of the homeless and emergency feeding) and wardens' sections.

Building Preservation Orders: The Greater London Council and London Borough Councils had power to make and enforce Building Preservation Orders for buildings of architectural and historic interest.

Control of Building Construction: The Greater London Council was responsible under the London Building Acts for the control of the construction of buildings in inner London. It delegated some of its functions to the inner London Borough Councils. The twenty outer London Borough Councils control the construction of buildings in their Boroughs.

Entertainments: The Greater London Council and the London Borough Councils had power to provide entertainment of any kind including the provision of theatres, concert halls and dance halls.

Education: See provision 6 on p. 82.

The standard attained by the councils in the provision of these services depends largely upon the degree of co-operation which exists between the thirty-two borough councils and the Greater London Council. The London Boroughs Committee was therefore formed as a voluntary association of all the London Borough Councils: (a) to provide a forum for the discussion of common problems and for the provision of common advice; (b) to enable the London Boroughs to speak with one voice when necessary to Government Departments; and (c) to provide a means whereby the Greater London Council can discuss problems affecting the Boroughs without having to go to each of them individually.

The remodelling of local government in Greater London by the 1963 Act constituted the first major reform in the structure of English local government since the late nineteenth century. The legislation was radical and its implementation fraught with major difficulties, particularly during the 1964–65 interregnum when many complex problems had to be resolved. The reorganisation was aided by Labour's council election successes which mollified the former political controversy and supposedly replaced it with "the gentle dew of constructive co-operation". (*The Times*, 1 April, 1965).

The Act was not without its critics, however, who questioned, for example, the reduction in the size of the Greater London Council area originally envisaged by the Herbert Commission; the decision to perpetuate the aldermanic system; the large constituencies and the limited responsibilities of the Greater London Council councillors; the reduction in the number of council seats within Greater London and its significance for democratic representation; the motivation behind some of the amalgamations; the division of responsibilities between the Greater London Council and the Boroughs; the role and future of the I.L.E.A.; or even whether the entire operation was too radical or not radical enough.

If, however, one accepts the Herbert Commission's assessment:

"that the choice before local government in Greater London is, in truth, to abdicate in favour of central government, or to reform so as to be equipped to deal with present-day problems",[12]

then the structure which emerged, despite any imperfections, was an endorsement of representative local government over centralised control. This was particularly significant at a time when local government faced a progressive diminution of its control over local services and their transfer to government departments or regional bodies. The reorganised London government system was therefore seen as "an act of faith"[13] which the Greater London Council and the London Boroughs would have to justify.

One appraisal of subsequent developments was made by the London School of Economics Greater London Group,[14] and it concluded that the two-tier system in Greater London had "some clear advantages over this system it replaced". The G.L.C. area was viable, its size and resources enabling it "to undertake certain overall functions essential in a great city", while the size and resources of the Boroughs were adequate for the exercise of their functions. The allocation of more important functions to the Boroughs had had an "invigorating effect" upon them and there had been "a general levelling up of standards". Where the respective responsibilities of the two tiers were clearly defined, the system appeared to be working satisfactorily. Differences had occurred, however, where functions had overlapped, more especially in housing, planning and highways, and the London Boroughs Association had played "a notable part" in securing inter-tier co-operation and resolving difficulties. Despite the "obvious merits" which had resulted from the change, however, the "reforms appear to have made little impact on the voting beha-

---

[12] The Herbert Commission, para. 707.
[13] *The Times*, 1 April, 1965.
[14] The Greater London Group, "The Lessons of the London Government Reforms", Research Study No. 2, H.M.S.O., 1968.

viour of the electorate, save in the outer boroughs for the G.L.C. elections". Nevertheless, the

> "general consensus of opinion among those most closely concerned with their implementation is that the London Government reforms are proving a success, though it must still be some time before their full potentialities are realised".

CHAPTER 4

Local Self-Government

1. The Local Government Franchise

The efficiency of our local government system rests largely upon the individual and corporate efforts of councillors to whom is entrusted the responsibility for translating community needs into public action. Responsible self-government demands a high degree of competency and integrity from those who undertake the manifold duties entailed in council membership. The councillor's role is nowhere defined and his interpretation of his functions will depend very much upon his own personality and experience. The Maud Report saw his role as that of a generalist manager, a decision-maker whose diffuse interpretation of democratic control had involved him in every small detail of day-to-day administration. The Bains Report, however, commented upon the diversity of the councillors' aims and interests: some would be more interested in constituency affairs, in service to the community and in welfare matters affecting the area and their constituents; others would concern themselves with policy formulation and the allocation of resources; while others would monitor progress and review procedures, critically evaluating the cost of departmental activities. Obviously his role is not fixed but will vary as his interests and experience develop. Whatever the preferred set of objectives, however, the relationship of the councillors with their officers is a vital factor in determining the efficiency and effectiveness of the local authority.

Much of the law relating to local government elections is consolidated in the Representation of the People Acts 1949 and 1969, and the Local Government Act 1972. British subjects and citizens of the Irish Republic of 18 years or over are entitled to vote at local elections, providing they are not legally disqualified and their names are on the Register of Electors for the authority. The Register is complied annually by the Electoral Registration Officer (often the chief executive to the local authority), who lists the names of those resident in the electoral area who are of voting age on the qualifying date, 10 October, and those who attain voting age during the subsequent twelve months (the date of attaining voting age being indicated). A preliminary register is issued and those who have been omitted may then apply for inclusion; in addition, objections will be heard against the inclusion of individuals. The registration officer decides upon these questions, but there is a right of appeal first to the County Court and then to the Court of Appeal. The final register is then published, coming into effect on the following 16 February and is tenable for the following twelve months.

Prior to the Representation of the People Act, 1969, people who lived outside the local authority but who occupied rateable land or premises of a yearly value not less than £10 within the authority, and were not disqualfied in any way, also qualified to be registered and to vote within that authority. The 1969 Act abolished, with effect from the 1970 register, the non-resident franchise and property qualification for candidates at local government elections. This did not apply, however, in the City of London. Service voters and Crown employees outside the kingdom and their wives may be registered as voters and may appoint proxies to vote on their behalf. Other absentee voters may apply to the registration officer for permission to vote by post, and since the 1969 Act this has been extended to voters who are unable to vote personally by reason of religious observance. The 1969 Act also changed the registration rules to entitle a person to be registered as an elector immediately on reaching the age of 18 and to vote in any subsequent election.

Persons not entitled to be registered or to vote include: persons under 18 years of age, aliens, persons convicted of treason or felony, persons of unsound mind, and, for a five-year period, persons convicted of corrupt and illegal practices at elections. Mental hospital patients and prisoners are not qualified as residents for voting purposes. Peers are not disqualified from local government elections.

2. Frequency of Elections

The Local Government Act 1972 required that all local elections in England and Wales after 1974 be held on the first Thursday in May or on such other day as may be determined by the Home Secretary by order made not later than 1 February in the year preceding the first year in which the order is to take effect.

County council elections will take place every four years, the whole council retiring together. Metropolitan district elections will take place in 1973 and 1975 and every year thereafter except in the year when a county council election is held.

Non-metropolitan district councils may, by resolution at a specially convened meeting, ask the Secretary of State to make an order (a) providing for whole council elections, all the councillors retiring together, or (b) for a system of retirement by thirds. Where (b) is chosen they may indicate areas, if any, which they wish to see divided into wards, each returning three members. Where the Secretary of State receives a request under (a) or does not receive a request under (b) before 1 April, 1974, he may order simultaneous elections. Where he receives a request under (b) he may ask the appropriate Boundary Commission for England or Wales to make proposals for a scheme. Where a system of simultaneous retirement applies elections will be held in 1973, 1976 and 1979 and every fourth year thereafter. Elsewhere, an election will be held each year except in the year of a county council election. Parish council elections will take place in 1976, 1979 and every fourth year thereafter, and the term of office will be three years for the councillors elected in 1976 and four years thereafter. All councillors will retire together. The elections of community councillors will take place in 1974, 1979 and every fourth year thereafter. Their terms of office will be five years for those elected in 1974 and four years for those elected at subsequent elections. All councillors will retire together in every ordinary year of election.

Occasionally there is need to fill a casual vacancy created by a councillor's death, his disqualification, his resignation, or his unauthorized absence from the authority's meetings throughout a period of six consecutive months. An election to fill a casual vacancy declared by the High Court or by the council must be held within forty-two days from the declaration, and a vacancy of which notice in writing has been given by two local government electors must be held within forty-two days of the notice having been given. Where a casual vacancy occurs within six months before the ordinary day of retirement from the office, it is not filled until the next ordinary election unless, on the occurrence of the vacancy, the total number of vacancies exceeds one-third of the council's membership.

3. Candidates for Election

Unlike Members of Parliament who may have no prior connection with the constituencies they represent, the law relating to local government elections requires a more positive identity of interest between the candidate and the area he wishes to represent. A candidate must be a British subject or a citizen of the Irish Republic, aged 21 or over and not subject to any disqualification under the Local Government Act 1972. He must also be qualified in one of the following ways:

1. by registration as a local government elector for the area of the authority for which he is a candidate; *or*

2. by occupation as owner or tenant of any land or other premises in that area during the whole twelve months preceding his nomination; or

3. by having his principal or only place of work during that twelve months in that area; *or*

4. by residing in that area for the whole of the preceding twelve months or, in the case of a parish or community council, within 3 miles of it.

Persons disqualified from election include anyone who:

1. holds a paid office or employment (other than the chairman, vice-chairman or deputy chairman) appointments to which are made or confirmed by the local authority or any committee or sub-committee or by any joint board or committee on which the authority is represented, or by any person holding such an office or employment; *or*

2. has been adjudged bankrupt, or made a composition or arrangement with his creditors; *or*

3. has been surcharged within five years before the election or since election by a district auditor to an amount exceeding £500; *or*

4. has within five years before or since the election been convicted in the U.K. of any offence and sentenced to imprisonment for not less than three months without the option of a fine; *or*

5. is a paid officer of the authority employed under the direction of a committee or sub-committee of that authority or a joint board or committee on which that authority is represented, and the authority to which he seeks election has a right to nominate a member to the committee or sub-committee concerned or is also represented on that joint board or committee; *or*

6. teaches in a school maintained but not established by a local education authority, i.e. in the same position as teachers in a school established by the authority.

Special exceptions from the provisions under 1 and 5 above apply in certain circumstances to teachers and other workers in educational institutions (see s. 81 of the Act).

4. Council Elections

For the purpose of the election of councillors counties are divided into electoral divisions, each with one member; metropolitan districts are divided into wards, with a number of councillors divisible by three; non-metropolitan districts are also divided into wards but each ward returns whatever number of councillors is provided for in the appropriate order. The number of parish councillors is determined by the district council but cannot be fewer than five in each parish, and elections may be held in respect of the whole parish or separately for each ward of a parish if it is so divided. Similarly a community which is not divided into wards will have one election, but if divided into wards will have a separate election of community councillors in each ward.

The election campaign formally commences when the Notice of Election is released by the returning officer who organises the local election. He sees that all statutory requirements are complied with and arranges polling stations and the requisite equipment, their manning, the swearing-in of staff and the announcement of the result. Each county council appoints an officer to be returning officer for the county, and each district council appoints a returning officer for the district and for parishes or communities within it. In London, each borough council appoints a returning officer for the borough and he acts as returning officer in the Greater London county elections. Elected members will not in future hold this office as was the case before the Local Government Act 1972.

Candidates for election may have a variety of motives for offering their services to the local authority, and they may be supported by a local political organisation. Nomination papers signed by a proposer, a seconder and eight other electors for that area must be handed to the returning officer by noon on the nineteenth day before the election; for parish council elections the nomination papers need only be signed by a proposer and seconder. Each "assentor" must add his electoral number. By the Representation of the People Act 1969 the nomination paper, and ballot papers, may contain a description of the candidate, subject to a maximum of six words, and the restriction prohibiting reference to a candidate's political activities is removed. Nominations must be accompanied by the candidate's written consent to his nomination, by a witness's signature and by a statement of the candidate's qualifications for election. The papers are examined by the returning officer who determines the validity of the nominations.

Each candidate is required to appoint an election agent to handle his campaign, although he may act as his own agent providing he informs the returning officer of his intention at least twelve days before the election.

At this stage, it may be apparent that there is no need for an election campaign because the number of nominations corresponds exactly with the number of vacancies to be filled, in which case the returning officer declares the nominated candidates elected. Alternatively, there may be fewer nominations than vacancies, in which case he declares the candidates elected and fills the remaining vacancies with the retiring councillors who, at the previous election, received the highest number of votes.

Where the nominations exceed the vacancies, a poll must be held by ballot, and the campaign is mounted in the days prior to election day. The agent and his voluntary workers organise support for their candidate by posters, speaking at election meetings and acting as polling or counting agents on election day. Prohibited practices include, amongst others, the indiscriminate sticking of posters, coercion, intimidation or bribery, and payment for cars to convey electors to and from the polls. The candidate, and particularly his agent, must record all election expenditure and ensure that the statutory limitation is not exceeded. The Representation of the People (No. 2) Act 1974 limits candidates' election expenses at local government elections, excluding election to the Greater London Council, to £45 plus 1p for every entry in the register of electors, and at ward elections in the City of London to £45 plus 1p for every elector taken according to the enumeration of the ward list. The limitation at G.L.C. elections is £200 plus 5p for every 4 entries in the register.

Despite the activity displayed by the voluntary workers and the high polls recorded at parliamentary elections, the local authority elector tends to display a remarkable reluctance to participate in the democratic process. The Registrar General's statistical returns for 1958 and 1967, years when triennial elections were held, show that on average in no type of authority did half the electorate exercise a vote. Even more perturbing, however, is the high number of uncontested seats (see Table 1). The result is that the proportion of the total electorate being able to record a vote is much lower than the number qualified to vote. The resultant minority councils cast doubt on such statements as "local government is the backbone of democracy".[1] Indeed the Maud Report commented (para. 39):

---

[1] Quoted in *The Municipal Journal*, 30 July, 1965, p. 2588.

TABLE 1. ANALYSIS OF LOCAL GOVERNMENT ELECTIONS HELD IN 1973

Area	Local government electors at 16/2/73	Total number of councillors	Number of councillors returned unopposed	Contested elections			
				No. of councillors returned	Electorate in contested divisions	No. of electors voting	% of electorate voting
Greater London Council	5,302,893	92	Nil	92	5,313,470	1,966,270	37·0
COUNTY COUNCILS							
Metropolitan	8,327,570	601	22	579	8,146,605	3,023,891	37·1
Non-metropolitan	19,354,642	3,129	396	2,731	17,386,510	7,399,655	42·6
Welsh	1,982,126	578	109	468	1,647,836	906,830	55·0
London Boroughs	5,302,893	No elections in 1973					
COUNTY DISTRICTS							
Metropolitan	8,327,570	2,514	66	2,445	8,204,197	2,744,195	33·4
Non-metropolitan	19,354,642	13,560	1,665	11,879	17,416,523	6,730,485	38·6
Welsh	1,982,126	1,521	281	1,240	1,690,233	847,131	50·0

Source: *The Registrar General's Statistical Review of England and Wales for 1973*, Part II, Table VI.

". . . our local government does not appear to be especially democratic".

The poll returns for individual authorities show a wide variation, for example, from 9·69 per cent in a new London Borough in 1964 to 84·3 per cent in a Welsh urban district in 1962[2]; and the general tendency is for the percentage voting to fall as the size of the authority increases, though this is not an invariable rule.

Apathy is the decisive factor and many commentators wonder how democratic local government can be when the poll is so low and uncontested seats so numerous. Yet, at the same time as the Local Government Information Office resolved to combat this "creeping paralysis", a contrary viewpoint was expressed by an Ipswich alderman at the 1965 annual conference of the Association of Municipal Corporations:

"Low polls usually mean the electorate is satisfied; high polls often occur when there is something to grouse about".[3]

There may be a degree of truth in this, but public apathy remains an eroding influence upon local democracy.

A number of remedial suggestions have been put forward to attract voters to the booths, and these include: the holding of all local elections on the same day with wireless, T.V., and newspaper commentary providing the necessary stimuli to increase turnout; the retirement en bloc of all councils; the dissolution of all councils when Parliament is dissolved and the elections of councillors and M.Ps. on the same day and on the same ballot paper.[4] The Maud Report recommended that in all authorities councillors should retire together and the system of triennial elections should be applied in all types of local authority. In the system advocated by the Redcliffe–Maud Commission it was proposed that all members of all main authorities should be elected on the same day, and that an inquiry should examine whether three years or four would be a better term of office for the main authorities and whether spring or autumn would be a better time for holding elections.

One further suggestion which has received considerable publicity and excited some controversy is the changing of the electoral system to that form of proportional representation known as the single transferable vote. Despite the alleged drawbacks of the system in

---

[2] *Ibid.*, 6 August, 1965, p. 2670.
[3] *The Municipal Journal*, 1 October, 1965, p. 3329.
[4] Professor J. A. G. Griffith, "Local Democracy: A Sorry State" in *New Society*, 14 February, 1963.

parliamentary elections, its advocates suggest that the disadvantages would not operate in local government elections.[5]

5. Councillors

Before the new councillor begins his term of office he has to make a declaration of acceptance which says:

> "I (name) of (address), having been duly elected to this office of councillor for the (local authority) hereby declare that I will take the said office upon myself, and will duly and faithfully fulfil the duties thereof according to the best of my judgement and ability."

Similar declarations have been made by over 24,000 councillors who direct the activities of over 2 million council employees and spend on the public's behalf more than Britain's defence budget.[6] Within their local authorities they are accorded the status and deference which one might expect from an office which, according to one opinion, "is one of the highest forms of voluntary service in the community."[7]

Yet of all society's roles that of the councillor would appear to be one of the most frequently maligned by the unsatisfied public. The following excerpt from an examiner's report reveals a sad stereotype which is all too prevalent an impression in the public mind:

> "Most saw him as little more than an incompetent ignoramus and were consequently somewhat handicapped in assigning him with anything but a very minor, for some even superfluous, place in local administration."[8]

The opinions of young students may not always be regarded as authoritative signposts to the truth, and one might question their objectivity. More validity may be attached to the following assessment, based upon a personal working knowledge, by a former President of the Society of Town Clerks, who wrote before the payment of allowances:

> "He (the councillor) receives no personal advantage from his office, but the demands on his time are ever increasing. He is

---

[5] For some of the main arguments see "Electoral Reform in Local Government", by E. A. Rowe in the *Municipal Journal*, 16 July, 1965 and J. Harvey and L. Bather, *The British Constitution*, Macmillan, 1963, pp. 71–72.

[6] Since 1965.

[7] *The Councillor's Handbook*, a guide for new councillors prepared by the Municipal Journal Ltd.

[8] Report on the Intermediate Examinations of the Institute of Hospital Administrators, *The Hospital*, vol. 61, no. 9, September, 1965, p. 498.

under closer scrutiny and more liable to be called to account for his actions. He invariably suffers financially from the time he gives to council work, and he can expect no public gratitude for his service. If the public realised the sacrifice, the honest endeavour, and the shrewd judgement which is put at their disposal, they would be less grudging in their thanks, and show more humility in their criticisms."[9]

The public's attitude towards their councillors reflects an amalgam of their own personal experience and assimilated local folklore, their perceptions being modified by the extent to which their expectations have been satisfied by the council. The public's attitudes are ambivalent: they accept the office as the keystone of the council's structure; they recognise him as a community leader who gives substance to the anonymity of the council's officers, and they may appreciate that without his voluntary acceptance of the time-consuming and enervating work there could be no semblance of democratic control over the administration of local services. Conversely, the councillor can be the focus of all criticism. He is arraigned for erecting incompetence into a system and indicted as a power-seeking, corrupt functionary by those who are incapable of accepting altruism as a valid motivation for community work.

Councillors are expected to help run the local authority in the best interests of its inhabitants, and this requires them to express community opinions in the council and committee meetings; to bring individual grievances to the appropriate departmental officers and follow up any subsequent action; to disseminate sound advice and communicate council proposals to the public; to promote the economic development of the authority by attracting new employment opportunities; to provide ample social and leisure facilities; to act as watchdog over the expenditure of public money by preventing excessive spending, by scrutinising chief officers' proposals, by evaluating priorities; to act as a local ombudsman; and generally to create a viable and efficiently administered community.

It is no small wonder that so many people are reluctant to stand for office, and in March, 1964, a committee under the chairmanship of Sir John Maud was appointed to look into this and related problems. Its terms of reference were:

"to consider how in the light of modern conditions local government might best continue to attract and retain people (both elected representatives and chief officers) of the calibre necessary to ensure its maximum effectiveness."

[9] *Guardian*, 3 June, 1965.

Reasons postulated for the reluctance to serve, and which the committee investigated, included distaste for party allegiance or publicity; the lengthiness of committee proceedings; the inconvenient times of meetings and transport difficulties; the feeling that local authorities have insufficient freedom to do what they should do; the financial loss involved and the absence at that time of any adequate arrangements for payment of members; and the unwillingness of some employers to release employees to serve on councils.

One frequent criticism of councillors is that many are too old and unrepresentative of the different age groups comprising the electorate. The Maud Report[10] confirmed earlier research[11] and showed that "members do not reflect the community in terms of age, sex, occupation or education. Members tend to be drawn from the older sections of the population; their average age is 55 and that of women members is somewhat higher. Over a quarter of the adult male population are in the 21–34 age group but only a twentieth of men members are of this age. Over half the men members, but less than a third of the adult male population, are over the age of 55. Members of rural district and county councils are on the average even older as are the aldermen. Comparatively few women serve on local authorities; over half the adult population are women but only about 12 per cent of members are women.

"A fifth of all members are retired people but the proportion of retired people who are members of rural district and county councils is significantly higher." There are also marked occupational contrasts with the population. "For example, employers and managers, and farmers and professional workers, occupy a larger proportion of seats in the councils than their proportion in the general adult male population. But the converse is true of skilled and unskilled manual workers."

The main obstacle to a balanced age and occupational representation is the reluctance of people to become candidates. The factors which affect recruitment are: the time involved[12] (although this covers a number of attitudes), inability to stand for election where

---

[10] *Management of Local Government*, Vol. 1, Report of the Committee, H.M.S.O. 1967, Chapter 6, and Vol. 2, *in toto*.

[11] For example, Mary Stewart, *Unpaid Public Service*, Fabian Occasional Paper, No. 3, 1964.

[12] In *Town Councillors* by A. Rees and T. Smith (Acton Society Trust) the authors, on the basis of a sample of thirty Barking councillors, comment on the effect of council work on family life. The councillors had an average of fifty main committee meetings annually as well as council meetings, sub, joint and consultative committees and about sixteen hours "homework" a month. The sort of people with whom they may perhaps be compared, in terms of the amount of time spent away from home, are heavy drinkers or commercial travellers.

one works because of residence elsewhere, the deterrent effect of party politics, absence of training, financial hardship involved, difficulties of release from employment, and the times of meetings.

It is possible that the current reformist spirit in local government may influence some of the more enlightened local authorities to modify those customary practices which tend to exclude the younger professional and manual workers and to introduce improvements in evening meetings, streamlined agendas, clerical assistance—which could make council service more attractive to these groups.

Many local authorities have embarked upon improvements which only a few years ago would have encountered opposition. One example is the increased attention which is being paid to training of councillors. The expansion of local government work and the complexity and scope of services rendered obviously requires well-informed councillors if they are to carry out the job they were elected to do. Sweden has led the way in this respect with its centralised school for councillors which was established in 1956 and in ten years had provided 27,000 delegates—45 per cent councillors and the remainder local government officers—with courses on local service legislation, administrative procedure, planning and anything else requested by their local authority associations.[13] There was no comparable body in Britain to provide formal training seminars for members, but since the 1960's there has been a slow but progressive build-up of interest in *ad hoc* courses provided by universities and technical colleges. An additional stimulus has been given by the establishment in 1967 of the Local Government Training Board whose provincial training officers have organised courses for members, officers and manual staffs. These have been well complemented by the training activities of such bodies as the Royal Institute of Public Administration, L.A.M.S.A.C., the Association of Councillors, the Institute of Local Government Administrators, and the Institute of Local Government Studies (Inlogov) at Birmingham University.

A further attraction to those who could not afford to stand for council service was the suggestion that a more adequate scale of remuneration should be paid. By the Local Government Act 1948 a councillor received a nominal allowance for food and travel, and a financial loss allowance which amounted to a maximum daily rate of £3·25. In December, 1969, the Government agreed to raise the amount to £4. This system was frequently criticised, particularly as it did not apply to councillors who were house-

---

[13] *The Municipal Review*, January, 1965 pp. 28–33.

wives or self-employed. Besides being unsatisfactory the law governing the allowances was ambiguous as to how far councillors could
claim for hypothetical earnings which they would have made had
they not been engaged on council duties. Whilst the above amounts
might have constituted a reasonable recompense for members of
small authorities, membership of large authorities often entailed
many hours of attendance weekly at various meetings and a disproportionate amount of travelling time;[14] in particular, committee
chairmanship could be a full-time occupation and thus deserving
of some greater allowance. As *New Society* had commented:

> "Our concept of local representation still seems to be rooted in
> the 19th century assumption of an inexhaustible supply of
> leisured gentlemen ready to undertake council work".[15]

A more realistic approach was taken in some other countries—
in 1963 a municipal councillor in Paris received £540 a year and
his opposite number in New York City received £2,500 a year. In
this country, political parties could make up the loss suffered by
councillors, and this could amount to a considerable sum. Mary
Stewart found that 29 per cent of her sample named sums between
£25 and £1,000 as their losses in one year.

The opinions presented to the Maud committee were mixed.
Lancashire County Council favoured financial recompense but
N.A.L.G.O. did not, and other opponents of payment have made an
exception for committee chairmen because of the responsibility they
bear. Meanwhile, the Greater London Council sought powers to
pay councillors an allowance and a bi-party group of members
discussed the idea at ministerial level and was assured of a sympa-
thetic reception when parliamentary powers were sought.[16]

The Maud committee's interim report on allowances for elected
members, published in June, 1966, pointed out that 87 per cent of
councillors questioned never claimed the existing allowance, probably
because they were unable to demonstrate financial loss. The committee proposed in lieu an annual expense allowance for councillors,
fixed by the local council, and a simplified quarterly claim for travel
expenses on which councillors would *not* be required to give details
of their journeys. In thus making the councils responsible for deciding

---

[14] Mary Stewart's survey indicated monthly average council work of 44 hours for
county councillors, 40 hours for county borough councillors, 20 hours for municipal
and metropolitan boroughs; travelling time: 19 hours and 9 hours for C.C. and
C.B. councillors respectively. See also Chap. 6.

[15] *New Society*, 14 February, 1963.

[16] *Municipal Journal*, 22 October, 1965, p. 3537.

the rates of allowances, the proposal, in words attributed to Sir John Maud,

> "runs counter to the general trend of practice in local government in Britain and does strike a blow for trusting the elected representatives of the country."[17]

The committee opposed the payment of salaries to council members but in its final report recommended that members of the Management Board should be paid part-time salaries. Additionally, it was not thought necessary to make recommendations on the payment of committee chairmen.

There is always some danger that payment might attract the job seekers who would be keen to grab the "spoils of office" but the benefits which might accrue from the attraction of a better age and occupational cross-section of the public to council service would more than compensate for the odd corporation carpetbagger who slipped through to committee chairmanship. Paul Smith, the former Town Clerk of Bognor Regis and the Secretary and founder of the Local Government Reform Society, wrote about the reform of local government and the need to protect the system from abuse:

> "In considering the problem as a whole, one must not forget the enormous contribution which most local councillors make towards the proper running of their towns by attending committees at all hours of the day and night and by looking into local problems and complaints on behalf of the public. This contribution is invaluable—it absorbs most of a councillor's spare time—yet it is unpaid and, to a great extent, not recognised by the vast majority of people.
> "As great as the need of local government reform is the duty of the public to realise the debt owed to its councillors. The status value of a monetary standard is accepted for almost all other forms of service: is this not the time to seriously consider the giving of appropriate financial recognition to these trustees of the public for all the sacrifices made in the interest of service to the community? This would not be a 'quid pro quo' but rather an earnest of our respect for their trust".[18]

Financial recognition was at last given by the Local Government Act 1972 which provided for the payment of an *attendance allowance* to councillors. The amount was to be determined by the local authority for all approved duties and could be claimed as of right, with no requirement to relate it to any loss of earnings. The

---

[17] *The Times*, 22 June, 1966.
[18] *The Times*, 16 August, 1965.

attendance allowance is taxable. Circular 16/74 prescribed the maximum amount as £10 for a period of twenty-four hours, including travelling time. A member is also entitled to receive a *travelling allowance* and a *subsistence allowance*, the latter being payable only in respect of duties performed at more than three miles from a member's home. Co-opted members are entitled to a non-taxable *financial loss allowance* for an approved duty, as are members who are not entitled to the attendance allowance. The maximum amount prescribed in the circular was £5·50 for each twenty-four-hour period and £2·75 for a period of less than four hours. Aldermen of the G.L.C. and the London Borough councils have a choice of either claiming the attendance allowance or the financial loss allowance.

The former restrictions on the payment of allowances to members attending conferences and meetings are removed and ministerial control is lessened. The authority will now decide on the conferences to be attended and the number of members authorised to attend. There are two limitations: (i) the conferences must concern the interests of the area; and (ii) the convenors may not be commercial or political. Councillors attending conferences are entitled to attendance allowance or financial loss allowance and travelling and subsistence allowances. The prescribed maxima for travelling and subsistence allowances do not apply to approved duty outside the United Kingdom.

For parish and community councillors the attendance allowance is payable only in respect of duties outside the parish or community; they are ineligible for attendance allowance, financial loss allowance, travelling allowance or subsistence allowance for any approved duty performed within the parish or community.

6. Indirect Election

Whereas councillors are elected by the public, a council's chairman or mayor is elected by the councillors.

(i) *Council Chairman or Mayor*

The first business to be transacted at the annual meeting of principal, parish and community councils is the election of a chairman or, in a borough or a successor parish, a mayor. He is elected annually by the council from among the councillors, and unless he resigns or becomes disqualified he will continue in office until his successor has made a declaration of acceptance of the office and becomes entitled to act as chairman. In the case of equality of votes in the election of a chairman the person presiding at the meeting shall give a casting vote in addition to any other vote he may have.

Principal, parish and community councils are also required to appoint a member of the council to be vice-chairman and he, unless he resigns or becomes disqualified, will hold office until immediately after the election of a chairman at the next annual meeting. Subject to any standing orders he will act in the capacity of the chairman during the chairman's absence.

Both the chairman and the vice-chairman of principal councils and the chairman of a parish and a community council may be paid a reasonable allowance by their councils to enable them to meet the expenses of their offices. The chairman of a district council will have precedence in the district, but not so as to prejudicially affect the royal prerogative.

In a parish which does not have a separate parish council the parish meeting will, subject to any provisions of a grouping order, elect a chairman at their annual meeting for the year and he will continue in office until a successor is elected. There is no such provision for a community meeting which, when it meets, will elect a chairman for that meeting.

The office of chairman or mayor combines the functional duties of chairmanship, mediation and guidance at council meetings with the ceremonial duties associated with being the authority's chief representative. To individual and groups from within and without the authority, he symbolises its corporate existence and it is the highest honour which a council can grant to its members. The majority of chairmen and mayors have exercised their duties with competence, and, conscious of their pre-eminent position and the responsibilities vested in them, have been able to dissociate themselves from party embroilment during their year of office. Unfortunately, as was the case with the aldermanic role, the incumbent can be influenced by party pressures. Since the passage of the Local Government Act 1972 the position can only be filled by a member of the council, whereas previously the honour could be granted to individual members of the public, but this rarely occurred. The tendency is for the office either to be allocated to the senior council member on the basis of a sharing arrangement between the respective political groups on the council or for the dominant party to monopolise the office. Succession to the chairmanship or mayoralty has not infrequently become an occasion for heated political wrangling and manoeuvring. The office then becomes a focus of grievance to the opposition and its incumbent the object of suspicion and antipathy.

These feelings may be intensified when the balance of power between parties is marginal and the chairman or mayor is required to give his casting vote on important issues of policy which have divided the parties. One of the main functions of chairmanship is to act impartially, but the influences acting upon a political appointee may be too great for him to remain neutral. Where power is the reward the opportunity to grasp it becomes a strong motivator to the unscrupulous.

To allay any public supicion of party involvement, some chairmen and mayors suspend their party membership and contact with local party executives during their year of office. Moreover, in order to minimise accusations of bias and to devote their full attention to a time-consuming office some relinquish their membership and chairmanship of council committees.

The offices of chairman and mayor can personify all that is good in local government, but it is the incumbent himself who, by his ability, self-discipline and awareness of his public responsibilities, will ennoble or discredit the image which the public receives.

(ii) *Aldermen*

The aldermanic office was a major feature of the composition of all county and borough councils until it was abolished by the Local Government Act 1972. Aldermen thus ceased to exist in England and Wales with effect from 1 April, 1974, but continued for a limited period on the Greater London Council and the London Borough councils until the fourth day after the G.L.C. election in 1976 and the London Borough elections in 1977.

Aldermen were elected by the councillors from existing councillors or persons qualified to be councillors. They comprised one-third of the number of councillors,[19] or a quarter of the full council, and served for six years; a half of their number retired every third year immediately after the election of new aldermen. Their duties did not differ from those of councillors, except that those in boroughs which were divided into wards acted as returning officers at local authority elections.

The aldermanic principle was introduced by the Municipal Corporations Act 1835, to provide borough government with an element of stability and continuity. Its introduction was violently opposed by the Whigs but the Conservatives feared that the

---

[19] In London the ratio was one alderman to six councillors.

councillors' tenure of three years in office was too short a time to guarantee stable local government and consistency of policy over a longer period. One-quarter of the council appointed for six years would provide, it was felt, the necessary consistency and continuity of experience. Whig opposition was blocked by the House of Lords and ever since the office has attracted controversy.

Not that the office was without advantages. The system did fulfil to some extent the original aim for continuity of personnel and policy. It was, moreover, an office of great status deriving added prestige from its antiquity and its association in the public mind with "elder statesmen". It allowed people of proved merit in many disciplines, and others with experience in various administrative capacities, but who did not wish to become involved in election campaigning or party politics, to be brought on to the council and to use their experience to the advantage of the public. Moreover, the office could be awarded by the council, on the public's behalf, to those who had distinguished themselves or brought benefit to the locality as industrialists, businessmen, social workers, etc. There was also the advantage, more theoretical than real, that in county councils where the elections were held trienially a completely new council could be elected, lacking in experience and detailed knowledge of their predecessors' policies; a half of the aldermen would continue in office for the following three years and could provide invaluable guidance.

Against these advantages, however, must be set the disadvantages:

1. The office, being filled by the choice of councillors, was plainly undemocratic in character.

2. The election of certain councillors or outsiders could cause jealousy among those not elected, and create grudges and vendettas which could only work to the detriment of council harmony and service to the public.

3. In boroughs where one third of the councillors were elected annually, there could be no sudden change of council to disrupt continuity. The prime justification thus broke down.

4. Appointments were rarely made from the electorate, the office generally being reserved for councillors.

5. Appointments were often allocated on the basis of seniority and not ability, with the result that many aldermen were very old. Mary Stewart's sample showed that 80 per cent of the aldermen on two county councils were over 60, more than a third over 70, and three were over 80 years of age.

6. Aldermen could dominate the council. Often the most powerful were elected aldermen and once elected they remained until they chose to retire. Because of seniority, they eventually sat on more

committees than did councillors and monopolised a disproportionate number of committee chairmanships.[20]

7. The system was abused extensively for party advantage, particularly when the party in control dead-heated or was defeated at the polls. Aldermanic votes were then used by that party "to entrench itself in power for a further term to flout the will of the people".[21]

This last aspect was the main source of controversy. In 1949, the Labour group in the L.C.C. retained control by packing the aldermanic seats although it had only sixty-four councillors against sixty-four Conservatives and one Liberal. In the metropolitan borough of Lewisham in 1959, the elections resulted in the Conservatives gaining twenty-eight seats and Labour twenty-seven seats; there was, however, a majority of Labour aldermen and their votes plus the casting vote of the mayor secured the election of an increased number of Labour aldermen, and Lewisham had a Labour-controlled council. A similar occurrence took place in Wolverhampton, but two High Court judges ruled that the election of seven aldermen, including the mayor, was invalid. Another practice was to bring back to the council councillors who were defeated at the elections; e.g. in the Huddersfield County Borough in 1961, when two former Labour councillors were defeated but returned as aldermen. *The Economist* wrote at the time of the Birmingham dead-heat in May, 1961, which resulted in a compromise between the two party leaders to allow Labour to retain effective power:

> "It is by no means unknown for local parties with an actual minority of elected councillors to hang on to office for three more years because they have enough aldermen to swing the vital vote."[22]

Such incidents as these should not be regarded as isolated cases, and there were frequent demands for legislative action to prevent the misuse of the system. Some local authorities joined in with cries for reform or abolition of the office. In 1964, Abingdon borough council passed such a resolution as did Oxford City Council.[23] Abingdon went further and circularised every member of the Association of Municipal Corporations to ascertain the degree of support for a memorandum to the Maud Committee, suggesting that if abolition were unpalatable, a number of reforms might be considered. These included making the title of alderman an honorary

[20] A. Rees and T. Smith, *Town Councillors*, Acton Society Trust, 1964.
[21] Henry Brooke, *Guardian*, 10 October, 1961.
[22] *The Economist*, 20 May, 1961, p. 755.
[23] *New Society*, 24 December, 1964, p. 17.

one, to be bestowed by the council at their discretion upon a limited proportion of senior members without altering their legal status as members of the council retiring every three years; reducing the proportion of aldermen to councillors, which was one to three outside London, to one to six; electing aldermen at the polls in the same way as senators in the American Congress; and ensuring that anyone defeated at the polls should be ineligible for aldermanic election during the following year.

Of the 247 replies to the Abingdon Memorandum, 121 were against change or offered no observations, forty were in favour of abolition or would welcome other reforms as an alternative, sixty-four were in favour of retaining the office subject to some change, and twenty-two were prepared to leave the matter to the Maud Committee or the Association of Municipal Corporations. In a supplement to the Memorandum, the Town Clerk of Abingdon Municipal Borough summed up the result and referred to a questionable attempt to regulate aldermanic elections:

> "It is interesting to note that a number of towns in opposing camps, for instance Abingdon and Preston, attempt to regulate aldermanic elections by Standing Orders. It is submitted that these are ultra vires in the sense that a person could be validly elected Alderman in contravention of such Standing Orders if the provisions of the appropriate statute have been complied with. The very fact that such towns have deemed it necessary to formulate Standing Orders repugnant to the statute to try to regulate these elections, suggests that the present law is in need of some revision.
>
> "The result may perhaps be fairly summed up in a single sentence by saying that there is an overwhelming majority for retaining the office of Alderman, since only 26 Cities and Boroughs are in favour of outright abolition; but that there is a strong and increasing demand for reform of the law relating to the nature, methods of election and tenure of the office."

It was not the office so much as the abuse of the system which made it imperative that some such legislative measure be undertaken. The office was undeniably undemocratic, but there were advantages to compensate for this. The temptation which the office afforded to the unscrupulous to manipulate aldermanic elections, however, could only tarnish the image of local authorities and contribute to a negation of the democratic principle upon which local government was founded. The view of the Maud Committee was that the system had "no logical justification" and that it should be abolished. The Redcliffe–Maud Commission reiterated the proposal and said that there would be no "place for aldermen on local councils, whose basic function is to be directly representative of local people". The opportunity to abolish the office was finally taken by the Local Government Act 1972. It also provided that a principal council could, by a two-thirds majority, confer the title of honorary alderman on former members who had "rendered eminent services to the council". These services could have been rendered to a predecessor authority.

7. Party Politics in Local Government

The foregoing account has made a number of references to the influence of party politics on the membership and balance of power in the council chamber, and it would be apposite at this stage to attempt to assess its contribution to local government. One opinion has appraised its influence in the following terms:

> "A new trend in local government theory can be drawn. . . . A majority of seats on a council, however small, is now taken to be a mandate for absolute control. It is the Parliamentary outlook. Everything follows logically from this. It is seen at its most consistent in places like Bristol, where Labour takes full control even with a majority of four; but, when in a minority, moves into straight opposition. The idea is—no sharing of responsibility, no co-operation."[24]

There is much evidence in the larger authorities to substantiate such a view; but the vast majority of local authorities are small and less tightly organised politically, and many have no political divisions at all. Moreover, one should not assume that political allegiances necessarily imply a continual atmosphere of party polemic and bitterness, for much council work, particularly in committee, is characterised by a spirit of co-operation and moderation.

Nevertheless party divisions do exist, and have been a significant feature of local government for many years. Local political associations came into being with each successive extension of the franchise in the last century, particularly after the Reform Act of 1867 increased the electorate by millions in the fast-expanding industrial towns.

At first the associations were most strongly organised in the larger

---

[24] Roy Perrott, "Whips in the Council Chamber", *Guardian*, 6 August, 1959. Note also the Maud Committee's comment (para. 367): ". . . in none of the other countries are the parties 'permanently embattled in the same way as in many English industrial authorities'."

provincial cities and industrial centres of the North and Midlands where, by the 1870s, municipal elections were being fought on party tickets. Soon such municipalities were also being run on party lines, as for example was Birmingham under the mayoralty of Joseph Chamberlain in 1873.

Local political associations were slightly later in developing in the south of England, but from its inception in 1889 the London County Council was organised on a party basis with the majority party, the Progressives, made up of Liberals and a few Fabians, and the opposition, the Moderates, being mainly Conservatives. The Conservative Prime Minister, Lord Salisbury, fulminated at the London County Council in 1894, as,

> "the place where Collectivist and Socialistic experiments are tried . . . a place where the new revolutionary spirit finds its instruments and collects its arms."[25]

By the time the Labour Party was formed in 1900, party political grouping was primarily rooted in the councils of most large towns. The non-payment of M.Ps. (until 1911) and the well-established national organisations supporting the Conservative and Liberal parties in Parliament, made the idea of a third and embryonic party achieving parliamentary control an extremely remote possibility. Earlier, local Independent Labour Party groups had turned their attention to local government and, primed with Fabian policies, the Labour Party joined in the local fray with no little success. In the 1919 local government elections Labour won 412 seats, gained control of the large county borough of Bradford and of twelve metropolitan boroughs; in contested elections in 1961 Labour gained 43·3 per cent of the votes in comparison with the 44·7 per cent won by the Conservatives and their supporters.[26]

An impression of the political alignment of local councils in England and Wales can be gained from Table 2 overleaf which shows the results of the first elections[27] to the new local authorities in 1973. This table gives no indication, however, of the vast diversity of political opinion and organisation which exists in each local council. An analysis of political activity in four English towns by J. G. Bulpitt confirmed the assessment of A. H. Birch that "local

---

[25] W. A. Robson, *The Government and Misgovernment of London*, Allen & Unwin, p. 86.
[26] Ivor Gowan, "Role and Power of Political Parties in Local Government", *Local Government Today—and Tomorrow* (ed. D. Lofts), *Municipal Journal*, 1962, p. 86.
[27] Compiled from data in *Keesing's Contemporary Archives*, pp. 25890 and 25961.

TABLE 2. PARTY CONTROL AT 1973 ELECTIONS

	Local authorities and election dates					
	12 April		*Welsh counties (8)*	*10 May*		*7 June*
Party control	*Non-metropolitan counties (39)*	*Metropolitan counties (6)*		*Metropolitan districts (36)*	*Welsh districts (37)*	*Non-metropolitan districts (296)*
Labour	7	6	4	26	19	71
Conservative	13			5	1	59
Independent	2		3		16	67
Conservative with Independent support	5					
Liberal						1
Democratic Labour					1	1
No party with overall control	12		1	5		97

Seats won	*12 April*			*10 May*		*7 June*
Labour	1,754			2,221		4,327
Conservative	1,533			835		4,286
Independent	642			618		3,534
Liberal	246			220		919
Plaid Cymru	18			43		
Others	17			91		449
Totals	4,210			4,028		13,515

parties are highly individual, conditioned more by their environment than by directives from central office and largely independent in managing their own business'.[28] In the four towns, only housing was consistently influenced by party politics, and in "other policy sectors no general pattern of party disagreement emerged". In the main, the "style of local party politics . . . seemed to be determined to a large extent by individual Councillors, the differences between them, and the past political histories of the local authorities". There was no evidence of bitter division between local parties on national party lines, but rather a desire to practise political restraint and avoid divisive issues. "With the exception of the Salford Labour Party all parties appeared embarrassed by their activities in local government. The predominance of patronage disputes suggests a preoccupation with the possession of power, not the use of it for policy purposes."

Bulpitt concluded his informative study with a tentative classification of party systems in local government into positive and negative systems. In the former, party representatives are in the majority and the parties accept a degree of political responsibility for Council work; the positive system can be further sub-divided according to the importance of (a) size and stability of the majority party, (b) the pattern of patronage distribution, and (c) the way in which Standing Orders are interpreted by the Labour Group. Negative systems are where two or more minority parties exist among a majority of Independents, there is little political responsibility for running the council, and "party is merely an electoral device".

Where party control is strongly organised, particularly on the councils of the larger municipalities and cities, "a kind of Parliamentary government in miniature" develops. Within that microcosm "a tougher, parliamentary outlook" prevails where,

> ". . . the party whips crack audibly off-stage; in which policy is decided out of sight and sound of press and public. . . in which there is often an informal 'Cabinet' of leading party men whose influence is unquestionable (or at least unquestioned); in which there is a clear division between the governors and the opposition, both tending to speak with one unified prefabricated voice from the depths of the party machine".[29]

The "voice" is "prefabricated" in that policy decisions are taken at party caucus meetings before the council meets. Here council members of the majority party, together with non-council members of the local party organisation, who may or may not have voting powers,

---

[28] J. G. Bulpitt, *Party Politics in English local Government*, Longmans, 1967.
[29] Roy Perrott, "Whips in the Council Chamber", *Guardian*, 6 August, 1959.

hammer out policy. Individuals may express their differing view-points in private, but once a line of action has been decided, individual members are expected to abide by the majority decision and to vote accordingly when the council meets. Failure to do so may result in expulsion.

The Labour group which controlled Leeds City Council had a highly organised party caucus which met at the "epitome" meeting before the council meetings and mid-monthly. This meeting "controls council proceedings", wrote Professor Wiseman who continued:

> "It shows also a group which devotes much time to study of the Council agenda and to minutes of committees other than those on which the inquiring member himself serves and which is determined to keep leader and chairman on their toes. The epitome meeting is essential if the majority party is to control the affairs of the Corporation."[30]

Thus the majority party caucus may be seen not only as the real decision-making body but also as an agency for the control of its own members. The council meeting, as a result, tends no longer to be "an instrument for decision but, like the House of Commons, an instrument for propaganda".[31]

Other results of majority party control will be seen in the emergence of the party leader as leader of the council, dominating its meetings, and the party's virtual monopoly of the chairmanships and vice-chairmanships of committees, aldermanic seats, mayoralties and council chairmanships. Sharing these offices on the basis of party strength, with the mayoralty/chairmanship alternating between Labour and Conservative nominees now tends in the larger towns and cities to have become more a residual tradition of the past than a convention to be perpetuated.

Opinions vary considerably as to the necessity and value of party politics in local government, and the following arguments for and against summarise some of these opinions. The case against political groups might include the following arguments:

1. Party politics are unnecessary and irrelevant in local government. Local authorities are primarily administrative, not legislative, bodies which are required to implement policies already decided in Parliament. The areas where local discretion is permitted are not so controversial as to require the confrontation of local party machines and should be decided on the basis of benefit to the community and

---

[30] H. V. Wiseman, "The Party Caucus in Local Government", in *New Society*, 31 October, 1963.
[31] Sir Ivor Jennings, *Principles of Local Government Law*, U.L.P. 1963, p. 129.

not political expediency. In this respect W. A. Robson has written: ". . . party alignments and loyalties tend to become a public nuisance when they are linked up with matters which have no bearing on the work of the Council".[32]

2. Acceptance of the party whip necessarily limits a councillor's freedom of decision and independence of action. Unlike the M.P., he does not have such extensive and tangible election support from the party to repay; his major obligation is thus to the electorate and their immediate, personal and local problems, not to the party machine.

3. The majority party caucus is an undemocratic institution insofar as its deliberations are influenced by the participation of party association representatives; the press and the public are excluded and the local authority's officers are never present to be consulted. Yet its decisions can exercise an important influence over the conduct of major community services.

4. Since the majority party caucus determines what the council does, the council meeting itself is an irrelevancy, and democratic control a hollow sham:

> "Local government is one of the sacred cows of the political mythology about the working of democracy in the United Kingdom. The idea that local government is essentially more democratic than central government lives on despite the singularly undemocratic working of local representation and of local elections."[33]

5. The majority party's decisions at the caucus meetings may be based upon a small majority vote of perhaps one. The image which is presented to the full council and to the public is, however, one of complete unanimity. The electorate will be unaware of the discussion preceding the vote, the alternative proposals expressed, and which council members took an independent line. These latter will be required to approve the narrow majority view, regardless of conscience or principles, at the council meeting, and may even have the additional embarrassment of having to defend as chief spokesman the party's final decision.

6. The majority party's monopoly of offices in the council and the committees may be interpreted by the public as a form of Tammany Hall corruption. Within the council the distribution of the spoils of office may cause jealousy, and the exclusion of worthy opposition members will add to their resentment.

7. Party politics contribute to the community's electoral apathy, help to dissuade able non-party men and women from standing for candidature or for co-option to council committees, and alienate the public from the council's members and officers.

---

[32] *Ibid.*, p. 87. Note also his comment on Clay Cross as "essentially a study of Tammany Hall politics applied to a small English local authority", *Political Quarterly*, October, 1974.

[33] *Public Law*, 1962, Editorial, p. 5.

8. In areas dominated by one party, its candidate is certain to be elected, whether opposed or not. The real selection will therefore be the "primary", where a candidate is chosen to stand for the party by the party leaders. They will almost invariably prefer conformists, and the electorate loses all direct influence over the type of candidate who is presented for election. The candidate will thus represent his party and not necessarily his ward.

9. The emergence of a party leader who "guides and controls his party's contribution to the business and debates of the council and . . . makes major pronouncements on council policy" may well become a form of autocratic dominance. Professor Gowan continues: "There is some danger that, surrounded by weak colleagues, and with an ineffective opposition, the leader can become the 'boss', and that the party system is then prone to degenerate into 'one-man' government. Such cases are fortunately rare . . ."[34]—but not unknown.

Those who defend the existence of party politics in local government have advanced the following advantages:

i. The party system, with a majority kept on its toes by an effective opposition, the local press and its own internal discipline, provides a local authority with strong and efficient administration. The alternative, a council composed of individualists, would result in compromise decisions which would satisfy no one, least of all the public.

ii. Party organisations give greater definition, vitality and coherence to the conduct of local matters, and "a proposal supported or opposed on party lines, gets a better and more zealous exposition and advocacy, and a more comprehensive discussion than otherwise might be the case".[35]

iii. To expect "the cut and thrust of debate" in the council chamber followed by a free vote to determine the outcome of disputed policies is to display a naïve interpretation of the purpose of a council meeting. The majority group's decision can be questioned in council, and after discussion matters can be referred back to committees for reconsideration, but debate will generally not change the majority group's earlier decision. This does not entail anything novel in our governmental process, and as Professor Wiseman has observed:

> "Debates are to educate public opinion and to enable parties to express their views and stake a claim for future support from the electorate. This argument may be even more valid in local government because the vast majority of decisions are on detailed administrative matters which a large meeting is incompetent to decide. At most it is competent to refer the matter back to the appropriate committee for further consideration."[36]

---

[34] *Ibid*, p. 74.
[35] H. Emerson Smith, "Party Politics in English Local Government," in *Secretaries' Chronicle*, March, 1955.
[36] *Ibid*, p. 10.

iv. Party politics educate the public and make local government understandable to the electorate. Without the spice of party strife in the council chamber, interest in the work of the local authority would be far less than it is; the exclusion of politics would increase the electorate's apathy and the number of uncontested seats. A study of local democracy by R. P. Lowry in "Micro City" in California showed that where personalities and not parties fight local elections, antipathy directed against a depersonalised party might be replaced by open hostility against candidates. An American study may not be strictly relevant to British experience, but a case may be made for the retention of political alignments in British local government. An editorial in *New Society*[37] commented:

". . . the problems of recruiting the right people to local government and arousing public interest are not solved by getting rid of organised politics. The party structure, to some extent, provides politicians with backing to offset personal abuse and enables issues to be seen in less personal terms. And if party politics are removed the electorate appears to feel even less involved in decisions than they do in Britain now. The achievement of effective grass roots democracy demands that local government should be made more, not less, a part of national political life."

v. The caucus meeting, far from rendering individual councillors politically impotent, provides them with an opportunity to speak their mind, without fear of misquotation in the press or mis-interpretation by the public or the council's officers, and to persuade their colleagues of the validity of their proposals. Similarly, they may ventilate constituents' grievances and those of local minority groups and make their leaders aware of ward or area difficulties. Such an opportunity is not available in the council meeting where a rigid timetable has to be maintained and "backbench" councillors have little opportunity to speak. Moreover, the caucus meeting's detailed analysis of the council agenda, which comprises the minutes of all committees, is not only personally valuable in providing councillors with a survey of the entire gamut of council affairs, but, more significantly, allows them to question committee chairmen on the content of their minutes so ensuring that proposals are dissected. If the replies of a chairman are unsatisfactory, the minutes may be referred back to the committee for reconsideration. Finally, where a party has a substantial majority on the council, leaders may become complacent or may assume oligarchic control; the caucus meeting permits members to exercise control over their leaders without committing the party to unseemly debate in the council before the opposition and the public.

It would thus appear that party allegiance need not be detrimental to the efficient working of local authorities, and may indeed

---

[37] 14 January, 1965.

make positive contributions to local government. The conclusion of the Maud Report (Vol. 1, para. 32–33) was that "The presence or absence of local parties does not determine the quality of local government. . . . England manages relatively well", but cautioned that "in the minority of authorities parties tend to have too much of a stranglehold in day-to-day operations. . . ."

The responsibilities shouldered by councillors obviously require of them the highest standards of personal integrity. Quite apart from the pressures imposed by party membership, there may be occasions when personal self-interest threatens to undermine a councillor's otherwise impeccable public record. The law requires that a member is precluded from taking part in the conduct of business in which he (or his spouse) has a pecuniary interest, direct or indirect, and he must disclose his interest and refrain from speaking or voting on the matter.[38] The penalty is a fine of up to £200. The Secretary of State has the power to remove the disability for speaking, or on principal councils, for speaking and voting. Widespread disquiet about the standards of probity in local government, particularly the revelations in the Poulson bankruptcy trial and the subsequent police investigations, led the Prime Minister (Edward Heath) to appoint in October, 1973, a committee of inquiry into the rules of conduct of members and officers in local government. Its chairman was Lord Redcliffe–Maud.

The committee's report[39] was presented to Parliament in May, 1974, and concluded that "the picture is still of an essentially honest public service" and that "standards of conduct in local government are generally high". In the period 1964 to 1972, when local authorities were served by some 48,000 members and over 2 million employees, there were 10 members and 22 employees convicted of offences under the Prevention of Corruption Acts, and 16 members convicted of failure to disclose a pecuniary interest under the Local Government Acts. Though the number of convictions is small, the committee stated that they "share the public concern that corruption exists" and "that unless corruption is stopped, it spreads. The only acceptable standard for British local government is complete honesty."

Rules of conduct derive from statute law, standing orders made by individual authorities, and conditions of service for employees. The committee proposed changes in all three sources. In addition, the committee proposed the establishment of a national code of

---

[38] Local Government Act 1972, ss. 94–96.
[39] *Conduct in Local Government,* Cmnd. 5636, May 1974.

conduct for all councillors, and offered a draft code for consideration. After discussion the following Code[40] was agreed.

NATIONAL CODE OF LOCAL GOVERNMENT CONDUCT

"This Code is a guide for all councillors elected or co-opted to local authorities in England, Wales and Scotland. It supplements both the law enacted by Parliament and the Standing Orders made by individual councils. It has been agreed by the Associations representing local authorities in all three countries and by the government.

1. *Law, Standing Orders and National Code*

"Make sure that you fully understand the rules of conduct which the law, Standing Orders and the national code require you to follow. It is your personal responsibility to apply their requirements on every relevant occasion. Seek any advice about them that you need from your council's appropriate senior officer or from your own legal adviser.

2. *Public duty and private interest*

"(i) Your overriding duty as a councillor is to the whole local community.

 (ii) You have a special duty to your own constituents, including those who did not vote for you.

(iii) Whenever you have a private or personal interest in any question which councillors have to decide, you must not do anything to let that interest influence the decision.

(iv) Do nothing as a councillor which you could not justify to the public.

 (v) The reputation of your council, and of your party if you belong to one, depends on your conduct and what the public believes about your conduct.

(vi) It is not enough to avoid actual impropriety; you should at all times avoid any occasion for suspicion or the appearance of improper conduct.

3. *Disclosure of pecuniary and other interests*

"(i) The law makes specific provision requiring you to disclose pecuniary interests, direct and indirect. But interests which are not pecuniary can be just as important. Kinship, friendship, membership of an association, society, or trade union, trusteeship and many other kinds of relationship can sometimes influence your judgment and give the impression that you might be acting for personal motives. A good test is to

---

[40] DOE Circular 94/75 *The National Code of Local Government Conduct*, October 1975.

ask yourself whether others would think that the interest is of a kind to make this possible. If you think they would, or if you are in doubt, disclose the interest and withdraw from the meeting unless under Standing Orders you are specifically invited to stay.

(ii) The principles about disclosure of interest should be borne in mind in your unofficial relations with other councillors—at party group meetings, or other informal occasions no less scrupulously than at formal meetings of the council, its committees and sub-committees.

4. *Membership and Chairmanship of Council Committees and Sub-committees*

"(i) You, or some firm or body with which you are personally connected, may have professional business or personal interests within the area for which the council is responsible; such interests may be substantial and closely related to the work of one or more of the council's committees or sub-committees, concerned with (say) planning or developing land, council housing, 'personnel matters' or the letting of contracts for supplies, services or works. Before seeking or accepting membership of any such committee or sub-committee, you should seriously consider whether your membership would involve you (a) in disclosing an interest so often that you could be of little value to the the committee or sub-committee, or (b) in weakening public confidence in the impartiality of the committee or sub-committee.

(ii) You should not seek or accept the chairmanship of a committee or sub-committee whose business is closely related to a substantial interest or range of interests of yourself or of any body with which you are associated.

5. *Councillors and officers*

"(i) Both councillors and officers are servants of the public, and they are indispensable to one another. But their responsibilities are distinct. Councillors are responsible to the electorate and serve only so long as their term of office lasts. Officers are responsible to the council and are permanently appointed. An officer's job is to give advice to councillors and the council and to carry out the council's work under the direction and control of the council and its committees.

(ii) Mutual respect between councillors and officers is essential to good local government. Close personal familiarity between individual councillor and officer can damage this relationship and prove embarrassing to other councillors and officers.

(iii) If you are called upon to take part in appointing an officer, the only question you should consider is which candidate would best serve the whole council. You should not let your personal or political preferences influence your judgment. You should not canvass the support of colleagues for any candidate and you should resist any attempt by others to canvass yours.

6. *Use of confidential and private information*

"As a councillor you necessarily acquire much information that has not yet been made public and is still confidential. It is a grave betrayal of trust to use confidential information for the personal advantage of yourself or of anyone known to you.

7. *Gifts and hospitality*

"Treat with extreme caution any offer or gift, favour or hospitality that is made to you personally. The person or organisation making the offer may be doing or seeking to do business with the council, or applying to the council for planning permission or some other kind of decision. Working lunches and other social occasions arranged or authorised by the council or by one of its committees or sub-committees may be a proper way of doing business, provided that no extravagance is involved. Nor can there be any hard and fast rule about acceptance or refusal of tokens of good-will on special occasions. But you are personally responsible for all such decisions and for avoiding the risk of damage to public confidence in local government. The receipt or offer of gifts should be reported to the chief executive.

8. *Expenses and allowances*

There are rules entitling you to claim expenses and allowances in connection with your duties as a councillor. These rules should be scrupulously observed.

9. *Use of council facilities*

"Make sure that any facilities—such as transport, stationery, or secretarial services—provided by the council for your use in your duties as a councillor are used strictly for those duties and for no other purpose."

Prior to the issue of the above Code a joint circular from the D.O.E. and the Welsh Office was issued on 31 July, 1974, to the chief executives of principal councils drew attention to those recommendations of the committee on which councils could take immediate action: they should have clear arrangements for the systematic review of their internal procedures from the point of view of probity; they should have clear and well publicised arrangements for receiving and investigating complaints; they should pursue vigorous policies of public communication, on both general and specific subjects; they should publicise the policies and procedures by which they carry out their statutory functions; they should adapt standing orders prohibiting canvassing for appointments and requiring disclosure of kinship; they should not permit their employees to undertake outside work, for payment by a member of the public, or any matter connected with their official duties, and a record of permissions given for approved kinds of outside work should be kept and should be open to inspection by councillors; and they should require senior or professional employees as a condition of service, not to take up within two years of retirement or resignation private employment in the authority's area without the authority's consent.

The Report and the Code were favourably received and their proposals generally supported, subject to the requirement for further consideration and clarification of certain items. The Association of Metropolitan Authorities, for example, commented on the division of opinion among its member authorities as to whether the procedure for written disclosure of pecuniary interests should be withdrawn. Other comments concerned: the proposal for compulsory withdrawal of an interested member from meetings and whether this should be left to standing orders rather than to statutory compulsion; the difficulty of enforcing the proposal on the misuse of official information for private gain; the disqualification of employees from membership; and the allegedly "unrealistic" and "illusory" proposal that officers should be banned from practising in the area for two years after leaving the authority's service. It was anticipated that if there was to be legislation on the report that these and other matters would be fully debated and that authorities and their associations would be fully consulted.

CHAPTER 5

The Local Government Service

1. Manpower Resources

Local authorities in England and Wales employed over two and half million people in 1975. These constituted one-tenth of the working population and included solicitors, architects, teachers, work-study officers, accountants, labourers, dustmen, engineers, park attendants and many others who are essential to the efficient provision of local authority services.

Within this diverse employment range a distinction is made between those in "the service" and the remaining employees. The "service" is made up of "those who participate in the administration and management of Local Authority services, and whose duties are of an administrative, professional, technical or clerical nature". Excluded from the "service" classification are manual workers, teachers and the police. These groups "are usually thought of as belonging to separate and well-defined services of their own".[1]

It is important to note this distinction between the "service" and the remainder, and to realise that while the efficiency and effectiveness of local authority services depends upon the many specialist abilities of its officers there is a larger body of personnel who perform essential duties, and more often under the critical gaze of the public. The accompanying table shows the number of employees engaged in separate departments or services which together cover the whole range of local authority activities.

2. "Proper officers"

Local authorities are empowered by s. 112 of the Local Government Act 1972 to "appoint such officers as they think necessary for the proper discharge by the authority of such of their or another authority's functions as fall to be discharged by them . . .". This provision is radically different from the requirements of the Local Government Act 1933 which required the appointment of officers

---

[1] J. H. Warren, *The Local Government Service*, Allen & Unwin, 1952, v.

with such specific titles as clerk, treasurer, medical officer of health, surveyor, and public health inspector. The approach embodied in the 1972 Act gives local authorities a much wider discretion in deciding what officer posts to establish. They need to decide which of their officers should be designated to carry out particular functions which are by statute to be exercised by a particular officer, and the legal device to achieve this is for a local authority to designate a "proper officer".

The exceptions to this general power, listed in the Act, are the

TABLE 3. JOINT STAFF WATCH SURVEY OF LOCAL AUTHORITIES IN ENGLAND AND WALES

Department or Service	Numbers employed at 31 March, 1975		
	Full-time	Part-time	Totals
Education: Lecturers and teachers	518,768	203,440	722,208
Others	220,862	481,968	702,830
Construction	136,458	808	137,266
Transport	22,494	391	22,885
Social services	127,300	146,551	273,851
Public libraries and museums	24,696	13,847	38,543
Recreation, parks and baths	64,995	11,762	76,757
Environmental health	19,991	2,202	22,193
Refuse collection and disposal	51,699	574	52,273
Housing	43,477	8,865	52,342
Town and Country Planning	19,502	485	19,987
Fire Service: Regular	30,934	—	30,934
Others	5,273	1,654	6,927
Miscellaneous services*	254,224	39,734	293,958
	1,540,673‡	912,281‡	2,452,954‡
Police: All Ranks	102,738	—	102,738
Cadets	4,856	—	4,856
Civilians	30,092	7,096	37,188
Traffic Wardens	6,162	—	6,162
	143,848	7,096	150,944
Agency staff	603	196	799
Magistrates' Courts†	5,687	1,105	6,792
Probation staff†: Officers	4,375	117	4,492
Others	2,421	865	3,286
	13,086	2,283	15,369

* Covers central support staff and other staff, not included in other departments or services, also school crossing patrols, staff on special functions, trading services and agriculture and fisheries.

† Excludes figures for outer London which were not available.

‡ Includes 505,061 full-time and 603,673 part-time manual employees.

requirements for non-metropolitan county councils and metropolitan district councils to appoint chief education officers and
directors of social services; for county councils to appoint chief
fire officers and members of fire brigades; in England, for county
councils and, in Wales, for some district councils and some county
councils to appoint agricultural analysts and inspectors of weights
and measures. Moreover, the freedom not to appoint prescribed
officers does not extend to committees of local authorities of which
some members are required to be appointed by a body or person
other than a local authority. Thus chief constables, deputy and
assistant chief constables must be appointed under the Police Act
1964, National Park officers must be appointed under s. 17 of the
Local Government Act 1972, and fishery officers under the Sea
Fisheries Regulation Act 1966.

Apart from these requirements local authorities now have the
general power to appoint the staff required to carry out their
functions and to establish their own mangerial and operational
structures. In addition, the statutory provisions which formerly
specified an applicant's qualifications for appointment, and the
requirement that specified statutory appointees could not be
dismissed without the approval of the appropriate central department, have, with certain exceptions, been removed by the Local
Government Act 1972. An officer appointed under the general
power holds office "on such reasonable terms and conditions,
including conditions as to renumeration, as the authority appointing
him think fit". However, most local authorities are members of
Whitley Councils which negotiate national salary scales and
conditions of service for most employees, while others (for example,
teachers and police) have their pay and conditions prescribed by
the appropriate government department.

There are twenty-two national negotiating bodies for conditions
of service in England and Wales (and a further three in Scotland)
and these are listed below together with the approximate number
of employees within the purview of each in 1974:

Administrative, Professional, Technical and Clerical Group

1. Joint Negotiating Committee for Chief Executives		450
2. Joint Negotiating Committee for Chief Officers		3,000
3. National Joint Council for Local Authorities Administrative, Professional, Technical and Clerical Services		375,000
4. Joint Negotiating Committee for Justices Clerks		460
5. Joint Negotiating Committee for Justices Clerks' Assistants		4,000

6. Joint Negotiating Committee for Approved Schools and Remand Homes — 1,500
7. Whitley Council for New Towns Staff — 6,000
8. Joint Negotiating Committee for the Probation Service — 3,600

Manual and Craftsmen Group

9. National Joint Council for Local Authorities Manual Workers — 920,000
10. Joint Negotiating Committee for Building and Civil Engineering Craftsmen — 180,000
11. Joint Negotiating Committee for Engineering Craftsmen — 10,000
12. Joint Negotiationg Commitee for Heating, Ventilating and Domestic Engineers — 500
13. National Joint Council for Blind Workshops — 900

Teaching Group

14. The Burnham Primary and Secondary Committee — 344,000
15. The Burnham Further Education Committee — 40,000
16. The Burnham Farm Institutes Committee — 600
17. The "Pelham" Committee (Colleges of Education) — 10,000
18. The "Soulbury" Committee (Inspectors and Organisers) — 2,500
19. Joint Negotiating Committee for Youth Leaders and Community Centre Wardens — 2,500

Uniformed Emergency Group

20. Police Council for Great Britain — 106,000
21. National Joint Council for Local Authorities Fire Brigades — 26,135 (whole time) 18,400 (retained)
22. National Joint Council for Chief Officers of Local Authorities Fire Brigades — 142

3. The N.J.C. for Administrative and Clerical Staffs

The National Joint Council for Local Authorities' Administrative, Professional, Technical and Clerical Services was formed in 1944 and is sometimes referred to as the National Whitley Council. The terms and conditions of employment of local government staff within its scope are negotiated at a national level by employer and officer representatives to the N.J.C. and these are implemented by the individual local authorities. The Council comprises seventy-one members, of whom thirty-six are appointed to represent the employers and thirty-five to represent the officers:

A. *Employers' Side*

Provincial Councils	16 representatives
Scottish Council	4 ,,
Association of County Councils	6 ,,
Association of Metropolitan Authorities	6 ,,
Association of District Councils	4 ,,

B. *Staff Side*

Provincial Councils (excluding Greater London district)	12 representatives 4 ,,
Greater London District Whitley Council	4 ,,
Scottish Council	4 ,,
National and Local Government Officers' Association	8 ,,
Union of General and Municipal Workers	3 ,,
National Union of Public Employees	2 ,,
Transport and General Workers' Union	1 ,,
Confederation of Health Service Employees	1 ,,

An independent chairman without voting rights is appointed for three years by the Secretary of State for the Department of the Environment.

C. *Functions of the National Joint Council:*

"To secure the largest possible measure of joint action for the consideration of salaries, wages and service conditions of officers within the scope of the Council and to consider such proposals in reference to these matters as are submitted to them from time to time by the Provincial Councils and the Scottish Council."

There are thirteen Provincial Councils and a Council for Scotland. Their membership varies from district to district, but N.A.L.G.O. representatives are in the majority on the staff side of each Council. Moreover, the Provincial Council representatives on the employees' side of the national council are all members of N.A.L.G.O. In addition, there are local joint committees within those local authorities where the employing authorities afford "facilities for regular consultation with representatives of their staffs on all questions affecting their conditions of service". The Model Constitution, determined by the National Joint Council, outlines the functions of such a committee: to establish regular methods of negotiation for the prevention of differences and their settlement should they arise, but excluding cases of individual discipline, promotion or efficiency; to consider any relevant matters referred by local authority committees or staff organisations; to make recommendations to the appropriate committee relating to the applicability of terms and conditions of service, training and education of officers; and to refer questions to the appropriate Provincial Council, provided the local authority approves, and inform it of any matter which is of more than local interest.

The Charter states that "Negotiations between individual local authorities and unorganised officers are impracticable" and consequently recommends local authorities to recognise the organisations which are represented on the National Joint Council, adding that "the interests of local authorities and their staffs are best served by individual officers joining an organisation representing them on the National Council."

The predominant union in local government is N.A.L.G.O. which was founded with 8,000 members in 1905 from the federation of the Municipal Officers' Association, a number of Municipal Officers' Guilds and the Association of Municipal and County Engineers, and was certified as a trade union in 1920. The Association's name was changed in 1952 from the National Association of Local Government Officers to the National and Local Government Officers' Association, "to take into account its newly extended membership to staffs in nationalised health, electricity, gas and other services". In 1964, affiliation to the T.U.C. was agreed by ballot after having been rejected by members on a number of occasions since 1921. It is the fourth largest trade union in Britain and the largest white-collar union in the world, with a membership which has grown rapidly in recent years to a total in 1974 of 518,000, of whom 329,658 worked in local government. It is organised in 1,211 branches in twelve districts. The union had a net asset value of nearly £4 million and its income, mainly from members' subscriptions, amounted to nearly £3 million at the end of 1973.

4. Conditions of Service

Employment conditions for A.P.T. & C. divisions are contained in the *Scheme of Conditions of Service*, known variously as "The Charter" or "The Purple Book". The categories of staff are:

A. *Clerical Division*

This division covers posts with duties of a clerical character and comprises three grades. Grade 1 is used as the general recruitment grade and for staff who undertake a range of tasks which can be carried out in accordance with well-defined regulations, instructions or general practice. The 1974 Salaries Agreement provided for the merger of the former Clerical Grades 1 and 2 and their extension by one point; for the abolition of the routine work bar and the introduction of a responsibility/supervisory bar; for the shortening of the scale by three points; and for improvements in the 21 age point.

B. *Administrative and Professional Division*

1. Trainee Grade: introduced in 1967 to secure a better share of the talented youngsters and university graduates needed to fill senior posts in the future. Trainees are normally required to undertake work of a clerical, administrative, professional or technical nature appropriate to the salary paid at the time.

2. A.P. Grades: a five-fold grading structure applying to posts involving professional work or concerned with the general administration of the local authority's work or the improvement of its organisation and to posts of a specialist nature not appropriately graded within other divisions.

3. Grades for Senior and Principal Administrative and Professional Posts: Senior Officers' Grades 1 and 2 are available for more senior administrative and professional posts filled by officers who are both fully qualified by examinations and also experienced in administrative or professional work. The extent to which the grades are used depends on the size of the authority and the scope of work undertaken, but the National Council envisage that these grades will include, for example, posts involving (i) advice on the formation of policy; (ii) the control of large or important sections of work; (iii) the leadership of teams of professional or technical officers; and (iv) individual work of a high order.

Principal Officers' Ranges 1 and 2 are for yet more senior posts than those above. The salary grading of posts above the level of P.O. 2 (excluding chief officers and their deputies) is at the discretion of the employing authority.

C. *Technicians and Technical Staffs Division*

This division of five grades covers officers undertaking work of a technical nature which requires a special training or expertise but does not need to be done by officers with full professional qualifications (or by officers studying for such a professional qualification). It will include, for example, draughtsmen, clerks of works, building inspectors, architectural technicians, engineering technicians, planning technicians, laboratory/workshop technicians, etc. It does not include posts of a professional nature filled by unqualified officers.

D. *Special Classes of Officer*

This section of the "Purple Book" contains a heterogeneous range of occupations including administrative staff, librarians, careers officers, public health inspectors, welfare assistants, staff in mental health training centres, home teachers of the blind, social workers, shorthand, audio and copy typists, machine operators, secretaries and telephone operators, laboratory/workshop technicians, and air traffic control officers.

E. *Miscellaneous Classes*

Seven salary grades for occupations including school meals supervisors, traffic wardens, telephone operators, and supervisory staffs in workshops for the blind.

The foregoing account provides an insight into the multiplicity of job designations and the range of abilities covered by just one of the main national negotiating bodies for local authority personnel. Referring to the general public's casual acceptance of the work of "town hall staff", B. J. Rusbridge, Secretary of the Local Authorities' Conditions of Service Advisory Board (L.A.C.S.A.B.), stated: "Few, indeed, comprehend the immense variety of occupations, skills and professions which keep alive the basic services upon which the community depends and which ironically are appreciated and valued only when they fail."[2] L.A.C.S.A.B. provides a service which covers all aspects of manpower and a full secretariat for the negotiating bodies which determine conditions for all local authority employees.

5. Committees on the Management and Staffing of Local Government

In response to a request from the Local Authority Associations the Minister of Housing and Local Government set up in 1964, two committees of inquiry. One, under the chairmanship of Sir John Maud, considered "in the light of modern conditions how local government might best continue to attract and retain people (both elected representatives and principal officers) of the calibre necessary to ensure its maximum effectiveness".

The terms of reference of the second committee, headed by Sir

---

[2] I.P.M. National Conference, October 1974.

George Mallaby, were: "To consider the existing methods of recruiting local government officers and of using them; and what changes might help local authorities to get the best possible service and help their officers to give it."

A circular issued by the Ministry of Housing and Local Government added that the Mallaby Committee was expected to examine "any special difficulties in getting and keeping staff for particular services; ideas for the greater employment of graduates; the career prospects; movement between authorities and the opportunities for promotion; any reasons for unwillingness of people to enter or remain in local government service. They will not be concerned with the pay of staff. Training schemes and the question in particular of administrative training for professional staff will certainly concern them; and also the desirability of a Staff College for local government."

The Mallaby Committee published its report *Staffing of Local Government* in March, 1967, having received information from a variety of sources during its three years' work. These included 145 submissions of written evidence (nine from local authorities), oral evidence from private individuals and various bodies, replies to postal questionnaires to a sample of local authorities and a sample of N.A.L.G.O. members, and visits to local authorities and other institutions at home and abroad.

After setting out the conditions of service and existing staffing situation, the bulk of the report analysed possible developments which would affect staffing in the context of the national shortage of manpower and particularly of skilled and trained personnel. The Committee detailed recommendations in the realisation that they would not all be applicable to all local authorities but "that action can generally be initiated on them without any new legislation and without awaiting the results of other enquiries which are now being conducted". The Committee thus recommended that local authorities should accept certain "propositions and responsibilities".

Regarding *recruitment* local authorities should recognise the growing need to recruit graduates as trainees for professional and administrative posts and the danger of not doing this. They should consequently place more emphasis on recruitment from universities and colleges. School-leavers should be attracted by good training schemes and opportunities to obtain administrative and professional qualifications. The necessity to offer comparable rewards and attractions to those offered by competing employers should be accepted. Consideration should be given to offering an extension of talks and lectures on local problems and developments to the schools, and to giving senior pupils the opportunity of seeing local authority work at first hand by means of holiday attachments. Close contacts should be maintained with schools' careers masters, youth employment officers, and registrars of technical colleges, supplemented by publicity for local government careers organised on a national scale. Attention should be paid to the timing of approaches to school leavers, undergraduates and the secretaries of appointments boards, and to the quality of their advertisements and publicity material. Local authorities need to note changes which affect the recruitment and use of medical practitioners in other branches of the National Health Service. Individual local authorities should consider making joint arrangements between themselves for the recruitment, appointment and training of staff.

With reference to *career prospects*, local authorities should ensure that the prospects of the school leaver trainee, are, when he has qualified, the same as those of his graduate counterpart, and that the technician is given a proper place beside the professional officer. Subject to the size of the local authority and the scope of its responsibilities, the lay administrative officer should be provided with a career which would take him to the second or third tier position in the department and he should be equal in salary and status with his professional colleagues at those levels. All senior posts in education departments, excepting that of Chief Education Officer and those concerned with advisory work with schools, should also be available to him. The Clerkship of an authority, being mainly an administrative post, should be open to all professions including the lay administrative officer.

On the matter of *selection procedure*, the Mallaby Committee stated that local authorities should consider seeking advice from outside assessors when appointing principal officers and their deputies. Interviewing panels of elected members for the selection and appointment of principal officers and their deputies should be small, while principal officers should be responsible for selecting and appointing their staff up to and including third tier level, making full use of the specialist advice available in the Clerk's Department.

Recommendations relating to *training* were extensive. Local authorities should accept responsibility for arranging training facilities and enabling their officers to make full use of them. It is the Clerk's responsibility to see that adequate training schemes exist. Adequate facilities for continued general education as well as professional training should be provided for direct entrants from schools, and selected well-qualified candidates should be sponsored for full-time university degree courses. When fixing departmental establishments allowance should be made for training needs.

Principal Officers should be responsible for ensuring that adequate arrangements are made for the training of their staff, and training officers should be of senior status. Local authorities should arrange for a Local Government Training Board to be established on lines suggested by the L.G.E.B. Working Party on the Cost of Training, with training levies and grants spreading the cost of training more equitably as with the Industrial Training Boards.

Induction training should be provided for new entrants, and local authorities which have the facilities should offer recognised courses of professional training by means of full-time, sandwich, block-release or day courses.[3] Professional officers should have opportunities to gain the widest possible experience in their own and related departments, and in selected cases receive periods of secondment to other local authorities, industry, commerce and public employment generally. The D.M.A. should be recognised as an "in-service degree" with a bias towards public administration, and its conduct should remain with the L.G.E.B. Training for the lay administrative officer should take into account both the work to be performed and the diversity of backgrounds of trainees, and should include practical experience, general studies and specialist studies in administrative subjects.

Facilities should be provided for clerical and machine operating staff to improve their educational standards and their technical proficiency, and able clerical staff should be encouraged to attain the standard necessary for entry to the trainee grade. Senior officers should receive formal training in management to suit their particular needs, and local authorities should consider the extent to which they can train their own staff for computer operation and for other specialist work in management services. Refresher training should be provided to keep officers abreast of developments, to retrain displaced officers and for married women or others returning to employment.

On the *use of staff* fourteen recommendations were made, some specifically directed to particular services or officers. More generally, the Committee recommended local authorities to examine their establishments to see whether and to what extent work could be done without loss of efficiency by staff without full professional qualifications; to draw on private resources for specialist services

---

[3] Note the comments in Reports Nos. 29 and 45 of the Prices and Incomes Board which emphasised the lack of an awareness in local government of the need for formal training in management, although there was evidence of low labour utilization, inefficiency, management which was remote, and lacking in quality, managerial expertise and cost consciousness.

when the flow of the particular specialised work is irregular; to recruit married women; and to facilitate the use of cars and to see that necessary ancillary assistance and equipment are provided. Greater use should be made of management services not only to assist decision-making but also to enable scarce resources to be used to the full, and smaller local authorities should enter into joint arrangements for the provision of management services.

With regard to *internal organisation* the Clerk was recognised as head of the council's paid service and had authority over all other departmental heads so far as this is necessary for the efficient management and execution of the council's functions. Clerkships should be open to all professions and occupations. Consideration should be given to reducing the number of separate departments by placing under one officer a group of departments with related functions; appointments of officers to such positions should have particular regard to their managerial abilities. Local authorities should devolve much wider administrative responsibility on principal officers, and make adequate arrangements for central establishment control. A central establishment organisation in a local authority should provide a number of executive services for individual departments and for the authority as a whole. The Maud Report, which appeared two months later, similarly emphasised the need for the reform of internal organisation, and the main proposals affecting the officers are considered in the next chapter.

Staff mobility should be encouraged between local authorities and other branches of the public service, with periods of secondment or attachment to government departments and statutory corporations. Qualified and experienced officers from the private sector should be recruited.

The Ministry of Housing and Local Government was recommended to examine the possibility of amending the law to permit the delegation of statutory functions to principal officers. Lastly, it was hoped that Local Authority Associations would give particular consideration to: setting up a Central Staffing Organisation to keep staff training needs under review and to perform a number of functions in relation to recruitment and training; determining how adequate facilities for training officers in establishment work could best be provided; establishing a central body to co-ordinate the resources of the various agencies concerned with the provision of, or advice on, the management services; establishing high level courses on the lines of those provided by the Imperial Defence College and making approaches to the Treasury and others likely to be concerned; and pressing for the implementation of the proposals of the Ministry of

Labour Committee on the Preservation of Pension Rights to assist in the recruitment of professional staff.

Few of the Mallaby Report's recommendations required changes in the law or in the structure of local government, and could therefore be implemented immediately. "There is no obstacle", said Sir George Mallaby, "except apathy. . . ."[4] Of all the recommendations, a major impetus was given to training by the creation from the L.G.E.B. of a Local Government Training Board which had its inaugural meeting in September, 1967. It initially adopted the grant and levy system operated by industrial training boards set up by the Industrial Training Act 1964. The L.G.T.B. remains a voluntary board, however, despite early demands from the T.U.C., N.A.L.G.O., N.U.P.E. and N.U.G.M.W. for a statutory board. Nevertheless, formal training increased significantly. Financial pressures on local authorities were reflected in a greatly reduced budget for the L.G.T.B. in 1975–6, dropping from an approved levy maximum of £5 million for 1974–5 to £1·45 million in 1975–6. The voluntary levy system was also abandoned and the board now receives its income direct from the rate support grant, so that from 1 April, 1975, all local authorities in England and Wales effectively contribute to the board's costs. At the same time, the board introduced a new limited grants scheme for certain manual workers (grants for training centres providing facilities for training roadmen, parks and playing field staff, and H.G.V. drivers) and for training staff, but all other grants ceased on 31 March, 1975. The L.G.T.B. emphasised that these changes did not imply a reduction in local authorities' training needs or in the scale of the board's own services.

Of the remaining Mallaby proposals, those relating to internal organisation were reiterated by the Maud Report and later re-stated by the Bains Report, so providing local authorities with guidelines for experiment and for giving the officers an effective responsibility for the day-to-day administration of services and a larger measure of decision and control. A greater awareness is also evident of the need, expressed by the Maud Report, for "a systematic approach to the processes of management", and in this respect the work of such bodies as L.A.M.S.A.C. in the areas of work and method study, job evaluation, computer usage, and all management service techniques; and INLOGOV in providing high-level managerial courses, can have a major influence upon the quality of local government personnel and consequently upon the service provided to the public.

---

[4] *Local Government Chronicle*, 20 May, 1967.

6. Management Structure

Local authorities are organised on a departmental basis, with each function, service or group of related services being the responsibility of a particular department. The department's hierarchy is headed by a chief officer who delegates sectors of work to his section heads, and is himself responsible to a committee of councillors for the detailed day-to-day work of the department and for long-term planning. Some departments such as that of the Treasurer provide a common service to all other departments; departments such as education or housing provide specific services. Certain departments may combine common and specific functions, e.g. the Engineer's department will be solely responsible for roads and also serve other departments.

Each local authority is unique in its departmental structure, and within each department the formal hierarchy reflects the chief officer's ideas of the best organisation to achieve his objectives, the availability of manpower, its efficiency and the persistence of customs, practices and procedures from the past. The creation of "shadow" local authorities between 1972 and 1974 provided an unique and unprecedented opportunity for existing departmental structures to be evaluated and modified to meet their new responsibilities. In May, 1971, a working party under the chairmanship of M. A. Bains, Clerk to the Kent County Council, was appointed by the Secretary of State for the Environment and the local authority associations to advise on management structures for the reorganised local authorities. Its report, generally referred to as the Bains Report, commented that whilst the best local authority management practice compared favourably with management in other enterprises, there was no cause for complacency. Bains condemned the many local authorities whose management structures "remain those which emerged from the development of local government in the 19th century", and proceeded to give practical advice for the newly reorganised authorities. The report strongly advocated a corporate approach to the management of local services in place of the traditional departmental attitude, and recommended certain basic structural features which should be common to all local authorities. These included a policy and resources committee supported by four resources sub-committees, and on the officers' side a chief executive supported by a management team of chief officers.

The report referred to the dual nature of management in local government, with both members and officers trying to "manage" but "too often suspicious and critical of each other's role". The resultant friction and competition combined to undermine morale and efficiency. The Maud Report had demonstrated the futility of regarding policy formulation as the exclusive preserve of members, and administration as the sole task of officers, and Bains reiterated the conclusion that neither members nor officers could regard the policy–administration dichotomy as an inflexible definition of their respective managerial roles. Officers must accept member involvement in administrative matters which affect their constituents, and members must accept that officers have a role in policy stimulation and formulation. Bains quoted J. B. Woodham, Treasurer of Teeside C.B., who saw the management process as a continuum extending from objective setting and resource allocation to the design of plans and programmes and finally to the execution of the plans at the far end of the scale. Throughout the process both members and officers are involved, with the balance of involvement changing from member control and officer advice in the formulation of policy to officer control and member advice in the provision of the service. Bains rejected the suggestion that delegation to officers undermined democratic control, stating that the member "should be concerned to ensure that the machine works, but he should not be required to operate it himself". The officer should have authority commensurate with his level of responsibility, should be able to use his own judgment and then should be accountable for his own decisions.

The Maud and Mallaby Reports' advocacy of one person as head of the authority's paid service was endorsed by Bains. The evidence suggested that there was little support for the all-powerful chief executive, but recommended one who "must act primarily as the leader of a team of Chief Officers and co-ordinator of activities". The following job specification was suggested:

1. The Chief Executive is the head of the Council's paid service and shall have authority over all other officers so far as this is necessary for the efficient management and execution of the Council's functions.
2. He is the leader of the officer's management team and through the Policy and Resources Committee, the Council's principal adviser on matters of general policy. As such it is his responsibility to secure co-ordination of advice on the forward planning of objectives and services and to lead the management team in securing a corporate approach to the affairs of the authority generally.
3. Through his leadership of the officers' management team he

is responsible for the efficient and effective implementation of the Council's programmes and policies and for securing that the resources of the authority are most effectively deployed towards those ends.

4. Similarly he shall keep under review the organisation and administration of the authority and shall make recommendations to the Council through the Policy and Resources Committee if he considers that major changes are required in the intrests of effective management.

5. As head of the paid service it is his responsibility to ensure that effective and equitable manpower policies are developed and implemented throughout all departments of the authority in the interests both of the authority and the staff.

6. He is responsible for the maintenance of good internal and external relations.

This concept of a chief executive is very different from that of the traditional clerk to the local authority who functioned as the authority's legal adviser and headed its secretariat. The clerk's conditions of service stated that he "shall be the chief executive and administrative officer of the council and shall be responsible for conducting the whole of the work of the council". His role, in a system which was regarded as a device for providing a number of separate services controlled by independent chief officers, was that of a co-ordinator with a comparative status invariably described as that of "first among equals". The office orginated in towns in the thirteenth century but there are few references to the post in borough charters before 1600. His duties were varied but he was commonly required to translate and convey all communications from Westminster to the townsfolk; he had to know the law and represent his borough in disputes with Westminster and other boroughs; he had to be able to write and spell in order to keep the town's rolls, and copy deeds, wills and charters; and he was sometimes required to manage the town's accounts. As his duties increased so did his influence, and the opportunities for various corrupt and irregular practices within a closed and self-perpetuating corporation were always present. The report of the Royal Commission of 1883 considered these irregularities and when the Municipal Corporations Reform Bill was drafted the town clerks' position and their tenure, generally for life, were acrimoniously debated. The 1835 Act embodied a compromise between the radical Whigs and the protective Tories and laid down that the town clerk would in future "hold his Office during (the Council's) pleasure", that he would be a "fit Person", and that he could not be a council member nor a treasurer, elected auditor or assessor. His duties were specified, the main being the counter-signature of orders for payment, responsibility for the compilation of the Freeman's Roll and the publication and distribution of Burgess Lists, and he was required to send a summons to each council member to attend council meetings.

Almost invariably, town clerks still continued to conduct their own private legal practices, but the addition of public health, sanitation and various other services in the nineteenth century made it increasingly difficult for them to maintain a dual role. Their statutory town duties were increased only slightly by the Municipal Corporations Act 1882, which made them responsible for keeping the charters, deeds, records and documents of the borough, and for supervising the nomination procedure for local elections and giving notice of election; they were also required to prepare and submit an annual return of receipts and expenditure to the Local Government Board. By the Local Government Act 1929, the Clerk became responsible for the supervision of the registration of births, deaths and marriages, while the Representation of the People Acts between 1918 and 1949, made him the key figure in the conduct of parliamentary and local elections; the Land Charges Act 1925, added to his responsibilities that of registering local land charges, and the Housing Act and Public Health Act, both in 1936, specified for the Clerk certain duties of a clerical nature.

The Clerk's duties were, consequently, manifold and important, and singled him out as the central figure in the chief officer echelon. However, overshadowing his three basic functions of lawyer, secretary and spokesman, was a fourth major function—that of co-ordinating the work of the different departments within the authority. Co-ordination is essentially an administrative technique, and the assumption that this talent was best exercised by legally trained Clerks was felt by many to be quite unwarranted. As the scope of local government became wider and more complex it became increasingly necessary that one official should be entrusted with the task of co-ordinating administration. The Royal Commission on Local Government (the Onslow Commission) concluded in 1929 that the most suitable co-ordinating officer was the Clerk and while "the balance of convenience points to the selection of a clerk with legal qualifications", the Commissioners also felt that it would be "regrettable if such a requirement were maintained to the exclusion of candidates who might bring into the services of an authority abilities of a high order".

In 1934 the Hadow Committee report on the qualifications, recruitment, training and promotion of Local Government officers, which "exerted a considerable influence in official circles"[5] as far as the local government service was concerned, took the same view as the Onslow Commission, stating: "The essential qualification of the clerk is administrative ability. He should be a person of broad and constructive outlook, interested in the wider issues of local government, skilled in negotiation, and he should ordinarily have had experience of administrative work". The report added that "too much importance should not be attached to the legal qualifications. We recognise its practical convenience, but we do not consider it essential where the Clerk's administrative duties are sufficiently heavy to occupy practically his whole attention, and a legal staff is employed." To insist on legal qualifications would exclude "persons of high administrative ability whose experience has been gained in other work".

The reports of the Treasury O. and M. Division on Coventry city council in 1953 referred to the need for a town clerk, acting in the capacity of a Chief Administrative Officer and to "changing the nature of the principal post", adding that it "would no longer be appropriate for the holder of the post also to be the Council's Legal Adviser because that would serve to obscure the purely administrative nature of the post and weaken it by the association of unrelated activities". It was felt that the effect of making the post wholly administrative would, incidentally, improve staff morale and corporate spirit by "throwing the post open for future generations on the basis of their administrative abilities and not primarily of their professional or technical qualifications".

The town clerk of Coventry disagreed with these views stating that "there is practical advantage and economy in the association of the administrative side of the office with the purely legal work. . .". Subsequently, however, the designation was changed to town clerk/chief administrative officer with power to intervene in administration where he considered it necessary in an endeavour to carry out the duties which the Council required him to assume.

The controversy over whether the town clerk should be trained as a lawyer or whether an administrator should be appointed, or whether two distinct offices should be created with the legal adviser subordinate to the chief executive has now largely abated. Tradition was first flouted with the appointment in July, 1965, of the Ford Motor Company product planning manager, who had no legal training, to become the "Principal City Officer with Town Clerk"

---

[5] J. H. Warren, *op. cit.*, p. 73.

of Newcastle upon Tyne, at a salary of £9,500. He headed the city's administration and co-ordinated a £175 million development programme. Nottingham followed with the appointment of a town clerk with the additional title of "Chief Executive Officer", and a salary in excess of £7,000; while at Basildon the late Alma Hatt, after twenty-one years as clerk to the council, was to become its first Chief Executive Officer paying "exclusive attention to the direction, promotion and co-ordination of the council's programme", and was succeeded by David Taylor, an ex-N.C.B. industrial relations officer. Stafford, Luton and Sheffield changed the town clerk's title to include "Chief Executive Officer".

Some of these designations were popularly referred to in the press as "city managers" and there was much speculation about the apparent similarity of the new appointments with that office and the applicability of that office to English local government. In 1966 there were approximately 2,000 city managers in America, increasing at the rate of seventy new adoptions each year,[6] and managers are appointed also in Ireland and West Germany. The U.S. City Manager occupies the same position as the president of a business corporation, which may be likened to the Board of Directors. He is the Chief Executive and theoretically "the council is responsible for policy, the Manager for execution and advice on policy".[7] The councillors are usually fewer than fifteen, however, and there are no committees, so that the Manager has wide discretion in matters of detail and is "in complete control of the executive arm of local administration". He appoints and may dismiss all technical officers, and can create, merge, dissolve, or rearrange departments to increase efficiency. The departments report to him and he "takes a particular interest in the financial matters of the administration. He supervises the budget preparation and the consideration of supplementary estimates". Financial management, as distinct from financial policy, is left to the accountant who is, however, responsible to the Manager and not to the Council.

The appointments in Britain of a chief executive, with uniquely wide powers of managerial control and direction over administration, have borne little resemblance to the dominant American city manager and have involved no radical disruption of the committee system nor a derogation of the chief officers' powers. The chief executive's role has invariably been enlarged as one integral aspect

---

[6] *Local Government Chronicle*, 12 November, 1966.
[7] T. E. Headrick, *The Town Clerk in English Local Government*, Allen and Unwin, 1962, p. 213.

of a number of changes in a council's internal administrative machinery which were felt to be needful. The widening of the area of recruitment to those who have no legal qualifications is a separate issue, and as the role becomes more administrative, and many clerks have within their own departments legal sections staffed with solicitors to deal with conveyancing, contracts, land charges and prosecutions, a legal training for the principal officer becomes irrelevant.

An INLOGOV research paper reported in 1971 that 81 per cent of county councils had a "principal officer", but that 89 per cent of them were designated "clerk", and 60 per cent had no formal authority over other chief officers.[8] From 1 April, 1974, all local authorities, with the exception of one non-metropolitan district, had appointed a Chief Executive Officer, with terms of reference approximating those described in the Bains Report.[9] The majority of C.E.O.s appointed when the Working Group was collecting its data were former clerks or occasionally treasurers, possibly a recognition of the need for a functionary with "across the board" experience. Particular professional qualifications were not regarded by Bains as significant, but it was recommended that young officers who had been identified as possible future C.E.O.s were to be given experience in different departments at appropriate stages in their careers. Bains felt that the balance of advantage lay with a chief executive free from departmental responsibilities, and most authorities appear to have agreed. However, the above research showed that 11 counties, 63 districts and 15 metropolitan districts had C.E.O.s with departments, but not necessarily heading the former clerk's department as the C.E.O.'s role does not generally encompass the traditional functions of the clerk. More frequently the C.E.O. heads a central department responsible for one or more of the main functions of personnel, management services, corporate planning, research and intelligence, and public relations.

The majority of local authorities have also accepted and implemented the Bains recommendation that each authority should establish a Management Team of about six principal chief officers whose corporate identity should be recognised formally within the management structure. It was intended to function as the

---

[8] Greenwood *et al.*, "New Patterns of Local Government Organisation", *Inlogov Occasional Paper 5A*, 1971.

[9] Greenwood *et al.*, "Contingency Theory and the Organisation of Local Authorities Part I: Differentiation and Integration", *Public Administration*, Spring 1975, p. 18.

counterpart of the Policy and Resources Committee and aid the management of the authority as a whole.

It would be responsible, under the C.E.O., for the preparation of plans and programmes in connection with the long-term objectives of the council and for the general co-ordination of the implementation of those plans. The Management Team might set up interdepartmental working groups, for example, a corporate planning group comprising the deputies of all departments, or a group for research and intelligence, or for manpower and management services.

Bains recommended that there was no need to appoint a deputy chief executive as each chief officer would function as the C.E.O.'s deputy within his own sphere of responsibility. The C.E.O. might have one or two personal aides selected from departmental high-fliers to serve for a limited period as part of their general career development. The necessity for each chief officer to have a deputy automatically appointed was also suggested to be a questionable practice, unless such an appointment could be justified. Additionally, emphasis was placed on the need to recognise the greater importance of management skills rather than professional qualifications as the determinant for advancement beyond middle-level jobs. Performance appraisal was given a cursory and exclusive reference in the suggestion of a systematic and annual review of chief officers by possibly the Performance Review Sub-Committee and of chief executives by the Policy and Resources Committee; there was unfortunately no suggestion of annual appraisals for other officers. However, financial rewards for exceptional performance were recommended.

The Working Group urged that departmental structures should continue to be based on the services provided by the authority, but that the traditional one department—one committee link should be severed by the amalgamation of allied services into corporate units comparable to the programme areas of the proposed committee structure.

Several possible departmental structures were suggested by Bains for county and district authorities. The reduction in the number of departments by merger has to some extent been achieved by the creation of directorates. In some local authorities this has entailed merging every department into one of a restricted number of directorates; in other authorities directorates have been limited to the line departments while the support services (e.g. clerk, treasurer, valuer and estates officer, planning officer, architect) have been

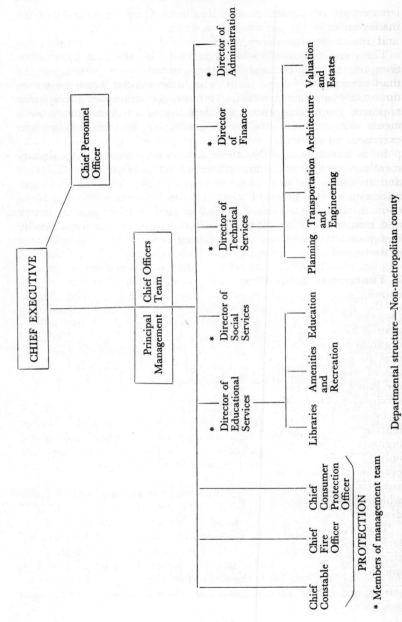

Departmental structure—Non-metropolitan county

CHIEF EXECUTIVE

Chief Personnel Officer

Principal Management | Chief Officers Team

PROTECTION

* Members of management team

Chief Constable

Chief Fire Officer

Chief Consumer Protection Officer

Director of Educational Services *

Libraries Amenities and Recreation Education

Director of Social Services *

Director of Technical Services *

Planning Transportation and Engineering Architecture Valuation and Estates

Director of Finance *

Director of Administration *

left as separate departments. The illustration[10] on page 146 from the Bains Report shows some departments grouped under directors and others remaining independent.

The completely integrated directorate pattern is rare, and some groupings (e.g. Educational Services) appear to be easier to effect than others (e.g. Technical Services) where difficulties of integration could produce conflict. The Report concluded that there appeared "to be substantial problems inherent in grouping departments together under 'directors', particularly if those directors exercise a co-ordinating role only". It added that there was "little point in forcing efficiently run departments into illogical groupings merely to provide an even balance of work between one director and another". An analysis of emergent structures in the new local authorities by INLOGOV members showed that only one county council had introduced a directorate structure, with four directors, and that most of the remaining county councils had rejected the directorate pattern for the traditional structure of ten or eleven departments.

7. Functional Specialisms

In 1967 the Maud Report referred (Vol. 1, para. 229–230) to the variable development and interest of local authorities in management services, and particularly the superficial use of organisation and methods investigations, but expressed the hope that its proposed organisation would give "greater scope for the use of management techniques of all kinds". Similarly, in 1972 the Bains Report pointed out the futility of limiting "management services" to O. & M. and work study only, and stressed the need to broaden the definition to include "all those services which help management to plan, control and improve the activities and organisation in a general sense". Such services would include not only O. & M. and work study but also operational research, job evaluation, management by objectives, network analysis, systems analysis, computer usage and a number of financial techniques which include management accounting, cost benefit analysis, discounted cash flow and planning programming budgeting systems.

This brief survey is not the place to deal systematically with such techniques, but each can contribute significantly to the more efficient use by local authorities of their increasingly scarce economic and human resources. Their application requires, however,

---

[10] *The New Local Authorities: Management and Structure*, H.M.S.O. 1972, pp. 103 and 105.

the recruitment of staff with specific training and more extensive experience in these separate disciplines than is available in the traditional Mangement Services Unit which undertook routine work study projects and, as Maud stated, "the review of elementary clerical procedures".

Bains expressed concern over the location of the various services to management within a local authority, feeling that they could "validly reside in various places and do not necessarily require to be administered within one monolithic management services unit" (p. 127). The Report added that some techniques could be most effectively utilised if they were located in individual departments, e.g. computers and finance-based techniques in the Treasurer's Department, while others would require to be centrally administered. Wherever they were located, the Working Group felt that there was increasing scope for teams made up from different departments to examine and appraise projects which were being examined by the management team.

Such interdepartmental working groups typify the spirit of corporate management which views local government as a system of interrelated activities requiring central direction and co-ordinated planning. In the past local authorities developed centrifugally, with responsibility diffused to a loose confederation of committees-cum-departments, and the resulting organisation was invariably weak at the centre and strong at the periphery. The Maud Report had condemned the disunity in internal administration and the divisive effect of departmentalism, and stimulated the many subsequent experiments by authorities to improve administrative co-ordination. The Bains Report is the most recent expression of the corporate approach and its recommendations for integrative mechanisms in the policy and resources committee and its sub-committees, the chief executive officer, the management team, directorates, programme areas and committees, interdepartmental groups and area offices have already been accepted widely by the reorganised authorities.

The rudimentary development of management techniques in local government has been matched by the lack of recognition given to the personnel function. This is not unexpected in mechanistic authoritarian structures, but in a labour intensive organisation which must nowadays adjust to changing social needs and problems "the major scope for improvements in efficiency and effectiveness must come through more effective use of human resources".[11] An

---

[11] Bains, para. 6.2.

authority's employees are the most scarce, costly and responsive of its resources, yet local government has been remiss in its failure to recognise the need to develop the complex of activities which constitute personnel management and has preferred to depend upon the intuitive man-management skills of its professional officers. Professor Stewart has observed how "Professionalism is assumed to replace the need for any recognition of the personnel function" and how "Professionalism places reliance on the professional loyalties and professional standards which can obscure real personnel problems".[12] Both he and the Bains Report also commented on the low status and restricted role of the establishment officer, local government's nearest equivalent to a personnel officer. He has been traditionally confined to record keeping and the day-to-day administration of pay and conditions of work, and acted as the council's watchdog in staffing claims and sometimes in disciplinary matters. He has had no opportunity to widen this accepted area of activity and has become "a prisoner of the role".

Recognition of these factors has prompted the new authorities to advertise for personnel managers with a higher status and organisational recognition to introduce and develop the full array of services which include manpower planning, selection and placement; education, training and career development; terms and conditions of employment; communications and consultation; negotiations on wages and conditions, and disputes procedures; and coping with the human and social implications of organisational and environmental changes. The complementary and more rigorous processes of advising on policy formulation, of co-ordinating manpower policies and assessing requirements, of problem diagnosis and prescription necessitate the appointment or secondment of experienced personnel managers from outside local government, for the required expertise has not yet been developed within local government.

The Bains Report recommended that the personnel officer should have access to the Chief Executive and not be subordinated to the Director of Administration or any other chief officer. It also stressed the need to keep the personnel function separate from management services at the operational level, with co-ordination exercised at a high level. Personnel management is essentially an advisory function, with responsibility for day-to-day personnel management resting with the appropriate chief officer, and the

---

[12] J. D. Stewart, "Personnel Management in Local Government", *Telescope*, December 1972.

Bains Report felt that chief officers should accept and act on the specialist advice of the personnel officer as they would accept that of the treasurer in financial matters.

Research conducted by INLOGOV showed that personnel and management services functions are now "widely recognised in almost all authorities", but the extent of development of the constituent elements varied according to the presence of inherited staff with previous experience, the availability of recruits and possibly the interest of individual authorities in developing the functions. By 1974, 90 per cent of the new counties in an almost complete sample had recognised the personnel function as meriting a separate department or specialist unit, 79 per cent had given departmental or specialist status to various management services, and "several" counties had created joint personnel and management services departments. Of the non-metropolitan districts in the sample 74 per cent and 58 per cent had created specialist units for personnel and management services respectively. In the metropolitan authorities 100 per cent of the counties and 97 per cent of the districts planned specialist units for personnel, and 20 per cent and 87 per cent were doing the same for management services.[13]

8. Relationship with Public and Council

"The Charter" requires that the conduct of local government officers be of the "highest standard" and adds that "public confidence in his integrity would be shaken were the least suspicion, however ill-founded, to arise that he could in any way be influenced by improper motives". He must ensure that he does not subordinate his duty to his private interests or put himself in a position where his duty and his private interests conflict." An earlier edition of "The Charter" added: "The public expects from the local government officer a standard of integrity and conduct not only inflexible but fastidious."

As a public servant an officer has to conform to a scrupulous standard of propriety in his relationship with the public and the authority which employs him. He is statutorily required to account for all moneys and property in his charge; he must declare any direct or indirect pecuniary interest in any contract into which his employing authority is preparing to enter or has entered; and he must

---

[13] Response rate for county districts was 64 per cent, for metropolitan counties 83 per cent and for metropolitan districts 92 per cent.

not exact or accept any fee or reward in his official capacity other than his due remuneration.[14]

The case of *Attorney-General* v. *De. Winton*[15] held that a borough treasurer is not a mere servant of the council but owes a duty to the public and stands in a fiduciary relation to the burgesses as a body. He must therefore disobey an order from the council which calls for illegal payment, and responsibility for such a payment rests on him personally.

In the case of *Re Hurle-Hobbs ex parte Riley and Another* in 1944 Lord CALDECOT, C.J. remarked that the Town Clerk "may be said to stand between the Borough Council and the ratepayers. He is there to assist by his advice and action the conduct of affairs in the Borough". If he sees the Council's actions may lead to an improper or unlawful act he must intercede with his advice.

Advice may sometimes be unpalatable, and an officer may lose the support of the elected representatives by his opposition to their wishes. He is nevertheless a servant of the council and is answerable to them for his actions. In the Bognor Regis inquiry of 1965, Mr. J. Ramsay Willis, Q.C., stated that the clerk to the council should express his opinion in a manner that would not embarrass his council, and once his view was known to them he should leave them to come to their own decision. It was the duty of councillors to formulate policy and they were directly responsible to the ratepayers at the polls.

Allegations of corruption and maladministration are not uncommon, however, particularly in connection with town and country planning and local authority contracts, but there is little evidence as to their incidence. In respect of councillors, the Maud Committee Report referred (para. 107 of Vol. 5) to "the general picture . . . of a high standard of honesty . . . even where members are subject to strong local pressures", although an attitude survey carried out for the Committee showed that 25 per cent of the electors felt that people became councillors "because they wanted to make money for themselves" (Vol. 3, Table 132). Yet there was no mention of officers although it has been said that "the scope for malpractice by officers is as great, if not greater, than that by members". The law relating to corrupt practices is the Public Bodies Corrupt Practices Act 1889, and of the nine persons prosecuted under this Act between 1964 and 1967 (inc.) seven were found guilty; and all of the eight prosecuted under s.76 of the Local Government Act 1933 were found guilty. The data relating to surcharges and irregularities reported by the

---

[14] Local Government Act 1972, ss. 115 and 117.
[15] [1906] 2 Ch. 106.

District Auditors show that between 1957 and 1966 there were 145 surcharges involving £67,707, of which only six were wholly or partly reversed on appeal to the minister, and 390 irregularities which led to 278 officers consequently ceasing to hold office. This latter number is small in comparison with the total numbers employed, but "it is not entirely negligible".[16]

The Report of the Prime Minister's Committee on Local Government Rules of Conduct, published in May 1974, showed that between 1964 and 1972 twenty-two local authority employees were convicted of offences under the Prevention of Corruption Acts 1906 and 1916. It recommended that officers should be required to disclose an interest not only in a contract but also in a "proposed contract, or other matter", and to disclose a pecuniary interest orally at meetings. Offences in respect of these requirements should be subject to the same penalties and limits on prosecution as those by councillors. The authority was also recommended to keep a record, open to inspection by councillors, of the pecuniary interests of chief and deputy chief officers, and of such other officers as the authority might require. A further recommendation was that the use for private gain of information received through employment in an authority should be a criminal offence.

The Prime Minister had previously announced in 1969 that the Government intended to extend the system for the investigation of complaints of maladministration by the Parliamentary Commissioner for Administration (the Ombudsman) to local government, the health service and the police. Support was provided by the "Justice" pamphlet *The Citizen and the Council* (November, 1969) which recommended a team of at least six commissioners. The White Paper *Local Government in England* (Cmnd. 4584), issued in February, 1971, stated that the Government thought that "there should be improved arrangements for investigating citizens' complaints", and a consultation document explaining the proposed system was sent to local authority associations and other bodies in 1972. A Health Service Commissioner for England, Scotland and Wales assumed the three posts on 1 October, 1973, and with effect from 8 February, 1974, ombudsmen were introduced into local government by Part III of the Local Government Act 1974.

Two Commissions for Local Administration, one each for England and Wales, were established. Each consisted of Local Commissioners appointed by the Crown on the recommendation of the appropriate

---

[16] D. E. Regan and A. J. A. Morris, "Local Government Corruption and Public Confidence", *Public Law*, Summer, 1969.

Secretary of State after consultation with the "representative body" for England or Wales. These bodies are representative of local authorities in England and Wales respectively and generally supervise the complaints machinery. Each Commission reports annually to its representative body which publishes the report. England is divided into areas, with one or more Local Commissioners responsible for each, and the same may be done in Wales if there is more than one Local Commissioner in Wales. Each Local Commissioner investigates complaints of maladministration brought by individuals or bodies of persons against any local authority (excluding parish councils and community councils), any police authority (excluding the Secretary of State), any water authority, and certain joint boards. Both members and officers are subject to investigation, as are committees of an authority, and agent authorities.

Complaints of maladministration must be made in writing to a member of the authority concerned who, with the consent of the complainant, may refer it to the Local Commissioner with a request that it be investigated. In general the complaint must be made not later than twelve months after the complainant first had notice of the matters alleged in the complaint, unless the Commissioner considers there are special circumstances which justify him waiving this condition. The Commissioner also has discretion to investigate a complaint, even though it has not been referred to him in the above manner, if he is satisfied that a request for investigation has been made by the complainant. In all cases he must be satisfied that the authority concerned has been afforded a reasonable opportunity to investigate and reply to the complaint. Only matters arising on or after 1 April, 1974, are subject to investigation, and no investigation can normally occur where the complainant could have had recourse to a tribunal, a Minister, or legal proceedings, nor in respect of actions affecting all or most of the inhabitants of his area. He is not authorised to question the merits of a decision taken without maladministration by an authority in the exercise of a discretion. Other matters specifically excluded from his jurisdiction are: court proceedings; matters concerning the investigation and prevention of crime; contractual or other commercial transactions; personnel matters; transactions connected with public passenger transport, entertainment, industrial establishments, markets, ports and harbours; and certain educational matters.

In investigating a complaint a Commissioner must give the authority concerned, and any person involved in the action complained of, an opportunity to comment on the allegations contained in the complaint. Investigations are to be held in private and conducted as the Commissioner considers appropriate. He may make such enquiries as he thinks fit and may decide whether any person may be represented (by counsel, or solicitor or otherwise) in the investigation or be awarded expenses or compensation for loss of time. The Commissioner has wide powers to require information to be produced and to compel the attendance and examination of witnesses.

After an investigation, or a decision not to conduct one, the Local Commissioner must send a report to the member of the authority who referred the complaint, to the complainant, and to the authority or persons about whom the complaint of maladministration was made. The report will be made available to the public, unless the Commissioner otherwise directs, for inspection for three weeks and public notice of this is to be given. In general, the report is not to identify or name persons.

Where the Commissioner finds a complaint has been justified, the report must be laid before the authority and be considered by them, and they must notify him of the action which they propose to take. If the Commissioner is not satisfied with the authority's response he will make a further report setting out those facts.

Apart from their reports on individual cases, Local Commissioners will make annual reports to their respective Commissions, which will review each year the operation of the complaints procedure and may make recommendations or express conclusions to local or other authorities or to Government Departments. The Parliamentary Commissioner for Administration will be a member of each Commission but will not conduct investigations under the Act.

CHAPTER 6

Administration by Committees

Schedule 12 of the Local Government Act 1972 regulates the meetings and proceedings of local authorities. It requires every principal council to hold an annual meeting and any other necessary meetings. Parish and community councils must hold an annual meeting, and parish councils are also required to meet on no less than three other occasions. Extraordinary meetings of principal, parish and community councils may be called at any time by the council chairman. A parish meeting must assemble at least once annually and, if there is no parish council, it must assemble at least twice; community meetings may be convened at any time. The extent of a local authority's work requires more frequent meetings than is suggested by the above, and most local authorities meet regularly at monthly intervals.

In the time available for these meetings, the members would be unable to exercise a close control over the volume and complexity of each department's responsibilities nor would they collectively have the expertise to do so; moreover, the full council is not structured for the purpose of close supervision over administration. Detailed consideration of the work of the authority is thus allocated by the council to committees comprising members of the council working in close collaboration with the permanent officers of the authority. The council determines the membership of each committee, their duration in office and the scope of its powers, and may co-opt on to committees (excepting the finance committee) persons who are not members of the authority.

Some committees are exclusively concerned with administering a single service, for example, education or housing, and these are frequently referred to as vertical committees; other committees, known as horizontal committees, administer a specialised function which affects a number or all of the authority's services, for example, finance, establishment or supplies. A committee which deals with a large area of responsibility may require the council to confer on it the right to delegate a section of its work to a sub-committee.

155

1. Types of Committee

Sir William Hart referred to the "several stages of development" of the committee system.[1] Initially the committees appointed are:

A. *Special Committees*

These deal with a particular task or problem of a temporary nature and are disbanded when their work is completed. Examples might include an unemployment relief committee during a local trade recession, or in Wales a National Eisteddfod committee to liaise with the organisers.

B. *Standing Committees*

These are permanent committees whose members are appointed annually to deal with a specific service of a continuing nature. Examples will include estates and libraries committees.

Neither special nor standing committees are executive bodies, their functions being to make recommendations to the council for approval. Standing orders sometimes confer a measure of executive authority upon such committees so that they may take decisions of a routine or programmed nature, but still subject to formal approval by the council. Copies of their minutes, reports and recommendations are made available to all council members before the council meetings so that members may call for discussion on specific matters. The quasi-executive power does not extend to unprogrammed areas, exceptional expenditure or matters of principle or possible political embarrassment.

At a later stage of development some acts permitted councils to delegate certain executive powers to committees. By s. 85 of the Local Government Act 1933 a council could at its discretion delegate all its powers to committees, except the power to levy, or issue a precept for, a rate, or to borrow money.

Where powers were so delegated the committee could act without reference to the council for approval and was at most only required to report its action. The committee itself could not further delegate its executive powers to a sub-committee—*delegatus non potest delegare* —but the committee could act without approval on its sub-committee's recommendations.

C. *Statutory Committees*

Statutes requiring the establishment of a particular service imposed on local authorities the duty of appointing these commit-

---

[1] Sir William Hart and Professor J. F. Garner, *Hart's Introduction to the Law of Local Government and Administration*, Butterworths, 1973, p. 136–8.

tees, and empowered the local authority to delegate to them all or any of their statutory powers excepting those relating to finance. The Local Government Act 1933 required the appointment of a finance committee in every county council; the Education Act 1944 required every L.E.A. to have an education committee; the National Health Service Act 1946 and the National Assistance Act 1948 required every county and county borough to establish a health committee and a welfare services committee. Sometimes an act required all matters affecting a service to stand referred to the Committee, and in some cases (e.g. Children Act 1948) the act required the local authority to appoint a special officer for the service. Certain statutory committees, for example police committees, have had executive powers conferred upon them, so that they alone exercise the powers and the council which appoints them has no control. In such cases the committee "is the real local authority for the service under its control" (Hart, p. 139).

The Local Government Act 1972 (s. 101) greatly extended the freedom of local authorities to "arrange for the discharge of any of their functions" by a committee, a sub-committee or an officer, or even by any other local authority. Statutory responsibility remains, however, with the authority upon whom the powers are conferred. Where powers are delegated to a committee the committee may itself delegate the powers to a sub-committee or to an officer. Having delegated a function, an authority is not prevented from exercising that function. The Act also removed many of the former legislative obligations by giving local authorities wider discretion in the appointment of staff and by repealing the provisions requiring the appointment of the following statutory committees:

Health Committee (National Health Service Act 1946)
Allotments Committee (Allotments Act 1922)
Diseases of Animals Committee (Diseases of Animals Act 1950)
Public Health and Housing Committee (Housing Act 1957)
Youth Employment Sub-Committee (Employment and Training Act 1948)

Local Authorities are still required to appoint the following statutory committees if they are responsible for the service:

Education Committee (Education Act 1944)
Police Committee (Police Act 1964)
Social Services Committee (Local Authority Social Services Act 1970)
A committee under Section 1 of the Sea Fisheries Regulation Act 1966

Children's Regional Planning Committee (Children and Young Persons Act 1969)

Special Planning Committee for a national park (Local Government Act 1972)

Joint Superannuation Committee (Local Authorities Social Services Act 1970)

The last four are Joint Committees.

D. *Joint Committees*

These may be formed by two or more local authorities to discharge any function in which they are jointly interested. A new provision introduced by the Local Government Act 1972 was that Joint Committees could include co-opted members, but at least two-thirds of the members must be members of the constituent authorities. The expenses of a joint committee are defrayed by the authorities in agreed proportions, but if there is disagreement it will be submitted to arbitration. Where the Joint Committee was formed from parishes or communities in the same district, the district council will arbitrate; in other authorities a single arbitrator will decide or, if they cannot agree, the Secretary of State will decide.

In the interregnum between the enactment of the Local Government Act 1972 and the changeover on 1 April, 1974, existing authorities were required to establish Joint Committees to consider matters affecting the new authorities, to plan for the changeover and resolve common problems relating to personnel deployment and conditions, management structures, accommodation, etc. Their composition and expenses were left to the merging authorities to determine, with recourse to the Secretary of State in case of disagreement. There was a power to co-opt.

E. *Advisory Committees*

S. 102 (4) of the Local Government Act 1972 gave recognition to a common practice by granting a new general power to local authorities to appoint advisory committees on any matter relating to the discharge of their functions.

2. Committee Membership

The composition of statutory committees is governed by the terms of the statute which establishes the service and there are wide variations in membership. Two-thirds of the membership of a county police committee must be members of the county council and the remaining third must be magistrates; the majority of the members of an education committee must be members of the L.E.A., but it must also contain co-opted members who have experience in education and are acquainted with educational conditions in the area (teachers may be members of the education committee of the L.E.A. which employs them); the majority of the members of a social services committee must be council members, but it may include co-opted members, and social services sub-committees are required to have at least one member of the local authority and the others need not be members even of the committee. Non-statutory committees and sub-committees may consist wholly of council members or they may have up to one-third of their membership co-opted from members of the public. Finance committees must consist exclusively of members of the appointing local authorities.

The council's standing orders will generally specify the method to be adopted for the appointment of committee members, and the procedure will vary from one authority to another. Members may be appointed by a selection committee which recommends names to the council; or there may be one representative from each ward, parish or area appointed to each committee; a system of proportionate representation based upon the respective strengths of the parties or some form of balloting may be adopted; or individuals may be left to persuade a consensus of the committee membership to accept them. Standing orders will usually specify also the minimum or maximum number of committees upon which a council member may serve, and it might vary from two to ten. Membership of the more "important" or "interesting" committees, such as Education, Finance, Planning, is coveted, and disappointment with not being appointed to these may cause friction and jealousy in the council chamber.

The key figure in the committee is the chairman. He controls its meetings, speaks on its behalf at council meetings and elsewhere and maintains a constant liaison with the chief officer of the department which executes the committee's decisions. He may be elected by the committee at its first meeting or by the full council, and his appointment is generally by seniority, on the dubious premise that long service produces administrative ability, or by merit based upon his familiarity with committee procedure and a long involvement and interest in the work of a particular committee, or as a reward for service to the dominant political group. There is no limit to his tenure of office, unless a term is stipulated in the standing orders, but an indefinite period should be avoided. It may be beneficial insofar as his experience should develop with each passing year, but he is also likely to become so "efficient" as to act independently of his committee, while meantime depriving enterprising committee members of the opportunity for advancement and chairmanship experience. For the same reasons, the tendency for the leading council figures to collect chairmanships should be avoided.

The chairman's relationship with his committee's chief officer and the senior departmental officers is critical, and should not be thought of in terms of a dominant-submissive partnership. The officers will execute the committee's instructions, but committee chairmen and members would be rash to ignore the advice of their officers or to attempt to impose excessive limits on their areas of discretion in making decisions on the committee's behalf. K. C. Wheare has stated that:

> "In practice the administrative function will be shared between the committee and the higher officials. It may be that in law the committee could make every decision and give every instruction; in practice it cannot be done. And it cannot be done, not only because no committee could give the time to cope with such detail, but because no good official could be expected to tolerate a situation in which he had no discretion, initiative or responsibility."[2]

The Treasury O. and M. Division's second report on Coventry[3] emphasised the need for the devolution of responsibility to chief officers:

> "To do so would . . . speed up and simplify administration without in any way weakening control."

The relationship between committee chairman and chief officer is

> "more subtle than the cliches about the distinction between policy and its execution".[4]

Ultimate responsibility will remain, however, with the committee and its chairman who will have to substantiate its recommendations and defend its actions, if it has delegated powers, to the full council.

Finally, a good committee chairman must be: experienced in local government, have served a lengthy apprenticeship, know procedure and be aware of precedent; have the welfare of the locality foremost in his mind; appreciate the mixed abilities of his committee members and the degrees of efficiency of his officers, get the best out of each

---

[2] K. C. Wheare, *Government by Committee*, Clarendon Press, 1955, p. 176.
[3] *Public Administration*, vol. XXXII, Spring 1954, p. 67.
[4] Sir William Hart, *Some Administrative Problems of Local Government*, I.M.T.A., 1965, p. 8.

and mould them into an efficient team; maintain good working relationships with his officers between meetings; and realise that his ability as a leader can directly affect the efficiency of his committee.

Disqualifications and disabilities

A person who is disqualified from being elected or being a member of a local authority is disqualified from being a member of a committee or sub-committee of that authority or from being a representative of the authority on a joint committee of the authority and another authority, but a teacher or anyone holding an office in a school or college maintained or assisted by that authority may become a member of any education committee or public libraries committee.[5]

If a member of a local authority has a pecuniary interest, direct or indirect, in any contract or proposed contract or other matter, and is present at any meeting of the local authority at which the contract or matter is being considered he must disclose the fact and must not take part in its consideration or discussion, nor may he vote on any question relating to it.[6]

3. The Council's relationship with its Committees

Whenever a council creates a non-statutory committee, the need to specify the extent of that committee's control over the service for which it is responsible poses an immediate problem. If the council delegates full executive responsibility for administering a service, the council faces the risk of relinquishing its overall control and becoming a mere rubber-stamp to the decisions of a committee which may come to regard itself as a separate *ad hoc* authority independent of the appointing council. The problem and its inherent dangers have been expressed thus:

> "It is most important that a right balance should be struck between the powers of a council and the powers of its committees. If too much power is given to committees, they will begin to act as independent bodies; they will be reluctant to co-operate with other committees of the council; there will be a lack of co-ordination in council work; and there will be attempts at empire building or committee imperialism at the expense of each other. This is, indeed, the great danger in administration by committees. . . . There are many reasons for it, but it is certain

[5] Local Government Act 1972, s. 104.
[6] *Ibid.*, s. 94.

that a good foundation upon which such difficulties and tendencies flourish is the grant of delegated powers of administration to committees of councils. It encourages them to believe that they are little councils in themselves."[7]

Appreciating the likelihood of such consequences, a council may hedge its delegation of executive powers with restrictions, requiring the committee to submit its reports to the council for formal approval, or not granting a committee the right to delegate its executive powers to a sub-committee. A council need not delegate any of its executive powers and may merely require from the committee recommendations upon which the council may base its decisions. This, however, would then necessitate the council itself having to re-examine all the facets of a matter under decision and apart from the time-wastage involved, the advantage of prior analysis at the committee level would be largely minimised.

Standing orders have thus tended to confer a limited executive power which permits a committee to make decisions on routine matters which are then formally approved by the council, whilst only matters of principle or those involving exceptional expenditure require council attention exclusively. Control is still retained over routine matters by the circulation to council members of committee minutes, reports and recommendations (these are also available to the press and the public), before the full council meeting; at this meeting also the committee chairman will rise to move that his committee's minutes, reports and recommendations be approved, and any member present, not being a member of that committee, may indicate his dissent and a discussion upon which a vote will be taken could follow.

In the case of statutory committees, these may have executive powers granted to them which only they can exercise and not the appointing council; nor may the latter express its disapproval of the committee's acts. A police committee for a county police force can compel a county council to raise the money it requires and obtain particular premises.

4. Co-ordination between Committees

A large local authority is likely to have over a dozen main committees and a large number of sub-committees, and in order to ensure that (a) the work of one is not duplicated by another, or (b) that a committee's actions are not contrary to council policy, or (c) that a

---

[7] K. C. Wheare, *op. cit.*, p. 175–176.

committee adheres to its terms of reference, or (d) that it does not deliberately work in isolation, jealously resentful of the encroachment of other committees upon its sphere of action, the council may exercise its overall control, achieve committee coordination, and integrate committee and departmental effort in a number of ways:

1. by clear definition of the functions and responsibilities of each committee and sub-committee;

2. by the establishment of a senior committee made up of the chairmen of all other main committees;

3. by the secretarial role of the Director of Administration's department and the work of the committee clerks, which lead to a standardisation of procedures. The integration of administration is facilitated by regular chief officers' meetings convened by the Chief Executive;

4. by such "horizontal" committees as the finance committee, co-ordinating all spending, and the establishments committee and planning committee which will provide common services to all departments and advice to all committees;

5. by the requirement that all committee reports and recommendations are submitted to the full council for formal approval;

6. by party political allegiances which may help to unite members and bind committees in support of party policy, while regular party group meetings should ensure co-ordination of effort.

5. Admission of the Public and the Press

In 1907 F. B. Mason, the proprietor of the *Tenby Observer*, printed an adverse report of a meeting of the Tenby borough council and later refused to leave a meeting of the aggrieved council when asked by the mayor. The council brought an action in the Chancery Division claiming a declaration that the council could exclude anyone who was not a council member from council and committee meetings and also sought an injunction restraining Mason from their meetings without their permission. Mason claimed that as a burgess, a newspaper representative and a member of the public he had a threefold right to attend a public meeting. The Court's decision, however, was that the council was a "creature of statute" and that there was no room for the application of the common law; moreover, the Municipal Corporations Act 1882, which governed meetings, gave no right to attendance. It therefore found in favour of Tenby corporation, and the appeal also went against Mason.[8]

There was public disquiet over the outcome as it had been generally inferred that there was a right in common law to admis-

---

[8] *Tenby Corporation v. Mason* (1908) Ch. 561.

sion to council meetings. Arthur Henderson responded by introducing the Local Authorities (Admission of the Press to Meetings) Bill to give journalists the right to attend local authority meetings, with the proviso that they could be excluded if the majority of members felt the exclusion to be advisable in the public interest. The bill was widely supported and enacted in 1908, and its provisions determined the relationship between local authorities and the press until 1960.

In the intervening years the limitations of the Act became increasingly apparent as the bodies to which it applied disappeared. By the terms of the Local Government Act 1933 the only local authority meetings the public had a right to attend were those of parish councils, "unless the council otherwise direct". Some authorities did nevertheless admit the public as a matter of grace. In 1949 and 1956 two bills were introduced which attempted to remedy the situation but both were unsuccessful. Finally in 1960 Mrs. Margaret Thatcher, in her maiden speech, presented a private member's bill which was enacted in a weakened form as the Public Bodies (Admission to Meetings) Act 1960. It provided for the admission of the press *and* the public to "any meetings of a local authority or other body exercising public functions", but the body could, by resolution, exclude the public "whenever publicity would be prejudicial to the public interest by reason of the confidential nature of the business to be transacted or for other special reasons". The Act's major deficiency was the restriction of the public and the press to those committee meetings which consisted of or included *all* the members of the authority.

The Local Government Act 1972 extended the right of access to meetings of local authorities to include access to the statutory committees constituted under s. 101 (9) and to committees, joint committees and advisory committees appointed by local authorities under s. 102 of the Act.

6. The Advantages and Disadvantages of the Committee System

The committee system is fundamental to local administration in England and Wales, but it is not without its defects. It is necessary, therefore, to evaluate the merits and demerits of the system in order to appreciate the experimental changes which are currently being made by some local authorities to their committee structure.

The main advantages of the committee system are said to be:

1. The division of a complex range of work amongst committees

and sub-committees ensures a more detailed and effective coverage of council services and responsibilities, and permits the full council, during the limited time of its meeting, to concern itself with policy matters without being overwhelmed by too much detail.

2. Division of the work amongst members, often according to their own interests, leads to specialisation in a narrow range of services (according to the number of committees a member serves). The consequent development of skill brings greater personal satisfaction and allows the member to make a more effective contribution to the work of the committee and to the community as a whole. The council officers serving the committee will thus be advising not uninformed amateurs but members who have some awareness of the technical aspects of the service and its problems, and also a knowledge of the relevant legislation.

3. As in the House of Commons, lack of time generally prevents the "backbench" councillor in the larger authorities from speaking at full council meetings, but he is given ample opportunity to participate in discussion at committee meetings. It is here that he will first prove his abilities and make his greatest contribution to the locality; for it is in the committee room that the spadework is done which will affect community services, not in the more formal and rarified atmosphere of council meetings where the public gallery witnesses only a rather sedate fraction of local government at work. Wheare says:

> "If there is to be any reality in the idea of democratic government, it is essential that as many people as possible should have an opportunity of taking part in governmental processes. Committees provide that opportunity".[9]

4. Co-option allows individuals who have a specialist knowledge of the committee's work to participate in its deliberations without having to stand for election or take on the full responsibilities of council membership. Moreover, where party organisation is strong, co-opted members have no need to toe the party line and may thus express their views with critical detachment. Authoritative opinion may more effectively lead the majority group to reconsider a matter than would the suspected opinions of the minority group's spokesman. Unfortunately, there is little use made of the power to co-opt, and a similar reluctance by members of the public to serve as co-opted members.

5. Committee members will represent different areas of the local authority, different shades of political opinion, different interests and classes. Such a cross-section of opinion should ensure that varying community interest will be taken into account before recommendations are framed or action taken.

6. The committee system brings into partnership the chief officers

---

[9] K. C. Wheare, *op. cit.*, pp.

experienced in their own sphere of activities, and the representatives whose uppermost concern should be their community's interests.

"Bureaucratic sense must justify itself before the questioning of common sense",

wrote Wheare, and the combination of specialist knowledge and community responsibility should produce administration which is at once efficient and personal, and sensitive to the needs and problems of groups and individuals in the area.

7. The informality of procedure and discussion at committee meetings, in contrast with the formal rules of debate observed at council meetings, the general absence of the press and the public, and thus the absence of any necessity to "speak to the gallery", enable members to discuss matters in a far more relaxed and uninhibited manner.

Against such merits should be balanced the alleged disadvantages of the system:

i. Delegation of executive authority to committees can give rise to such abuses as "committee imperialism", lack of co-operation between committees and co-ordination between services, and independence of council control which may ultimately affect the quality of the service and result in a tarnished image of the council in the public's eyes.

ii. The power to co-opt is rarely used because of the reluctance of council members to have a meritocracy critical of their perhaps unsophisticated efforts or their unquestioning acceptance of party group decisions. Co-option also offers opportunities for abuse by allowing fellow-travellers, defeated councillors, or even acquaintances to take a part in committee work when they may know little and care less about the service administered by the committee. Where co-option is obligatory, for example on the education committee, academics could provide what would amount to a gratuitous consultancy service, but they may still be regarded with suspicion by the elected members. Finally, co-opted members may be disruptive of genuine group harmony, may be intolerant of the financial restrictions which frequently bedevil a committee's work, and carry no responsibility as far as the public is concerned if their specialist schemes misfire.

iii. Council membership is a part-time activity which makes extensive demands upon time. Lack of time coupled with membership of several committees means that committee meetings must be arranged at intervals of perhaps four to six weeks or more. In the meantime, decisions are awaited by the council's officers and action is being delayed, departmental work is being disrupted and the public becomes increasingly more resentful of apparently unjustifiable delays in routine matters. As an administrative technique, the committee system in local government creates bottlenecks, frustration and inefficiency, which will increase when sub-committees are involved in the chain of delegation.

iv. The extension of the council's functions stimulates the creation of extra committees and sub-committees, which in turn make greater demands upon the council members' time. The alleged advantage that committee membership increases a member's opportunity to specialise in segments of the council's work may in fact be more of a textbook dream than reality, for the division of a member's energies over a range of services and his attempts to keep abreast of legislative and technical developments may place too great a burden upon him. He is, when all is said and done, generally a part-timer with a living to earn elsewhere, and his committee work may lead to an excessive involvement in detail and a deterioration in the quality of his work, particularly where policy decisions are required. Additionally, committee work may leave him little time to meet his constituents with any regularity and prevent him from following up their complaints and keeping a watching brief over his constituency.

v. The creation of separate committees for separate services tends to isolate the operation of departments. Basildon Urban District Council, for example, felt "it important that as the size of their administration grows they continue to maintain a common service with a common aim, namely the benefit of the community". As committees increase in number, problems of co-ordination increase unless a council attempts to rationalise its committee structure by grouping services which have a broadly similar purpose. Such rationalisation, however, will entail the reduction in the number of committees and the consequent surrender of chairmanships, together with their status, prestige and power, and these are not lightly forsaken.

vi. Committees produce a vast amount of paperwork which members should assimilate. Basildon Urban District Council found that their committee members received 350 pages of reports in six weeks, plus internal progress reports, government publications and policy documents from outside bodies. All this reading, if conscientiously done, makes further inroads on time.

vii. Committee meetings in many authorities are held during the evening and require the presence of officers who have already completed a full day's work. Even when meetings are held during the day, senior officers often have to make time to attend and to have reports prepared, which then have to be produced by typists, clerks and machine operators. The cost involved in such operations is not inconsiderable, and in terms of energy expenditure and frustration the cost may be incalculable!

viii. The monopoly of committee chairmanships and the holding of a majority of seats on the more important committees by the dominating party introduces a further element of discord between the majority and the aggrieved minority. Commital to a party line and the leadership of a strong chairman could also stultify discussion within a committee and undermine its purpose.

ix. The lack of information emanating from committee meetings because of the exclusion of the press and the public has caused much dispute and can prompt public suspicions of committee corruption. Of the complaints received by the Local Government Reform Society during 1965, 13 per cent of them related to secrecy over council committees and documents,[10] and after the Bognor Regis inquiry in November, 1965, there were newspaper recommendations that committee meetings at which councillors voted on tenders and planning decisions should be open to the press and the public, and receive publicity.[11] Many councils feel, however, that reporters are only seeking items for sensational criticism, or that meetings are often treated as routine calls for junior reporters. For their part, the press are irked by the absence of information and feel they have a public duty to gain entry to committee meetings or at least to receive early statements after committee meetings, instead of after council meetings which have ratified committee decisions. There is a need here for councils to study the 1961 circular on the Public Bodies (Admission to Meetings) Act, and for a sensible arrangement to be worked out between senior editorial staff and council members and officers in each locality.

Such features of the committee system are clearly detrimental to effective administration. The Committee on Management was similarly critical, commenting that: "The virtues of committees are, at present, outweighed by the failures and inadequacies of the committee system" (para. 128). Its report refers to the absence of a co-ordinating and unifying central body comprising a selected few members to provide an authority with overall direction and control. Instead there is a proliferation of committees constituting a system which is "a contrivance for decentralising the various functions of the council and for creating a number of microcosms of it to meet problems as they arise". Such dispersal of direction and control among committees, with each committee in turn having its own supporting departmental hierarchy, results in a general lack of unity in the authority's work—"There may be unity in the parts, but there is disunity in the whole" (para. 97).

The report adds that the committee system also contributes to the misuse of the authority's officers. The requirement that statutory functions cannot be further delegated to officers is extended in some authorities where "a vast range of administrative decisions are

---

[10] *The Times*, 13 December, 1965.
[11] *Ibid.*, 24 November, 1965.

taken by members in committees". The effect is to inhibit the devolution of administrative discretion on officers, which "in practice
means that any member or officer has convincing arguments for
insisting that matters, however minor, shall be considered at committee level". There is a reluctance therefore to attempt to distinguish
between major issues and day-to-day matters, between "policy",
which is the province of the members, and "administration", the
province of the officers. "We believe that the lack of clear recognition
of what can and should be done by officers, and of what should be
reserved for decision by members, lies at the root of the difficulties
in the internal organisation of local authorities" (para. 101). Such
a lack of distinction between the respective roles and responsibilities
of members and officers leads to overlapping, waste of time and
energy, and constitutes a gross misuse of skills, manpower and money,
and further acts as a disincentive to qualified people entering the
local government service.

The difficulty, and perhaps impossibility in some cases, of dis-
tinguishing between policy and administration in the social and
political context of the locality is stressed. Where members and
officers are doubtful, they will "play safe", particularly where there
may be possibilities of appeal against decisions, and the matter will
be added to a committee's agenda. Further reasons for increasing
the agenda would include the sensitivity of members to neighbours'
reactions, a desire to appear to have a full knowledge of what the
authority is doing, a sentimental or personal interest in particular
matters, or to fill in the detail of caucus decisions; officers may also
put up issues for discussion "'just to create an interest', for 'tactical
reasons' or because of an unwillingness to accept responsibility"
(para. 111).

The Parkinsonian tendency of committees to concentrate on the
trivial is also noted, "because they come easily within the reach of
their understanding and to avoid discussion of major questions
because of the difficulties which they involve". This, however,
highlights the problem of determining at what level of decision-taking
a committee can relinquish direct responsibility because of the principle that members are ultimately responsible for the conduct of
affairs in the authority. "The committee system . . . does not lend
itself to the careful selection of the key-points at which control should
be exercised by those who are ultimately responsible; it leads to the
indiscriminate submission to committees of material for information,
mingled with material for deliberation or for decision—a hugger-
mugger of the important and the trivial."

Reference is also made to the demands and the cost of the committee system. The number of committees in authorities varies, averaging nineteen in county councils and twenty-one in county boroughs; the average number of sub-committees is high, with forty-seven in county councils and forty in county boroughs, one authority having 160 sub-committees! Wide variations are found in the nature of sub-committee work and the number of members on each. Demands upon members' time are great, with an average of over six council and committee meetings a month in counties and over nine per month in county boroughs; the duration of each meeting could be an hour or as much as five and a half hours. Total time spent on council business for the member could vary from over thirty-four hours per month in a rural district to seventy-six hours in a county borough, but with only a quarter of this time actually in attendance. This was seen to be another disincentive towards offering oneself for local authority service. Lastly, the volume of paperwork was noted, with one county borough sending out 700 sheets a month to each member (1,000 if he were on the education committee), at an estimated total cost of £2,000 a month.

7. Modifications to the Traditional System

Dissatisfaction with such characteristics of the committee system had already stimulated a few councils to pioneer radical modifications in their internal organisation. Newcastle upon Tyne appointed a "city manager" or "Principal City Officer with Town Clerk" (Mr. Frank Harris) in 1965. He envisaged a change in the traditional relationship between members and their chief officers, the latter being delegated "complete responsibility for running his own show . . . (and) . . . responsibilities shall be widened so that far less committee time is devoted to detail and more time is available for well-considered policy decisions".[12] He planned to reduce the number of committees from thirty-six to eight, and of these two would be key committees or "planning bases" at which controversial party issues would be determined by political party groups before being presented for debate. The two committees would be (a) the *Municipal Relations Committee*—with responsibility for internal organisation, parliamentary work and by-laws, public relations, registration, administration of justice and the sole control of staff; and (b) the *Resources Planning Committee*—responsible for the general control of long-term planning, budgeting, town and development planning, financial control and administration. The remaining six committees would be responsible

---

[12] *Local Government Chronicle*, 24 July, 1965.

for public safety, health and social services, education and leisure, housing, public works and transport, and civic enterprises.

Basildon U.D.C. also appointed a Town Manager, abolished all sub-committees (excepting three education sub-committees) and approved the creation of an *Executive Committee* of nine members which would occupy a structural position between the council and all normal committees. Tamworth M.B. proposed a *Resources Planning Committee*, working through a management group of ten members, and a reduction of committees from nine to four. Bedford M.B. established a *Management Committee* to guide the authority's overall strategy and to permit better control and direction of all committees within that strategy. Similarly, Camden borough set up an *Advisory Committee* to exercise overall co-ordination.

In addition to reducing the number of committees the need for allocating co-ordinating and directive powers to a central committee is given explicit recognition in the above proposals. The Committee on Management said that committees and sub-committees should be kept to a minimum, with no more than six committees in the larger authorities, that they should be deliberative and not executive or administrative bodies, except for exceptional purposes, and that they should each deal with a group of subjects. Additionally, all but the smallest authorities should appoint a *Management Board* of between five and nine members which would have wide powers delegated to it.

The functions of the management board would be: (a) To formulate the principal objectives of the authority and to present them together with plans to attain them to the council for consideration and decision; (b) to review progress and assess results on behalf of the council; (c) to maintain, on behalf of the council, an overall supervision of the organisation of the authority and of its co-ordination and integration; (d) to take decisions on behalf of the council which exceed the authority of the principal officers, and to recommend decisions to the council where authority has not been delegated to the management board; and (e) to be responsible for the presentation of business to the council subject always to the rights of members under standing orders.

The significance of this body for the existing committee organisation would be: (a) Committees should not be directing or controlling bodies nor should they be concerned with routine administration; (b) no committee should have more than fifteen members (including co-opted members); (c) committees should be deliberative and representative bodies; (d) committees should take executive decisions only in exceptional circumstances when the management board requires them to do this—these fields of decision-taking should

172

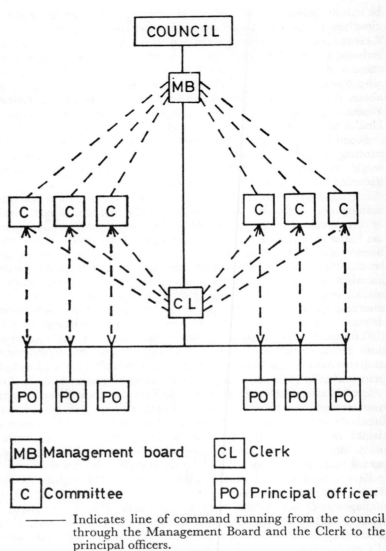

| MB | Management board | | CL | Clerk |
| C | Committee | | PO | Principal officer |

——— Indicates line of command running from the council
through the Management Board and the Clerk to the
principal officers.
– – – – lines of contact and advice only.

This diagram does NOT imply that one committee has only
one principal officer associated with it or that each principal officer
has necessarily a single committee to refer to.

be strictly defined by the management board and it should be made clear that the committees issue instructions to the officers only on these matters; and (e) the number of committees should be drastically reduced and similar or related services should be grouped and allocated to one committee. Para. 168 states: ". . . we believe that in an all-purpose authority it should be possible to reduce their number to about six", and suggests—Planning and development, Housing, Works—including highways and traffic, Education and culture, Health and welfare, and Public protection.

Board members would individually assume responsibility for the running of a particular service, as well as for speaking for a particular service and department on the Board and in the council; they could become "municipal ministers". The advantages were suggested to be: the establishment of a close working arrangement between the management board and principal officer; and difficult issues could be brought rapidly to his notice and decisions swiftly taken. On the other hand, some serious disadvantages were visualized: the board member could become so involved in affairs that he might become full-time and require an office and supporting staff to do his work; he could become the real, but untrained, head of department, with the principal officer his subordinate, so reducing the discretion and responsibility of the principal officer; the present dispersal of responsibility among committees would be replaced by the fragmentation of "ministerial responsibility"; and perhaps most serious was the impossibility of reconciling "the supervisory and co-ordinative role of the Clerk with the primary allegiance of principal officers to individual management board members".

Certain safeguards were therefore necessary: the board's chairman must ensure that his colleagues, by acting independently, did not break the unity of the board; and secondly, the relationship between the Clerk and the principal officers which creates organisational unity must not be thwarted by the development of independent arrangements between a principal officer and a board member.

Reactions to the proposed organisation were varied. The presidential address to the Institute of Baths Management attacked the management boards which "were likely to provide a Tammany Hall type of control".[13] On the other hand, Sir Andrew Wheatley, a member of the Committee on Management, agreed with the concept of a management board but felt that the proposal went further than was necessary. It would invest "far too much power in the small number of members" and "will deprive the greater majority . . . of

---

[13] *Local Government Chronicle*, 21 September, 1968.

the opportunity of participating effectively in the formulation of policy and the development of services . . . without the committee system local government could not work". He wished to retain standing committees and invest them with executive powers, "but on any major issue of policy or new scheme involving capital expenditure they should first report to the management board".

Both A.M.C. and C.C.A. opposed the idea of a management board, the former finding that the proposal left no room for a participating role for elected members if committees were to lose their executive function, and the latter thought it unlikely that candidates for election would contemplate serving for years on non-executive committees. The R.D.C.A. felt the idea was suitable for rural district councils and certain of them (e.g. Wrexham, Grimsby and Newport Pagnell) had gone some way to the establishment of a management board, but had retained committees with more than merely deliberative powers. Many cities and boroughs favoured the creation of a policy advisory or co-ordinating committee, some strengthened or adapted the functions of an existing committee (generally the finance committee), whilst almost all had accompanied the change with a reduction and simplification in the committee structure.[14] The Secretary of the A.M.C. commented: ". . . the board would effectively import cabinet government into local government. . . . By and large, local government has sided with Wheatley . . . very few authorities indeed have been prepared to try the 'full Maud' management board".[15]

Supportive weight was given to this evaluation by a later analysis of organisational changes which had occurred.[16] This showed that although many local authorities had accepted Maud's analysis of the problem, they had not accepted the proposed solution and had favoured instead Sir Andrew Wheatley's proposal. Of the eighty-three county boroughs asked for information, forty-two of the seventy-seven respondents rejected the management board proposal "either implicitly by adopting some other approach to the problem of policy co-ordination, or explicitly by giving reasons for rejection", and the reasons were fairly consistent: "(1) Conflict with collective responsibility of councillors; concentration of power; undemocratic. (2) Divisions of councillors into two classes (those on the management board and the remainder). (3) Discontent and frustration of

---

[14] B. C. Smith and J. Stanyer, "Administrative Developments in 1967: A Survey", *Public Administration*, Autumn 1968, Vol. 46.

[15] J. C. Swaffield, "Local Government Changing", *New Society*, 19 September, 1968.

[16] R. Greenwood, A. L. Norton and J. D. Stewart, "Recent Changes in the Internal Organisation of County Boroughs: Part 1 Committees", *Public Administration*, Summer, 1969, Vol. 47.

councillors not on management board. (4) Effect on recruitment of councillors of high calibre. (5) Inappropriate to local government because based on commercial or central government practice."

Regarding the reduction in the number of committees recommended by Maud, of the thirty-four county boroughs which had completed a revision only Bradford had achieved reduction to six committees, whilst the remainder largely operated with ten to fifteen committees. The size of committees had barely changed from pre-Maud days, but most were in line with the Maud recommendation of a maximum of fifteen members. As far as the allocation of functions to committees was concerned some authorities had barely altered the basic structure, while others had made "incisive analyses of their organisation" and amalgamated related functions, but the "common pattern still differs little from that revealed by the Maud Committee research". There was, however, indication that where committee structures had been reformed "there has been a great saving in members' time and, in so far as officers also attend meetings, of their time too".

Generally local authorities accepted the Maud Committee on Management's diagnosis of the organisational problems which resulted from their committee structure, and also accepted that greater internal co-ordination was required and could be achieved by allocating wide functions to a policy committee; but it was not accepted that reorganisation should entail a radical change in the powers or functions of existing committees. Although not bound by the recommendations of the Committee on Management, the Report of the Royal Commission commented that its members were "firmly of the opinion that the new main authorities must have a central committee, board or body of some kind, by whatever name it may be called". Additionally, "the case is surely cast-iron for a central body to advise the council on its strategy and priorities, co-ordinate the policies and work of the service committees, and ensure that the best managerial methods are adopted in each department and in the work of the council as a whole". Each of the new authorities should therefore work out the form of central committee most suited to its requirements, and also the division of duties between the central committee and the service committees "which would continue to be at the heart of affairs". "It is, however, a radical change from traditional practice that we seek. The central committee must be at the core of the administration; and the proliferation of committees must be ended".[17]

---

[17] *Royal Commission on Local Government in England* 1966–69, Vol. 1, paras. 486, 489, 493–5.

8. The "Bains Report"

The Working Group set up to advise the new local authorities on management structures, chaired by M. A. Bains, found that in a number of authorities the central policy committees were "in fact not concerned with central policy and strategic discussions at all".[18] Some of them had become "the council's waste paper basket" and were "operating as a low-key general purposes committee"; others were "responsible for any matter which comes up between meetings of other committees". To provide the council with comprehensive and co-ordinated advice on which to base its policy decisions, the Working Group advocated the establishment of a Policy and Resources Committee. It would aid the council in setting its objectives and priorities and, once the major policy decisions had been taken by the council, co-ordinate and control the implementation of those decisions. It was recommended that its membership should not be restricted to the chairmen of other committees but should include other members and, where possible, minority party representation. To be effective, it "must . . . reflect the power structure of the majority party".

The Policy and Resources Committee was to have ultimate responsibility under the council for the authority's three major resources of finance, manpower and land (including buildings), and for each of these resources there would be set up a resource sub-committee to exercise day to day control. The membership of these sub-committees should not be limited to the members of the Policy and Resources Committee but should include a "substantial proportion" of the authority's members. Bains felt that it was essential that the chairmen of the sub-committees should be members of the Policy and Resources Committee. To fulfil the need for an independent monitoring system which would possess sufficient status and formal authority to make detailed investigations of any project, department or area of activity, and to call committees and officers to account, a fourth sub-committee named the Performance Review Sub-Committee was recommended. It was to report directly to the Policy and Resources Committee and would be chaired by a member of the parent committee.

The reduction in the number and size of the service committees since the Maud Report was not seen as the cure for "all the ills of an ineffective management structure", and could even exacerbate the problem of giving members adequate opportunities to participate. The Working Group concluded that there was "no 'best buy'

---

[18] *The New Local Authorities: Management and Structure*, H.M.S.O. 1972.

when it comes to deciding the number of committees which a particular authority requires". The Maud recommendation to reduce the number of committees had been achieved by grouping together certain linked services and by substantial delegation of executive powers to committees and to officers. The Working Group therefore urged that the committee structure should be based upon the objectives of the authority and the programmes necessary to achieve those objectives, rather than upon the provision of particular services. Each programme committee so established would be served by the skills and experience of a number of different departments, so encouraging a corporate rather than a departmental approach.

The committee structure which emerged from this analysis was capable of adaptation to the needs of individual authorities, and one of the possible committee structures suggested for a non-metropolitan county was as follows:

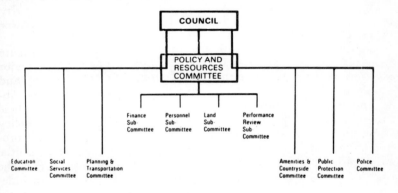

Committee structure — Non-metropolitan county

Notes 1 A separate National Parks committee will be required in appropriate counties.
      2 The Police committee is the police authority, but by convention it is expected that it will use the same lines of communication as other committees. The diagram reflects this.

In this diagram the programme committee for Education combines education, libraries, museums and art galleries; the programme committee for Planning and Transportation encompasses planning, highways and transport planning, traffic, parking, road safety, lighting, aerodromes, and public transport co-ordination; the programme committee for Amenities and Countryside links country parks, footpaths and bridleways, commons, caravan sites, recreation and tourism, small holdings,land drainage, refuse disposal, and entertainment; and the programme committee for

Public Protection includes consumer protection, emergency services, health education, and registration and licensing.

The Report also discussed the need for area committees with delegated powers from the council to run services in parts of the new and geographically larger authorities. Devon C.C. has area social service committees and Basildon U.D.C. suggested integrated area offices in the new counties comprising sections of all the departments of the county council and area committees for member involvement. The Working Group found no substantial body of support for such area committees operating under delegated authority. However, the Report did recommend that within programme areas, working groups of members should be set up, without the constraints of formal sub-committees, to provide members with opportunities to identify themselves with areas of activity in which they had a particular interest and also to provide officers with an immediate point of reference at member level.

Since the publication of the Bains Report in 1972, research by members of the Institute of Local Government Studies has shown that almost all the authorities in their sample had a central policy committee, with functions closely related to those specified by Bains for the Policy and Resources Committee.[19] There is, however, less consistency in adopting the four resource sub-committees. Some authorities have decided that the four functions should come within the deliberations of the Policy and Resources Committee, others have recognised their importance by according them full committee status, while others argue the case for additional central committees and/or sub-committees. The picture generally is of local authorities agreeing on the necessity for policy co-ordination and resource management but disagreeing on the number of committees and sub-committees required.

The Bains proposal that no authority should require more than six programme committees is best reflected in the districts where three-quarters of the sample of 212 non-metropolitan districts have five or six committees, but the counties and metropolitan districts range widely between four and twelve committees. The overall reduction in the numbers of committees has tended to increase the number of members per committee. This is the inevitable result of the compromise between the numbers or size of committees predicted by Bains, but it may yet have a deleterious effect upon individual member participation in group discussion and decision

---

[19] R. Greenwood *et al.*, "Contingency Theory and the Organisation of Local Authorities. Part 1: Differentiation and Integration", *Public Administration*, Spring 1975, Vol. 53.

making, and may in turn lead to an increase in the number of sub-committees. The number of sub-committees being set up appears, however, to be relatively few at present.

Whereas the majority of authorities appear to have endorsed the principle underlying programme committees, they have not necessarily accepted the specific committees proposed in the Working Group's report. Counties showed the lowest degree of acceptance with 21 of the 39 counties in the sample having three or fewer of the recommended six committees, at least a half of the counties having the committees for social services, public protection, planning and transportation, and where appropriate, police. A third of the metropolitan districts (13 from 36) had five or six of the proposed committees, while over a half of the 212 non-metropolitan districts had all four of the committees recommended by Bains for that type of authority, viz. housing services, recreation and amenities, development services, and environmental health and control.

Area committees were rare, being established by only ten counties, two metropolitan districts and seven county districts. As units for linking communities, interest groups and councils in large areas, as forums for the expression of community needs, as operational bodies functioning as territorial sub-committees to the council's service committees, the area committees suggest one of the most significant and potentially useful innovations.

CHAPTER 7

Functions of Local Authorities

I. ALLOCATION OF RESPONSIBILITIES

Local authorities provide a comprehensive range of environmental, protective and personal services which are essential to community life. A local inhabitant may not realise their full extent, yet directly or indirectly they affect almost every aspect of his existence, from the time he is born to the moment he dies.

1. Services provided by Local Authorities

The following pages (see Table 4) itemise the major functions of the principal authorities in England and Wales and those of the English parish councils and Welsh community councils. Apart from the changes necessitated by the reorganisation of the National Health Service and the water services, which are described elsewhere, the reorganisation effected by the Local Government Act 1972 entailed no change in the overall scope of local authority functions. Reorganisation presented an unique opportunity to see the range of services in their entirety and to allocate them between the two operational tiers. A general formula for the allocation of functions was laid down in s. 179 of the Act whereby the functions of former county, urban district and parish councils became the functions of the new county, district, parish and community councils. The general formula was subject to the specific allocation of particular functions. Strategic services which needed to be provided and administered over large areas were allocated to the new county councils, as were the police and fire services. Services which are essentially local, such as housing or refuse collection, were to be run by the district councils. In the conurbations, education, personal social services and libraries were allocated to the metropolitan district councils, which are generally responsible for populations of 250,000 or more, but elsewhere were allocated to county councils. The functions of authorities in Wales are generally the same as those of their equivalents in England, but the differences are noted separately. Also itemised separately are the parish and community council functions, which were increased by reorganisation. In addition to their statutory functions, all local authorities have a general power to spend up to the product of a rate of 2p a year on other provisions which will benefit their area or its inhabitants.

Although each tier is independent of the other, many of their duties are interrelated and it is essential that in these matters the authorities work together. To facilitate co-operation the previous system of statutory arrangements between county and county districts for delegating and claiming functions were repealed and replaced by the simpler provision of an *agency arrangement*. Thus, by mutual agreement, local authorities can arrange for one to carry out functions on behalf of another, for example, a district can act as the agent of the county in highway maintenance. Such an arrangement is available for all the functions on the accompanying table except education, police, social services and national parks. Agency powers apply also to parish and community councils which may act as agents for principal councils and also arrange for a principal authority to act as their agent. In no case may the financial responsibility for a function be made the subject of an agency arrangement.

The accompanying table is not wholly comprehensive as it excludes a number of minor functions such as the powers conferred on individual authorities by local acts. It also excludes those cases where an authority may have the right to be consulted or to make representations on a function which is the responsibility of another authority. In some cases too, the responsibility for discharging a function may be vested in a joint board (e.g. a port health authority) which will act in place of the local authorities for its area.

The extent of provision will vary according to public need and the authority's financial resources. All the powers are conferred by Parliament and no local authority may provide a service or exercise any powers without statutory authority. Should it exceed the statutory requirements, it will be judged to have acted *ultra vires* and various sanctions may be applied.

The table set out on the following pages is an extract taken from Circular 121/72 issued by the Department of the Environment.

TABLE 4. ALLOCATION OF FUNCTIONS IN ENGLAND

County Councils (Outside Metropolitan Areas) and Metropolitan District Councils.

Education
Youth employment
Personal social services
Libraries

All County Councils	*All District Councils*
Museums and art galleries (a)	Museums and art galleries (a)
Housing—	Housing—
Certain reserve powers	Provision
	Management
	Slum clearance
	House and area improvement
Town development (a)	Town development (a)
Planning—	Planning—
Structure plans	Local plans (c)
Development plan schemes (b)	
Development control (d)	Development control (d)
	Advertisement control
Derelict land (a)	Derelict land (a)
National parks	
Country parks (a)	Country parks (a)
Conservation areas (a)	Conservation areas (a)
Building preservation notices (a)	Building preservation notices (a)
	Listed building control
Tree preservation (a)	Tree preservation (a)
Acquisition and disposal of land for planning purposes, development or redevelopment (a)	Acquisition and disposal of land for planning purposes, development or redevelopment (a)
Footpaths and bridleways—	Footpaths and bridleways—
Surveys	
Creation, diversion and extinguishment orders (a)	Creation, diversion and extinguishment orders (a)
Maintenance (a)	
Protection (a)	Protection (a)
Signposting	
Transportation—	Transportation—
Transport planning	
Highways (e)	
Traffic	
All parking	Off-street parking (f)

All County Councils	*All District Councils*
Public transport (g)	Public transport undertakings (h)
Road safety	
Highway lighting	
Footway lighting (a)	Footway lighting (a)
Environmental Health— Animal diseases	Environmental Health— Food safety and hygiene Communicable disease Slaughterhouses Offices, shops and railway premises (j) Factories Home safety Water and Sewerage (k)
Refuse disposal	Refuse collection
Consumer protection (e.g. weights and measures, trade descriptions ex- plosives, food and drugs)	Clean air Building regulations Coast protection Cemeteries and cremation
Police (1)	Markets and fairs
Fire (1)	Byelaws
Swimming baths (a)	Swimming baths (a)
Physical training and recreation (a)	Physical training and recreation (a)
Parks and open spaces (a)	Parks and open spaces (a)
Smallholdings	Allotments Local licensing
Airports (a)	Airports (a)

Parish Councils

Parish councils broadly retained their previous functional responsibilities. In relation to the functions listed above they have powers in connection with:

Footpaths and bridleways—
  Maintenance
  Signposting
	Cemeteries and crematoria
	Swimming baths
	Physical training and
	   recreation

Transportation—
  Off-street parking (f)
  Footway lighting
	Parks and open spaces
	Allotments

The Act provides parish councils with a right to be consulted about planning applications affecting land in their areas.

Allocations of Functions in Wales

The distribution of functions in Wales broadly follows the distribution of functions in England, except that the following fall to district councils or may in certain circumstances be exercised by them: refuse disposal, disposal of abandoned vehicles, libraries, on and off-street parking, food and drugs, weights and measures, and certain functions relating to agriculture listed under s. 200.

The functions of parish councils in England are exercisable in Wales by community councils.

NOTES

(a) Concurrent powers exercisable by county and district councils.

(b) In consultation with district councils.

(c) Except in national parks where counties would be responsible. Responsibility for local plans subject to development plan schemes or structure plan.

(d) Primarily a district council function except in the case of a national park or of "county matters" as defined in Schedule 16 of the Local Government Act 1972.

(e) District councils may claim maintenance powers for footpaths, bridle-ways, and urban roads which are neither trunk roads nor classified roads.

(f) In accordance with the county transportation plan.

(g) Metropolitan counties will be Passenger Transport Authorities, non-metropolitan counties have co-ordination functions.

(h) Some non-metropolitan districts under local act powers.

(j) Fire precautions under the Offices, Shops and Railway Premises Act will be a county council responsibility.

(k) Subject to water reorganisation.

(l) Subject to amalgamation schemes.

2. Joint Provision

Two or more neighbouring authorities may combine voluntarily or be combined by statute or ministerial order to provide and maintain a joint service for reasons of economy, territorial convenience or administrative efficiency. There were examples of joint action as long ago as 1696 when Bristol replaced the separate Poor Law administrations of nineteen city parishes with a "Corporation of the Poor" which combined all parishes and their churchwardens. This precedent was followed by several other towns and urban parishes, and legislation in 1722 permitted parishes to combine for poor law purposes. The principle of combination found a number of advocates and many towns, parishes and rural counties established joint authorities. The Poor Law Amendment Act 1834, adopted the principle by creating unions of parishes under the aegis of elected Boards of Guardians and a further major example in the nineteenth century was the forty-five-member Metropolitan Board of Works

(1855) providing an array of drainage and highway services for London's vestries, district boards and the City.

After the Public Health Act 1875, which empowered districts to form themselves into a united district for public health purposes, a number of acts included clauses providing for the combination of authorities for housing, education, mental care, electricity supply, town planning, sea fisheries, libraries, cemeteries, fire brigades, etc. The power to establish joint committees and boards was generally neglected, however, and between 1875 and 1939 there were only sixty-five set up by local acts and 190 by provisional orders, 111 of the latter being for isolation hospitals.[1] The *Municipal Year Book* 1966 lists thirty burial boards or committees, twenty joint sewerage boards, one conservancy catchment board, eighty-nine water boards and sixty port health authorities, and in 1967 included a section on educational building consortia and housing groups.

One might have assumed that the convenience and economy attainable by joint action would have appealed to cost-conscious councils, but local authorities were generally not anxious to participate in joint undertakings. They were reluctant to forsake any part of the services which they administered and jealously preserved their autonomous control. Many of the smaller authorities were unwilling to enter into agreements where their minority representation might be subordinated to the larger authorities, while mistrust of "big brother" and his future intentions also served to limit effective co-operation. The equitable sharing of costs also became a contentious issue. The result was that many local authorities preferred to administer their own services rather than amalgamate for economy and efficiency.

Governmental attitude to amalgamation has varied, depending on whether it has been contemplating a radical reconstruction of local government or not. In the latter case, in 1945 for example, the government believed it "to be inexpedient to contemplate drastic innovations" preferring "to rely on the existing structure . . . with appropriate machinery, where necessary, for combined action";[2] but the Maud Report (1967) compared the situation unfavourably with foreign practice where there existed "a more relaxed and pliant state of affairs." In Britain, joint action was "not popular", and one effect of the difficulty "of inducing local authorities to act together, or to combine with outside agencies" was to reinforce "the central

---

[1] Elizabeth Howard "Joint Authorities" in *Essays on Local Government*, ed. C. H. Wilson, p. 212.
[2] *Local Government in England and Wales during the Period of Reconstruction* (Cmd. 6579).

government's liking for provisions which allow little latitude". The implication was clear: unless local authorities were prepared to join forces to provide services, and in the process surrender a measure of individual sovereignty, central authorities would be more tempted "to lay down the ways in which duties are to be discharged".

S. 101 (5) of the Local Government Act 1972 gave local authorities the general power to combine to "discharge any of their functions jointly" and to appoint joint committees to which they might delegate powers to the same extent as they would to their own committees. The general power did not include a local authority's functions with respect to levying, or assessing a precept for, a rate, or borrowing money, or for the discharge of any of its functions under the Diseases of Animals Act 1950. The composition of joint committees, their terms of reference and proceedings, and the appointment of sub-committees, are the same as those laid down for the appointment of committees by a local authority. Thus at least two-thirds of their members must be members of the appointing authorities, and the co-option of non-members now has statutory backing.

The expenses incurred by a joint committee, whether appointed or established voluntarily, are defrayed by the authorities in agreed proportions. Where there is disagreement, the act requires (s. 103) that in any case where parishes or communities in one district are in dispute that the district council will arbitrate; in any other case, a single arbitrator agreed on by the appointing authorities or, in default of agreement, appointed by the Secretary of State, will determine the issue.

The general power to appoint joint committees gives local authorities added choice in determining appropriate arrangements for the most economical and efficient provision of services over combined areas. In addition to joint committees there are also joint boards which are composed of nominees of two or more local authorities. These have been established to administer services in which several local authorities are concerned, and may be created by local acts, e.g. the Derwent Valley Water Board, set up in 1899, or they may be constituted under provisions contained in general acts, e.g. the Secretary of State may by order constitute a joint board comprising members of public health authorities as a port health authority, or create a joint board for water supply, or for securing greater efficiency in the discharge of all or any of the sewerage functions of local authorities, or set up a joint board as the county planning authority for two or more county councils. The Passenger

Transport Authorities set up under the Transport Act 1968 and comprising representatives of the appropriate local authorities to control policy and finance, but with autonomous operational powers vested in the technical experts of the Passenger Transport Executives, are an extension of the joint board principle.

Joint boards are generally bodies corporate, with perpetual existence and a common seal; they may sue and be sued, have the power to hold land and to raise loans either independently or through their constituent authorities upon whom they may issue precepts. They are invariably formed for the running of more permanent services. Whereas joint committees are completely dependent upon their constituent authorities, the joint board is independent of control by its constituent authorities. The distinction is simple but important, and this "dependency test" will help to identify those joint boards which are loosely referred to as joint committees, e.g. the Mersey Tunnel Joint Committee.

II. LOCAL AUTHORITY SERVICES

Figures published by the Chartered Institute of Public Finance and Accountancy show that the total estimated expenditure to be met from rates and grants for 1974–5 rose by more than £1,000 million to £7,380 million. The total to be met from grants rose by 18 per cent to £4,321 million, and the total met from rates by 27 per cent to £3,002 million. Only £57 million was to be met from balances. The distribution of expenditure is shown below:

Service	£ million	%	Increase % over 1973–4
Education	3,282	47·0	+12
Housing	746	10·7	+67
Social Services	549	7·9	+32
Police	546	7·8	+13
Highways	537	7·7	+13
Refuse collection and waste disposal	177	2·5	+25
Fire	134	1·9	+24
Town and country planning	121	1·7	+49
Parks and open spaces	114	1·6	+15
Libraries, museums and art galleries	112	1·6	+18
Other services	665	9·5	+16
	6,983	100·0	
Provision for inflation	397		
	7,380		+26

In the three years after 1971–2 current expenditure by local authorities increased by 7 per cent to 8 per cent per year in real terms, and this growth rate far outstripped the 2 per cent annual growth in national resources. The joint circular *Rate Fund Expenditure and Rate Calls in 1975–76* (D.O.E. 171/74) examined the economic prospects and the implications for individual services of the 1975–6 rate support grant settlement which provided for no growth over the best estimates of expenditure for 1974–5 plus an allowance for inescapable commitments. In September 1975 further limitations on local authority spending were outlined in *Local Authority Expenditure in 1976–77: Forward Planning* (D.O.E. 149/75) which said that in 1976–7 "there will inevitably be a reduction in the standard of local services". Local authority spending in 1975–6 had exceeded the level set in the R.S.G. settlement by about 2 per cent, which was originally the amount of growth allowed for the following year. Education would be one of the worst affected services, where there will be "no scope for improvement of standards for the education service at any level". On housing, rent increases averaging 60p a week were expected, and the government intended to pay a special housing subsidy in 1976–7 to reduce the amount of the rate fund contribution to housing revenue accounts that would otherwise be necessary. Police, probation and after-care services faced stringent economies. There was to be no extra spending on "youth, recreation and community services" and increased charges for trading services such as swimming pools. Social services escaped relatively unscathed but the circular suggested savings by leaving finished buildings empty and cutting the number of people due to go into residential homes.

It is unfortunately impracticable in the available space of this book to discuss each local authority service, and five only of the major services—education, housing, town and country planning, police, and health and welfare services—will be considered within the framework of the appropriate legislation.

1. Education

The education system in England and Wales is administered by the Secretary of State for Education and Science through the Department of Education and Science. In 1970 the functions of the Secretary of State relating to primary and secondary education in Wales were transferred to the Secretary of State for Wales, except those relating to the qualifications, training, supply, salaries and superannuation of teachers.

The local education authorities are the councils of the non-metropolitan counties and metropolitan districts. They assumed full responsibility on 1 April, 1974 for the education functions carried out by the councils of the former counties and county boroughs. On the same day the power of the former county councils to delegate administrative functions to divisional executives was repealed and existing schemes of divisional administration were abolished. No further schemes for excepted district status can be made. The Secretary of State is empowered to constitute a joint board to act as L.E.A. for the areas of two or more councils. In the Greater London area the outer boroughs are L.E.A.s, but the inner boroughs, the City and the Temples come under the administration of the Inner London Education Authority, a special committee of the G.L.C.

Education constitutes the largest single item of a local authority's expenditure and its cost is continually rising. As L.E.A.s have little control over centrally imposed standards of school design, construction and staffing, and no control over staff salaries or the number, nature and timing of new schools, it has been suggested by such bodies as the National Union of Ratepayers' Associations that the cost of education should be borne by the Exchequer while its administration could remain with the L.E.A.s.

A. Development

Poverty and ignorance among the lower orders of society attracted the attention of voluntary reformers from the S.P.C.K. in 1700 through to John Wesley and the voluntary schools of Lancaster and Bell in the early nineteenth century. The State did nothing to remedy the vast educational deficiencies until Parliamentary Committees were appointed in 1816, and their inquiries revealed the "existence of tractless wastes of educational destitution"[3]. In 1833 parliamentary funds of £20,000 were paid to the National Society and the British and Foreign Schools Society, and very gradually an administrative structure was pieced together until in 1839 the Committee of Council on Education was set up to administer government grants.

The main development in publicly provided primary education dates from the Education Act 1870 which set up directly elected school boards in areas which were short of schools and empowered them to raise a rate in order to finance their work. The country was divided into school districts, which were boroughs or civil parishes,

---

[3] J. S. Maclure, *Educational Documents, England and Wales*, 1816–1963, Chapman & Hall, 1965, p. 18.

and the principle of compulsory education from 5 to 13 was accepted. The success of the School Boards in supplementing the work of the voluntary schools pointed the need for a similar leaven in secondary education. This was done by the Education Act 1902, which made the counties and county boroughs education authorities. Under Part III of the Act borough councils with a population of 10,000 and urban districts with 20,000 population became authorities for elementary education only.

The Education Act 1918, strengthened local authorities, reformed the grant system so that not less than 50 per cent of the cost of education was met by central government, abolished elementary school fees and all exemptions from the leaving age of 14, and extended the local education authority's range of permissive services. The Act had laid the duty of establishing "a national system of public education" on the councils of counties and county boroughs, where it remained until 1944.

B. *The Education Act* 1944

The principal act which governs public education in England and Wales is the Education Act 1944.[4] Its main provisions were:

1. The Ministry of Education superseded the Board of Education and the Board's president became a Minister.

2. The Minister of Education was made responsible for the education of the people of England and Wales and the local education authorities were required to perform their part "under his control and direction".

3. The former division into "elementary" and "higher" education was replaced by primary, secondary and further education—"a continuous process conducted in three successive stages".

4. County and county borough councils were made responsible for all stages. Local education authorities were given the duty of ensuring "adequate provision of primary and secondary education" including nursery and special schools, and to prepare development plans showing how this was to be done. Tuition fees at maintained schools were forbidden. Part III authorities were abolished.

5. The dual system, i.e. the co-existence of local education authority schools and voluntary schools, was modified considerably. The financial settlement was made more generous to the voluntary bodies. Church schools could choose "Aided" status, with capital grants of 50 per cent (raised to 75 per cent in 1959) or "Controlled" status, where the local education authorities appoint a majority of the managers.

---

[4] As amended by various Education Acts since 1946, the Local Government Act 1958, the London Government Act 1963, and the Local Government Act 1972.

6. The leaving age was raised to 15 (came into effect in 1947) and provided for it to be raised to 16 by Order in Council "as soon as it has become practical". A general principle was laid down concerning the right of the parent to have his wishes taken into consideration over the choice of school.

7. Part-time day attendance at County Colleges was to be required at some future date for those who had left school before the age of 18.

8. The obligation and powers of the local education authorities in connection with such ancillary services as medical, school meals, transport, provision of school clothing and the award of scholarships for higher education, was extended.

9. In all primary and secondary schools the day should begin with a corporate act of worship and religious instruction should be given in county schools according to a syllabus agreed by representatives of the religious denominations.

C. *Classification of Schools*

The three stages envisaged by the 1944 Act, which were.to be the responsibility of the local education authorities, were:

1. *Primary Stage* (up to the age of 11 years) which included Nursery (to age 5), Infant (from 5) and Junior Schools (age 8 to 11).

2. *Secondary Stage* (11–15 years, to be raised to 16) which comprised Secondary Grammar, Secondary Technical and Secondary Modern Schools; all intended to be of equal status.

3. *Further Stage* which included County Colleges, Technical Colleges and Colleges of Art and Commerce, Evening Institutes, Services for Youth, Adult Education and Community Centres.

Since 1959 a number of reports have detailed certain of the inadequacies of educational provision in the three stages. The *Crowther Report*, 1959, on the educational needs of youngsters between 15 and 18 years of age recommended: the raising of the school-leaving age to 16; compulsory part-time further education for those leaving school at 16; improvements in further education for technicians, craftsmen and operatives, including "sandwich courses"; the recruitment of more teachers; and the revision of syllabuses to prevent pre-specialisation. The *Albermarle Report*, 1960, advocated: the adoption of a ten-year programme for the youth service, with the service to be available for the 14 to 20 age group; priority for training professional youth leaders; a generous building programme; and the establishment of a Youth Service Development Council to advise the Minister of Education in refashioning the service.

The Newsom Report, 1963, entitled "Half our Future", considered the education of pupils aged 13 to 16 of average and below-average ability. It recommended: raising the school-leaving age for secondary modern pupils from 1965; longer school hours, some of which were to be spent on "extra-curricular" activities; a curb on examinations and the provision of a school-leaving certificate for 16 year olds; the replacement of inadequate buildings; the relief of overcrowding; the arrangement of an experimental building programme to try different forms of school organisation and teaching methods in purpose-designed schools; specific attention for schools in slum areas; and an emphasis on spiritual and moral development.

In 1967, the *Plowden Report*, "Children and their Primary Schools", recommended: special assistance ("positive discrimination") for schools in slum areas in the form of more teachers, additional finance for school buildings, and more generous supplies of equipment; the recruitment of over 50,000 "teachers' aides" by 1973–74; a large expansion of nursery schools; smaller classes; the abolition of corporal punishment; regular parent-teacher contacts; more teaching aids; and special attention to the teaching of English to immigrant children.

In July 1968 the Report of the Public Schools Commission, under the chairmanship of Sir John Newsom, recommended *inter alia* that: independent boarding schools should take at least 50 per cent assisted pupils from maintained schools after a period of about seven years; the cost of assisted places, subject to parental contribution, should be met by L.E.A.s on a pooled basis; the only justification for public expenditure on boarding education should be the need for boarding, for either social or academic reasons; independent schools should take pupils of a wider range of ability; they should be encouraged to work closely with each other and with maintained schools; there should be more co-educational boarding schools; and schools that are charities but which serve no truly charitable purpose should lose any financial reliefs.

With effect from September, 1972, the school-leaving age was raised to sixteen. A report published by the D.E.S. in April, 1975, stated that schools had made a good start in the first year with almost every secondary school reporting some degree of success. It said that too much emphasis had been put on the failures of R.S.L.A., particularly on the "hard core of dissidents, probably less than 10%, who have created problems out of all proportion to their numbers". Examination courses had been more successful than non-examination courses, but "the danger of creating a distinct 'R.S.L.A. group' somehow outside the corporate life of the school has not entirely been avoided". Link courses in brick-laying, plastering and secretarial skills with local technical colleges had operated in three out of every four L.E.A.s, with one in every ten L.E.A.s making very extensive use of them, but "arrangements have not always worked smoothly". Work experience was not a major feature of the first year. Additional examination work and the need for more pastoral care and guidance had placed extra burdens on teachers and there was a greater demand for in-service training. Staffing was sufficient to deal with the extra pupils though there were shortages of specialists such as handicraft teachers. L.E.A.s generally provided extra staff but policies varied with some staffing ratios "as low as 1:20 or even worse". A special building programme spread over 1970–73 amounting to £125 million was allocated to provide accommodation for the extra pupils. Most schools had sufficient materials, equipment and accommodation to implement their curricular plans.

In December, 1972, a White Paper *Education: A Framework for Expansion* (Cmnd. 5174) set out the government's educational objectives and priorities for the decade to 1981. Five areas of education were examined with attention being directed at scale, organisation and cost rather than on educational content, and a flexible programme was laid down to provide a framework for future action: (i) *Nursery Education*: to be provided without charge to all children at the age of 3 and 4 whose parents want them to have it, with priority being given initially to the deprived areas; (ii) *School Buildings:* by the mid-1970s to replace or improve many of the oldest primary schools and to launch a secondary school improvement programme in 1975–6, and also to spend more on the building of special schools for handicapped children; (iii) *Better Staffing Standards*: to achieve an increase in the number of teachers from 364,000 in 1971 to about 510,000 in 1981; (iv) *Teacher Training*: to achieve several of the objectives of the James Report *Teacher Education and Training* (January 1972) so that from 1974–5 there should be regular in-service training for teachers for periods equivalent to one term every seven years, more help during a teacher's probationary period, development towards an all-graduate teaching profession, and encouragement being given to a new three-year training course leading to qualified teacher status and a B.Ed. degree; (v) *Higher Education*: to increase the number of students taking full time or sandwich courses so that by 1981 about 22 per cent of 18-year-olds would be taking higher educational courses as against 15 per cent in 1971 and 7 per cent in 1961; to introduce new two-year courses leading to a Diploma in Higher

Education; and to expand colleges providing these advanced courses of study.

The White Paper suggested that in the ten years between 1971–2 and 1981–2 total expenditure on schools was likely to rise from £1,475m. to £2,000m. (at 1972 prices) and on higher education from £687m. to £1,120m. Thus total annual expenditure on schools and higher education, which together account for 75 per cent of education expenditure (both capital and current), was expected to rise by £960m.

A team of examiners from the Organisation for Economic Co-operation and Development in Paris reviewed "educational development strategies" in England and Wales in 1974 and studied the D.E.S. planning methods by taking the 1972 White Paper as the operational model. In a detailed critique published in 1975[5] they stated that: decentralisation of educational decision-making in England and Wales does not necessarily result in a high level of participation; civil servants have a power in their own right, often giving them authority over their political masters; the D.E.S. are unnecessarily secretive about their decision-making and prefer to rely on informal methods; this system of planning means goals and priorities escape regular scrutiny; and the education White Paper was narrow in outlook and had important omissions, particularly in the 16–19 age group and adult education. The O.E.C.D. Report and the report of the formal confrontation between the examiners and three senior civil servants from the D.E.S. raise several fascinating questions about the relationship between civil servants and politicians, about the character of the D.E.S. as "pragmatic, conservative and evolutionary, not theoretical, futuro-logical and revolutionary" and the radical politician's drive for change and discontinuity, and about the degree of openness attending the planning process.

A Committee of Inquiry chaired by Sir Alan Bullock produced its report *A Language for Life* in February, 1975. It recommended *inter alia* a system of monitoring to assess a wider range of attainments than has been attempted in the past and allow new criteria to be established for the definition of literacy. There should be positive steps to develop the language ability of children in the pre-school, nursery and infant years by involving parents, improving staffing ratios in infant schools, and employing teachers' aides whose training had a language element. Every school should have an organised policy for language across the curriculum, should

---

[5] *The Times Educational Supplement*, 9 May and 13 June, 1975.

establish every teachers' involvement in language and reading development, and make a suitably qualified teacher responsible for advising colleagues in language and the teaching of reading. English in the secondary school should have improved resources. L.E.A.s should appoint a specialist English adviser and establish an advisory team, should introduce early screening procedures, give additional assistance to children retarded in reading, establish a reading clinic, provide tuition for adult illiterates and the children of families of overseas origin. Teacher training should include a course on language in education and there should be an expansion in in-service education in reading and the teaching of English.

In September, 1975, a Schools Council report *The Whole Curriculum 13–16* called for a system of assessment that did not perpetuate the divisions in the present curriculum between the academic and the non-academic. Every pupil should be given a documentary record of their attainments, interests and aspirations when they leave school, and examination boards should widen their responsibilities to validate these documents and offer a comprehensive assessment service to replace the present system of examinations at 16-plus. The assessment should differentiate between different kinds of achievement rather than different levels.

D. *Comprehensive Secondary Education*

In July, 1965, the Department of Education and Science, which replaced the Ministry of Education in 1964, issued its now-famous Circular 10/65 which stated:

> "It is the Government's declared objective to end selection at eleven-plus and to eliminate separatism in secondary education. ... The Secretary of State accordingly requests local authorities, if they have not already done so, to prepare and submit to him plans for reorganising secondary education in their areas on comprehensive lines".

The plans were to be prepared within a year.

The Labour Party defined the comprehensive school in the following manner:

> "It is a secondary school which is intended for all normal children in a district without dividing them into grammar, technical or modern departments". (*Fair Deal for Kids*, 1975)

Circular 10/65 described the main forms of comprehensive organisation. These were (i) the orthodox comprehensive schools with an age range of 11–18; (ii) "two-tier" systems of various kinds, under which pupils transfer at the age of 11 to a junior comprehensive school, and thence at 13 or 14 some or all transfer to a senior school; (iii) comprehensive schools with an age range of 11–16, combined with sixth form colleges for those over 16; and (iv) a system of "middle schools" under which pupils transfer at 8 or 9 to a comprehensive school with an age range of 8 or 9 to 12 or 13, and thence to another comprehensive school for older pupils.

All children leaving primary school would enter the comprehensive school for their area without taking a streaming or selection test (11 + being abolished). The first year or two would entail diagnosis of abilities and aptitudes, and by the age of 13 (believed to be a better age than 11 to assess abilities) would be allocated to their "sets", i.e. the classes for which they are best suited in the appropriate subjects. Children would be transferred to higher or lower streamed classes on the basis of teachers' assessments.

Since 1965 comprehensive education has been the centre of controversy in a number of L.E.A.s, with public protests in Liverpool, Bristol, Luton, Sunderland, Cardiff, Newport, Westmorland, Surrey, Bournemouth and the inner London Boroughs culminating in "the triumph of the village Hampdens"[6] in the case of *Bradbury and others v. London Borough of Enfield* in 1967. As a result the Education Act 1968 clarified and amended the law relating to changes in the character and premises of county and voluntary schools so as to prevent the Court of Appeal's decision in the above case invalidating changes effected since 1945 by L.E.A.s.

The editorial in the Comprehensive Schools Committee's bulletin (Spring 1968) showed how the Government's request to L.E.A.s to submit reorganisation plans was being thwarted in a number of ways and how as a result, it was alleged, at least half of the 103 schemes approved by the D.E.S. were unsatisfactory. A Parliamentary reply in November 1968 showed that 116 plans had been implemented or approved, and of the remaining forty-seven, sixteen were under consideration by the D.E.S., the proposals of seven had been rejected and revised schemes were awaited, seventeen had not submitted schemes, and seven—Bournmouth, Bury, Kingston upon Thames, Richmond, Rutland, Westmorland and Worcester—had refused to submit schemes. To deal with the "recalcitrant" authorities, the Queen's Speech in October 1969 referred to the government's intention to introduce legislation to compel L.E.A.s to submit schemes for comprehensive organisation. The return of a Conservative government to office in 1970 interrupted this intention, and in Circular 10/70 it withdrew Circular 10/65 and allowed

---

[6] "Enfield and the law", *The Times Educational Supplement*, 1 September, 1967.

authorities to decide for themselves whether to prepare reorganisation schemes.

E. *The Comprehensive Debate*

The supporters of the comprehensive school system claim the following advantages:

1. The comprehensive school will rescue those children whose future would otherwise be jeopardised by the eleven plus examination. It is an examination which some claim is not scientifically valid or discriminating, and is taken on one day when a child may perform below par; additionally, 11 is too early an age for such an important decision to be made.

2. The comprehensive school will make for fluid movement within and among streams.

3. It will equalise and extend educational opportunity for all children. The grammar system is unfair in that the availability of places varies from area to area, e.g. in 1963 33 per cent of all Welsh secondary scholars were in grammar schools, 22·6 per cent in the eastern counties. Even more important, "parity of esteem" is a myth because differences in class, parental attitudes and home conditions affect a child's progress and middle class children have a better chance of getting into a grammar school (research in 1946 showed 54 per cent of upper middle class children got grammar school places, 11 per cent of lower manual class). Therefore, parental affluence is a determining factor.

4. It will allow good students to move ahead as well as they would in a grammar school and at the same time encourage the less able by their example.

5. It will develop everybody's capacity for intelligence and make the most of the nation's "pool of ability".

6. It will allow economies of scale in buildings, schools and teaching staff.

7. It will make the services of the best teachers available to all instead of to a narrow band of top students in the grammar school, where the best qualified teachers generally gravitate.

8. Most of all, the protagonists allege, the comprehensive school will overcome social barriers, snobbery and inequality and put an end to the social divisiveness of the present system.

The opponents of the comprehensive schools put forward the following counter-arguments:

i. All the above claims seem attractive on paper, but are based on little more than theoretical assumptions, e.g. Dr. J. D. Koerner, an American educationist, wrote:

> "The comprehensive school will not necessarily do any of these things, certainly will not do all of them and probably can never

do some of them. Moreover, none of them really has much to do with how schools are organised and administered. Most of the things that need doing in British education could be done through the existing school system" (*Daily Telegraph*, 25 February, 1966)

ii. The grammar schools and the direct grant schools, many of which are the admiration of the Western world, will be swept away on the basis of unsubstantiated theory. In America and Russia, where almost all schools until recently have been comprehensive:

"Separate schools for the children at the very top of the ability range seem to be an inevitable consequence eventually of all otherwise fully comprehensive systems". (K. Ollerenshaw in *The Sunday Times*, 6 March, 1966)

Why not use the experience of these countries and keep our "proved" schools? The fate of these schools, their traditions, their effectiveness are in the balance, and fears of their abandonment have led one public school headmaster to comment: "Nowadays there are only two types of secondary school—comprehensive and apprehensive!" Britain should preserve her unique and in many cases unrivalled educational establishments, "avoid massive standardisation and leave room for heterodoxy and choice and dissent". In addition, what happens to the denominational schools in this standardisation?

iii. The secondary modern schools and their students have not been given a fair chance; they have been allowed to become "custodial institutes" which contain "the submerged three-quarters". Greater research needs to be undertaken and greater efforts need to be made to develop these children by orientating the teaching to more positive practical, realistic and vocational subjects. Where academic ability is shown, the children can be prepared for the appropriate examinations and the high incidence of "O" and "A" level successes is proof of what can be achieved by enlightened teaching in these schools.

iv. The argument that social distinctions would be eradicated is more theoretical than realistic. In any case, school is primarily a place for education and not social reform. Putting all children in a comprehensive school is no more valuable than in three schools, and may positively serve to emphasise social distinctions: "The social effect of such schools is to reinforce rather than combat class consciousness" (Koerner). "There is no easy way in a free society to achieve a true social *and* intellectual mix in each school" (Ollerenshaw). Social distinctions would also be emphasised by the fact that "grammar" stream students would take the leadership posts.

v. The cost of conversion is prohibitive. The change has never been worked out in terms of finance, buildings or manpower. Existing buildings (including the Newsom "slums") and the existing short supply of teachers will have to be pressed into service. Said the *Sunday Times* (18 July, 1965):

". . . to spend money on reorganisation when about £1,250 million is needed to bring school buildings up to standard and when the school population is growing fast . . . is wrong. Obviously existing school buildings cannot be discarded. There are now about 6,000 secondary schools with an average of 500 pupils".

The raising of the school-leaving age in 1972–73 will aggravate teaching and accommodation difficulties, but in order to offset the necessary extra building costs the D.E.S. announced that £36 million would be allocated for each year from 1968 to 1971 to local authorities.

vi. Comprehensive schools, to stand a chance of success, require purpose-built buildings. These are not generally available, and any scheme thus necessiates patched compromises. Yet even if such buildings were available, size becomes a major problem and serves to destroy the pupil/teacher relationship which is so essential in the education process. The children become members of a vast impersonal and anonymous empire, and the teachers, perhaps confined to the lowest streams, may become disillusioned and inclined to neglect the backward pupils. The best teachers (particularly the science graduates) may leave and so aggravate the teacher shortage.

vii. The lowest streams may tend to drag down the better.

"The greatest problem of the American comprehensive school has been to escape mediocrity—to avoid having the standards and the ethos of the school established by the average instead of the best" (Koerner).

viii. Many parents are worried by the lack of choice and the feeling that education is being subordinated to political expediency. Their fears are not lessened by the complexity of the prototype schemes and the failure of local education authorities to prepare acceptable schemes. It is, as Lord James of Rusholme has said,

"an area characterised by prejudice and misconceptions, by inconsistencies and an enormous amount of sheer ignorance".

ix. There is no surety that comprehensive schools are educationally better. What if theory does not work out in practice—a generation of student guinea-pigs will have been sacrificed. Why not have purpose-built comprehensive schools in new towns and not tamper with the existing system? Allow them to run side by side for a decade, compare results and then decide.

Circular 4/74 withdrew Circular 10/70 and asked every L.E.A. which had not already done so to submit plans for developing a fully comprehensive system and for ending selection at eleven-plus or any other age. Before the Secretary of State (then Mr. R.

Prentice) had received all the replies a survey conducted by *The Times Educational Supplement* in February, 1975, showed that only twenty of the 104 L.E.A.s in England and Wales were truly comprehensive and that a quarter of the pupils (35 per cent in Greater London) still sat selection examinations. Forty L.E.A.s claimed to be either completely comprehensive or said they would be by September, 1975, and twenty of these had a fully comprehensive intake in both county and voluntary schools. The remainder had converted their county schools to a comprehensive system, but most had no plans for changing their voluntary schools, which were often partially, if not wholly, selective. Many of them, particularly in the metropolitan districts, were Roman Catholic schools.

At least seven L.E.A.s, and possibly fourteen, had little or no intention of going fully comprehensive unless forced to by legislation. The seven L.E.A.s (Bexley, Buckinghamshire, Essex, Kingston, Redbridge, Trafford and Sutton) had declined to commit themselves to complete comprehensive reorganisation. Buckinghamshire, Kingston and Trafford had no plan to abolish selection, while the remainder wanted to retain a few of their grammar schools alongside their comprehensives. Other L.E.A.s which may refuse to go fully comprehensive include Cumbria, Devon, Dorset, Kent and Bury.

Of the remaining L.E.A.s, twenty-five have had programmes approved to introduce comprehensive schools and expect to be fully comprehensive by 1980, and thirty-two authorities have no firm date mainly because local government reorganisation upset their comprehensive plans. Many of the thirty-two (e.g. Avon, Berkshire and Suffolk) have had radically to readjust their programmes to take account of the constituent authorities; others' (e.g. Devon and Dorset) have had small enclaves of entrenched opposition to comprehensive schools in their new boundaries. A general complaint from this group, composed mainly of counties and a few metropolitan districts, was the lack of money to develop and complete comprehensive plans. Difficulties also occurred where populations are static or declining, and these areas were hit by the Government's decision to give building money for basic needs only. Moreover, the *T.E.S.* survey showed that this group of thirty-two L.E.A.s was not wholly committed to a fully comprehensive system. Among them are Bury, Calderdale, Salop, Warwickshire, Bolton and Lancashire. Bolton, with 29 per cent still in grammar schools and taking up 1,300 places in local direct grant schools each year, and Lancashire with a 62 per cent comprehensive school population and maintaining more than 6,000 pupils in direct grant and independent schools, could possibly qualify, in the *T.E.S.*'s phrase, as "covert rebels".

Failure to reorganise on non-selective lines could lead to ministerial pressure being applied. Circular 4/74 states that the Secretary of State would "not propose to include in future building programme projects at non-comprehensive schools". This would be a major problem for those L.E.A.s (e.g. Buckinghamshire) with growing school populations who needed new schools. The Secretary of State preferred not to legislate to end selection in secondary education, but by March, 1975, a short bill was being drafted by the D.E.S. to be introduced in the 1975–6 parliamentary session "if any authority still insists on retaining selection thus frustrating nationally agreed policy". It was also suggested that the fiscal benefits enjoyed by independent schools as charities would be removed by the same bill.

Mr. Prentice had already announced that the direct grant would be phased out from 1976 and that by the end of the summer of 1975 the governing bodies of the 1,973 direct grant schools (with 120,000 pupils and costing the state £13m. per year) had to tell him whether they intended to close down, go independent, or seek to join the maintained system as non-selective schools. Particular difficulties are likely to arise over the direct grant boarding schools which provide places for 10,000 boarders, many of them paid for by local authorities on the grounds of boarding need. It is assumed that most of these schools will go independent. Where the direct grant schools have traditionally filled the role of local grammar school (particularly in Lancashire), fitting them into the comprehensive system should be fairly straightforward. If the schools opt for independence, the local authority may continue paying fees but recover some of the money from parents.

The political debate over the three Labour Party manifesto priorities of comprehensive education, ending the direct grant, and taking away the charitable status of independent education will undoubtedly persist. Meantime L.E.A.s must continue to provide an educational service within an environment of conflicting political ideologies. The Opposition spokesman on education (N. St. John-Stevas) in March, 1975, referred to "the battle to preserve the good schools in Britain . . . against the greatest act of educational vandalism since Henry VIII dissolved the monastries four centuries ago". He urged Conservative councils to help direct grant schools by taking up places and assisting parents with fees out of the rates, and they should continue to do this if the schools went independent. Similarly, voluntary aided school governors should "keep their heads" and present a united front with voluntary controlled schools against authorities such as Inner London.

Within this context of rhetoric and doctrinaire convictions the respective roles of the L.E.A.s and the Secretary of State should be noted. The Education Act 1944 requires L.E.A.s to "afford for all pupils opportunities for education" while the duty of the Secretary of State "shall be to promote the education of the people . . . and to secure the effective execution by local authorities, under his control and direction, of the national policy for providing a varied and comprehensive educational service in every area". It is debateable whether these roles suggest a relationship in which the Secretary of State is in a position to deprive local education committees of autonomy in determining the form of secondary education, or to have his power construed as "the power to overrule local democracy and impose the central will". Unfortunately, education has become a political shuttlecock, characterised in the secondary stage by dogmatism and absolutist beliefs in either a universal system which allegedly provides equality of opportunity but excludes choice, or a selective system which allegedly perpetuates social inequalities. Perhaps the local authorities who refuse to conform to central government's dictates "are not only defending local democracy but also reminding us of the need for humility and scepticism in education".[7]

2. Housing

Nineteenth-century industrialisation left Britain with a heritage of speculatively built dwellings grouped in squalid and dilapidated ranks around the mines and factories which originally attracted the workmen and their families. Problems of sanitation, water supply and drainage were all tackled before any attempt was made to improve housing conditions, and not until the Labouring Classes Lodging Houses Act 1851, was there legislation empowering borough councils and local boards of health to provide tenement houses for the working classes and to regulate and control common lodging houses. In 1868 local authorities were enabled to compel landlords to repair their property, and Manchester in 1867 procured a local act which permitted the closure, without compensation, of houses unfit for human habitation. The Artizans' and Labourers' Dwellings Improvement Acts of 1875 and 1879 introduced slum clearance by authorising local authorities to condemn, demolish and reconstruct areas, and in 1884 the Government appointed a Royal Commission on Housing.

---

[7] Dr. John Rae, *The Times Educational Supplement*, 16 May, 1975.

The Housing of the Working Classes Act followed in 1890 which consolidated and amplified previous legislation and gave local authorities the permissive power to purchase land and raise loans for housing the working classes. Nevertheless, only 5 per cent of working class houses built between 1890 and 1914 were built by local authorities.

Slum clearance aggravated overcrowding and slum conditions in other areas, while the First World War worsened the housing problem. Drastic remedial action was required and the government responded with the Housing and Town Planning Act 1919, whereby the entire loss of local authorities' housing schemes in excess of a penny rate was met by the Exchequer. Approximately 176,000 houses were then built, but the cost to the Exchequer led to the Act's discontinuance in 1921 and subsequent Housing Acts in 1923 and 1924 gave less extravagant financial assistance to encourage building by local authorities and private builders. Between 1919 and 1930, one and a half million new houses were built, amounting to a 20 per cent increase in the nation's housing.

The Housing Act 1936, consolidated all previous housing legislation and became the principal Act. It defined the powers and duties of local housing authorities—the repair, maintenance and sanitary condition of houses, the clearance of unfit houses and the redevelopment of the area, the abatement of overcrowding, and the provision of new houses. The local housing authorities were to be the councils of county boroughs and county districts.

During the 1939-45 war one-third of Britain's houses were destroyed or damaged, and the population increased by $2\frac{1}{4}$ million. The housing situation was critical, and building during the war (only 220,000 houses) had fallen behind the 1934-39 average of 360,000 houses per year. The Housing (Financial and Miscellaneous Provisions) Act 1946, brought housing within the scope of the Minister of Health (Aneurin Bevan) and he placed the responsibility for meeting the demand squarely on the local authorities. A ratio of four local authority houses for one private dwelling was established, and local authority rentals were to be subsidised. At first a subsidy of £22 per annum for sixty years was specified, but increasing building costs necessitated a revision of the subsidy and rents rose above the 10s. level.

The Housing Act 1949, empowered local authorities to make improvement grants to private owners to improve and convert existing property, to advance loans for the improvement and purchase of freehold property, and encourage local authorities to build houses for all sections of the community and not only, as formerly, for the working classes. The Housing Act 1952, increased subsidies to local housing authorities for every house built and readvocated the sale of council houses; this latter matter was further clarified in 1960 with the minister's circular 5/60 encouraging local housing authorities to assist council house tenants to become owner-occupiers. The Housing and Repairs Act 1954, stimulated the improvement and conversion of old houses by emphasising the existence of grants, brought into prominence the slum clearance powers of the local housing authorities and required them to make five-year plans for slum clearance, and facilitated the acquisition of slum areas for clearance and redevelopment. Under the Housing Subsidies Act 1956, the Minister repealed all subsidies for the building of houses for general purposes, and retained only those for dwellings to rehouse households from slums, for houses for overspill population from congested areas, and for one-bedroomed houses.

The Housing Act 1957, consolidated the law relating to housing, excepting financial provisions which were consolidated in separate legislation in 1958, and defined Local Housing Authorities in England and Wales as the councils of county boroughs, boroughs, urban districts and rural districts. The Act makes provisions for securing the repair, maintenance and sanitary condition of houses, clearance and redevelopment, the abatement of overcrowding, and details their general powers and duties in providing housing and for its management. Part VII deals with a number of general matters including the Central Housing Advisory Committee, building byelaws, acquisition of land, joint action, etc.

The Housing Act 1961, proposed to redistribute housing subsidies in such a way as to encourage the introduction by local housing authorities of differential rent schemes based on "realistic" rent policies towards council house tenants able to pay. This remains, however, one of the most controversial aspects of housing finance. It also made provision for £25 million to be paid in advances to non-profit making housing associations for the construction of small houses to rent. The modernisation of older homes was also encouraged by permitting the landlord to receive a greater return on his share of modernisation expenditure.

The Parker Morris Committee recommended housing improvement standards in its report *Homes for Today and Tomorrow*, published in 1961. Local authorities were expected to incorporate the recommended standards, which were subsequently more precisely defined, in new designs, and schemes submitted to the minister after 31 December, 1968, would qualify for subsidy or loan sanction only if they complied with the standards.

The 1963 White Paper *Housing* (Cmd. 2050) made particular reference to these older dwellings which were becoming obsolescent although not yet unfit for habitation. Towns already faced the twin tasks of slum clearance and building for current need, but plans for the redevelopment of the older areas, for "twilight area renewal", were also necessary.

The Housing Act 1964, established a Housing Corporation to stimulate, through non-profit-making housing societies, the building of new houses and flats either for letting at cost rents or on the basis of group ownership in order to meet the demand of persons who did not wish, or are unable, to rent or buy in the ordinary way and cannot expect help from local authorities. Other parts of the act were framed to accelerate the modernisation of older houses, in some cases compulsorily, and to give local authorities greater powers to combat squalid conditions in houses in multiple occupation.

The Housing Subsidies Act 1967, gave effect to the Government's proposals in its White Paper *The Housing Programme* 1965 *to* 1970. Part I of the Act provided for the payment of housing subsidies to public authorities in England and Wales. These comprised (a) *a basic subsidy* which took the place of the £24 per house normally payable under existing legislation and calculated in respect of all approved dwellings completed in a financial year. It took the form of a contribution towards the loan charges incurred in financing their capital costs and broadly had the same effect as if the local authority had been able to raise a loan at 4 per cent per annum; and (b) *supplementary subsidies* where appropriate for expensive sites high flats, building in special materials, town development, extra cost of precautions against subsidence and special needs. Part II provided for assistance to owner-occupiers on mortgage payments on houses, and was designed to help those in lower income groups by providing for a new type of loan—an option mortgage—at a reduced rate of interest.

The Government aimed to redress a long-felt grievance of occupying leaseholders with the passing of the Leasehold Reform Act 1967, which was based on the principle "that the freeholder owns the land and the occupying leaseholder is morally entitled to the ownership of the building which has been put on and maintained on the land." Consequently the Act stipulated that tenants (with five years tenancy) of houses held on long leases (twenty-one years or more) at low rents were enabled to enfranchise the property by purchasing the freehold, or alternatively to obtain a fifty years' extension of the lease. Part I implemented substantially the proposals of the White Paper *Leasehold Reform in England and Wales* (Cmnd. 2916), and Part II amended previous legislation by extending the protection of the Rent Acts to long tenancies.

A housing survey in 1967 showed that there were more unfit houses and substandard houses, with 3·7 million needing repairs and 2·3 million lacking one or more of the basic amenities. It was considered that this housing was worth saving and a White Paper *Old Houses into New Homes* (Cmnd. 3602), published in April 1968, made proposals for general improvement areas and for the raising of the discretionary grant and the standard grant.

These proposals were put into effect by the Housing Act 1969, which increased the discretionary limits of the improvement grant to private owners from £400 to £1,000 and the conversion grant from £500 to £1,200, with a minimum cost of works of £100. The standard grant limit was raised from £155 to £200, and basic amenities were not all required to be provided at the same time. In addition, a special grant of one half of the cost (up to a maximum of £200) could be paid by a local authority for the provision of standard amenities in a house in multiple occupation. Part II enabled authorities to declare general improvement areas where "living conditions . . . ought to be improved by the improvement of the amenities of the area or of dwellings therein or both" (s. 28). Thus authorities became responsible for the improvement of whole areas and not just individual houses. The authority must inform residents and property owners of the action they propose to take and the assistance available for the improvement of amenities. The local authority has powers to carry out works, to acquire and to let land, and may be authorised by the minister to acquire compulsorily any land. Part III provided a procedure whereby houses let on controlled rents and satisfying certain conditions became regulated tenancies on the issue of a qualification certificate.

Rent Control

Since the Rent and Mortgage Interest Restrictions Act 1939, the majority of house rents in Britain had been frozen at the pre-war level. Their tenants, often paying a lower rental than the market value of the property, were obviously disinclined to move out of accommodation which they perhaps no longer fully utilised, while others found it almost impossible to rent accommodation. The landlords of rent-controlled property were losing from the low rentals, and, with the increased costs of maintenance, were allowing their property to deteriorate.

The Minister of Housing and Local Government consequently introduced the Rent Bill which was enacted in 1957. Houses let unfurnished, with a rateable value above £30 (£40 in London and Scotland), were decontrolled (totalling about 390,000 houses in England and Wales), while the rents of the remaining 4½ million rent-controlled properties could be increased to a maximum of generally twice the 1956 gross value,[8] exclusive of rates and services, and would also become decontrolled when the sitting tenants left. All houses which were let after the Act were free from control. The Labour Party opposed the Bill because it feared that many tenants would experience hardship, and they kept up their attack whenever housing was subsequently debated. In 1963 an opposition motion deplored "the intolerable extortion, evictions, and property profiteering which have resulted from the Rent Act 1957", and Mr. Harold Wilson referred to the "disease of Rachmanism" and to instances of alleged intimidation. The persecution of tenants by unscrupulous landlords was not unknown in London, but there was little evidence of such pressure being applied in the provinces, or for that matter of the increased rentals being used to improve properties or of tenants moving to more suitable accommodation.

The Milner Holland Committee's Report on *Housing in Greater London* (Cmd. 2605), published in 1965, commented upon the acute housing shortage in London and the abuse of tenants by bad landlords. It observed that fifty years of rent restriction had hidden the real cost of housing provision and maintenance and that neither rigid rent restriction nor random decontrol would alleviate the situation. The Report also referred to the lack of security of tenure as one of the main problems facing tenants. Three months earlier some protection had been afforded by the enactment of the Protection from Eviction Act 1964, restricting the right of the landlords of furnished or unfurnished property to regain vacant possession without a court order.

The Rent Act 1965, restored rent control, in the form of rent "regulation", over most unfurnished lettings which were not controlled on 8 December, 1965. A new system for reviewing and registering rents was introduced and principles for determining "fair" rents were laid down. Severe penalties were imposed for harassing, or evicting without a court order, the residential occupier of any premises. The law relating to furnished dwellings, mortgages, and premiums was also amended.

Thus tenants in decontrolled unfurnished dwellings who felt their rent was too high[9] could approach a rent officer who would investigate and fix a "fair" rent. If this rent were unacceptable to

---

[8] This could vary from 1⅓ times to 2⅓ times the 1956 gross value dependent upon the liability for repairs.

[9] Or landlords who felt the rents to be too low.

either tenant or property owner the case would go before a rent assessment committee of three independent persons who would review all relevant factors and fix a "fair" rent. This would then be entered on a register and remain fixed for three years. The act also froze immediately all rents for unfurnished property of a rateable value of up to £200 in the provinces and £400 in London, subject only to the landlords' and tenants' rights of application for the fixing of fair rents.

From October 1966 rent tribunals were integrated with rent assessment panels, and rent officers, whose duties under the Rent Act 1965 had previously concerned only unfurnished lettings, were authorised to answer queries about furnished lettings as well and also to issue forms of application to Rent Tribunals. Owing to pressure of work, the integration did not take place in the Greater London area until April 1969. The Rent Act 1968 consolidated previous rent legislation, except for certain provisions affecting tenancies under rent control and other tenancies. These exceptions referred to protection against harassment and unlawful eviction, and to s. 16 of the Rent Act 1957, which required the minimum length of a notice to quit to be four weeks.

A White Paper *Help towards Home Ownership* (Cmnd. 3163) outlined proposals for "option mortgages" whereby one million house buyers with relatively low incomes might pay reduced rates of interest on their mortgages. This was implemented by the Housing Subsidies Act 1967 which also made provisions for government guarantees for mortgage loans of up to 100 per cent of valuation for people taking out option mortgages, and for the payment of more favourable rates to local authorities in England and Wales for housebuilding. This was an important change, for in place of the previous flat-rate annual subsidies of either £8 or £24 per dwelling (under the 1961 Housing Act), the subsidy would now vary with capital costs and current borrowing rates and so help those authorities with the highest costs and the biggest housing programmes.

In the politically controversial area of council house rents, the Prime Minister announced in November, 1967 that rent increases in twenty-two local housing authorities would be referred to the National Board for Prices and Incomes. Having examined fifteen of the schemes, the Board required a larger sample to determine broad trends and the result of their inquiries was published in Report No. 62 (Cmnd. 3604) in April 1968. It referred to the great variation in standard rents and rent increases between authorities, stemming partly from increasing costs. The Report therefore proposed "a set of uniform principles for the determination of rents which could conduce to a greater uniformity in rents for comparable dwellings". The Board favoured raising local authority rents, but that it should be effected gradually and not exceeding 7s. 6d. per dwelling in a twelve-month period; when this amount was inadequate equalisation account funds should be used for the benefit of the housing revenue account. The Board also advocated local authorities to adopt rent rebates for low income tenants and to extend rebate schemes to tenants in the private sector.

There were protests against the Government's approval of the N.B.P.I.'s findings from, for example, the local authority associations, the G.L.C. and the London Boroughs Association and those authorities which were trying to bring rents "up to a more realistic level" (e.g. the G.L.C. scheme was based on the "fair" rents for private tenancies assessed under the 1965 Act). Nevertheless the Prices and Incomes Act 1968 introduced certain restrictions on the freedom of housing authorities to fix rents by imposing a degree of central control up to the end of 1969 and for a further year for rents registered during its currency. Ministerial approval had to be sought to increase the rents of local authority houses, while the minister could require local authorities to reduce rents if they were increased after 31 March and before 10 July, 1968, when the Act came into force.

After the expiry of the powers under the 1968 Act, the Rent (Control of Increases) Act 1969 laid down that increases registered for regulated tenancies should be phased over a period to 1972, with initial increases limited to 7s. 6d. a week; that increases in individual council rents might not exceed 10s. a week up to 1 July, 1971, without ministerial consent; and that where the rents of more than 10 per cent of a local authority's dwellings were increased in any twelve week period the average increase might not exceed 7s. 6d.

On assuming office in 1970 the Conservative government's plans for reshaping housing subsidies and rents were first expressed in the 1971 White Paper *Fair Deal for Housing* (Cmnd. 4728). The Secretary of State for the Environment (Peter Walker) stated that under his proposals $2\frac{1}{4}$ million tenants in the private sector would for the first time have a rebate scheme available and that council house tenants of the 40 per cent of all local authorities which did not operate rent rebate schemes would in future be covered. He added that only 10 per cent of subsidies went to those in need through the operation of rent rebate schemes. The increases for council dwellings whose rents were below the fair rent would be phased in annual steps, with an average annual increase of 50p a week.

The Housing Finance Act 1972 implemented these proposals and effected a radical reform of housing finance. Its principal provisions were:

(a) In the private sector the 1·3 million premises still subject to rent control would be brought into the fair rents scheme over a $2\frac{1}{2}$-year period. Private landlords and tenants might agree rates between themselves subject to certain safeguards for the tenant.

(b) In the public sector fair rents would be assessed by local authorities for their own houses and flats, and these would be submitted to a special rent scrutiny board drawn from the appropriate rent assessment panel. The increase to a fair rent would take place by annual instalments from 1972/3, with an average annual rise of £26 for those below fair rent. Fair rents would be redetermined at three-yearly intervals. Council tenants would receive the same protection against summary eviction as that enjoyed by other tenants.

(c) Rent rebates would be provided for council tenants and cash rent allowances for private tenants of unfurnished but not of furnished dwellings based on income and family circumstances. Local housing authorities would be responsible for operating and meeting the cost of rebate and allowance schemes.

(d) Existing housing subsidies would be replaced by a number of new subsidies which included: residual subsidy, transition and rent rebate subsidies, rent allowance subsidy, rising costs subsidy, slum clearance subsidy.

(e) Housing associations and societies providing rented accommodation would be brought within the fair rents scheme and might raise existing rents to the fair rent level by annual amounts not exceeding 75p a week beginning not earlier than January 1973. Tenants would be eligible for rent allowances.

(f) If a local authority failed to implement the act's provisions, the government might declare the authority to be in default, and if the authority did not comply with directions made by the Secretary of State he might appoint a housing commissioner to carry out all or certain of the authority's housing functions.

Anthony Crosland had described the bill as "the most reactionary and socially divisive measure that is likely to be introduced in the lifetime of this Parliament", and as "harsh . . . inequitable and inflationary". The provision of the Act stipulating an average increase of £26 in council rents for 1972–3 had not been implemented in anticipation by most authorities in April, so that they were obliged to introduce an increase of £1 a week from 1 October for the remaining six months of 1972–3. As a result several Labour-controlled local authorities said in July and August that they refused to implement the act in this respect. At the same time a number of authorities applied to the Secretary of State for permission to make increases of less than £1 on the grounds that the rents of more than 2 per cent of their dwellings would thereby be brought above the fair rent level. By mid-September seventeen authorities had expressed their intention not to implement all or parts of the act, and by December, 1972 default orders had been made for five authorities. Continued opposition led to the appointment of housing commissioners for Bedwas and Machen U.D. and Merthyr Tydfil C.B., while district auditors were asked to make extraordinary audits of the accounts of Conisborough U.D. and Clay Cross U.D. The Clay Cross councillors may have "succeeded in putting up the most sustained challenge to central government from a recalcitrant local authority since Poplar and 'Poplarism' half a century ago".[10] But their defiance also led to North-East Derbyshire District Council, the successor to Clay Cross after reorganisation, inheriting a deficit of £67,707 on the general rate fund account partly owing to the council's refusal to implement the 1972 Act, and a further deficiency of £270,092 on the housing revenue account caused mainly by the council's failure to obtain subsidies under the same act. It also cost the council £30,810 in rent income in 1972–3 and £78,835 in 1973–4. By refusing to grant rent rebates the council denied some tenants financial benefits of up to £100 a year, and the cost of sending in a housing commissioner to administer the act was assessed at £7,528.[11]

The Rent Allowances (Furnished Lettings) Act 1972 provided for rent allowances to tenants in furnished accommodation. Not all "furnished tenants" were eligible and priority was to be given to those tenants "who are at present most disadvantaged in the market for furnished accommodation". In April, 1973 a White Paper *Widening The Choice: The Next Steps in Housing* (Cmnd. 5280) pointed out that a number of people preferred to rent their homes or could not afford to buy, and their choice had become increasingly more restricted as the privately rented sector contracted. The government thus wanted to increase the total of houses for co-ownership by strengthening the Housing Corporation whose function was to promote the development of housing associations. Lord Goodman was appointed chairman of the Housing Corporation and of the National Building Agency to see how best the voluntary movement could make the required expansion in the

---

[10] Austin Mitchell, "Clay Cross", *The Political Quarterly*, Vol. 5, No. 2, April–June, 1974.
[11] Interim report of Sheffield District Auditor, *Local Government Chronicle*, 15 November, 1974.

provision of homes for renting. Under the Housing Finance Act 1972 the Housing Corporation was empowered to lend to all housing associations. Moreover, the Corporation was required to promote the development and effectiveness of the voluntary housing movement as a whole, particularly where housing conditions were worst and the needs greatest. It was to seek out housing land and support housing associations in its purchase, and help them to convert and improve existing houses.

In June, 1973 a White Paper, *Better Homes*: *The Next Priorities* (Cmnd. 5339), showed that there were about a million unfit houses in England and Wales in 1971, of which some 355,000 were owner-occupied, 58,000 were council houses and some 645,000 were held on other tenures, notably privately rented. Nearly 70,000 unfit houses were being dealt with annually by slum clearance and the remaining slums—less than one million—should "with rare exception" be dealt with by 1982. Land hoarding and gains by property developers were also covered. A Housing and Planning Bill was introduced in January, 1974, to deal with the substance of the two white papers but the General Election intervened soon after its second reading.

The new local authorities came into being on 1 April, 1974, and by s. 193 of the Local Government Act the housing authorities outside London are the district councils. Certain reserve powers in relation to housing may be exercised by county councils. In the same month the Labour government's Housing Bill was introduced, broadly following the provisions of the Conservative Bill, and was enacted in July. The main provisions of the Housing Act 1974 were:

(a) The Housing Corporation received additional powers to sponsor and control voluntary housing associations and to provide accommodation for renting and for sale for owner-occupation, and would also have extended facilities for borrowing and lending. The Corporation's borrowing powers would be raised from £300 million to £400 million, with provision for its increase by order to £750 million.

(b) "Housing action areas" might be declared by local authorities by reference to physical and social conditions, and would be designated for a period of five years with a possible extension for a further two years. In respect of these areas local authorities might (i) make improvement grants at increased rates; (ii) require private owners to make improvements in housing; (iii) acquire housing accommodation, compulsorily if necessary and subject to the Secretary of State's approval; (iv) provide, convert, improve, repair, manage and furnish housing on land acquired in such areas. They should also publicise proposed action and the assistance available for improving housing accommodation.

(c) Improvement grants were not to be available for second homes or for developers who wished merely to sell for profit, but would be available only to owner-occupiers and to landlords who undertook to keep their dwellings for letting. Provision was made to stop discretionary improvement grants going to more expensive owner-occupied property and to houses built within the past twelve years. An owner who received an improvement grant and sold the house or left it unoccupied within five years (seven in housing action areas) would have to repay the grant.

(d) Local authorities might serve provisional notices of proposals for securing the compulsory improvement of dwellings in certain circumstances in a general improvement area or a housing action area.

D.O.E. Circular 70/74 outlined initiatives for increasing housing programmes and proposed that local authorities should: negotiate contracts with private builders with land to build houses for the authority on their land; negotiate favourable prices for completed and almost completed but unsold private houses; draw up plans for the progressive extension of social ownership of rented property; sell council houses for owner-occupation in areas where there was no unmet demand; build for sale to owner-occupiers and for long-lease to housing co-operatives; help housing associations to deal with area housing problems. The March, 1974, Budget had increased public expenditure on housing to allow local authorities to increase their programmes of building for rent, to acquire new unsold private houses and to make a start on municipalisation in the worst areas of housing stress. With the above initiatives it was envisaged that local authority expenditure on housing would rise by £350 million in 1974–5 over and above the figure of £1,963 million specified in the Public Expenditure White Paper of December, 1973.

To deal with the steady decline in the supply of private rented accommodation and the danger of existing tenants losing their homes, the Labour government introduced the Rent Act 1974 which (a) provided full protection under the Rent Acts of 1965 and 1968 for tenants of furnished accommodation other than tenants of resident landlords; (b) extended the duration of rent tribunal security for six to twelve months for categories not covered by full protection; (c) raised the rateable value limits of furnished lettings subject to control from £1,000 in Greater London and £500 elsewhere to £1,500 and £750 respectively—i.e. to the limits applicable for unfurnished lettings; (d) enabled tenants against whom an order for possession had been made to apply again to a court, which would have power to rescind the order if it would not have been granted had the Act been in force; and (e) gave tenants access to rent officers for the fixing of fair rents, and gave them indefinite security of tenure. The act did not apply to lettings to students by specified educational institutions, to lettings for holidays, or to furnished and unfurnished lettings created after the passing of the Act.

When Anthony Crosland moved the second reading of the Housing Rents and Subsidies Bill in November, 1974, he said that its purpose was "to cut the throat of the Tory Housing Finance Act at a stroke". It was enacted in February, 1975, and certain provisions of the Housing Finance Act were repealed and new provisions relating to rents and subsidies were introduced. The main provisions were:

(1) *Rents.* Parts V and VI of the 1972 Act, which provided machinery for determining fair rents for local authority dwellings and required authorities to increase their rents, were repealed and freedom to fix reasonable rents was restored to local authorities. However, in determining rents, a local authority was to have regard to the terms of its rent rebate scheme under s. 18 of the 1972 Act which was retained, as was the rent allowance scheme. The authority was empowered to review rents and make such changes as circumstances required, and to make provision for a working balance, but not a surplus, in its housing revenue account "which is no larger than is reasonably necessary having regard to all the circumstances".

(2) *Subsidies.* The following new subsidies are payable to local authorities and new town corporations:

(a) A housing subsidy comprising five elements:

(i) A basic element which is the aggregate of the amounts payable for 1974–5 in respect of the residual, transition, rising costs and operational deficit subsidies of the 1972 Act which are superseded (as are the rent rebate and town development subsidies).

(ii) A new capital costs element of 66 per cent of new reckonable loan charges.

(iii) A supplementary financing element of 33 per cent of the excess of reckonable loan charges over those for 1974–5.

(iv) A special element if the H.R.A. shows a deficit.

(v) A high costs element if an authority's relevant expenditure exceeds the standard level of expenditure.

(b) A modified rent rebate subsidy equal to 75 per cent of the authority's standard amount of rent rebates for the years 1975–6 onwards. An authority is required to make a rate fund contribution for each year equal to the balance plus the costs for the year of administering the rebate scheme.

(c) An expanding towns subsidy payable for ten years to a receiving authority in respect of qualifying dwellings for letting. The amount and the circumstances in which, and the conditions subject to which, it is payable will be determined by the Secretary of State.

(d) A transitional town development subsidy payable from 1975–6 to any authority which was entitled to receive a town development subsidy under the 1972 Act for 1974–5. The Secretary of State may reduce or discontinue this subsidy if the dwelling in respect of which it is payable has been demolished, disposed of, is not fit to be used, or is not being used, for letting as a dwelling, or in any other relevant circumstances.

(3) *Housing associations and co-operatives.* The Housing Act 1974 was amended so that housing associations whose rules restrict membership to tenants or prospective tenants and preclude the grant or assignment of tenancies to persons other than members are eligible for housing association grant and revenue deficit grant. If property is disposed of to an approved housing co-operative, the authority's housing subsidy will continue to be paid. Grants will be paid to co-operatives which are registered housing associations.

(4) *Private sector.* A new scheme of phasing rent increases for private sector housing was introduced and was set out in schedule 2 of the Act. Fair rents will continue, but annual increases in registered rents above 40p will be phased. The decontrol of tenancies by rateable value was terminated; dwellings without basic amenities will remain controlled, but landlords will be able to recover as increases in the rent 12½ per cent of expenditure on repairs.

(5) *Miscellaneous.* (a) Part II of the 1972 Act was amended to provide allowances to almspeople. (b) The Central Housing Advisory Committee, appointed by the Housing Act 1957, was abolished. (c) Concealed in Part IV of Schedule 6 (Repeals and Revocations) was the repeal of ss. 95 to 99 of the 1972 Act which referred to default powers and the appointment of housing commissioners and the withholding of housing subsidies.

The Housing Rents and Subsidies Act 1975 was intended as an interim measure to cover a three-year period while a longer-term inquiry into housing finance was being carried out within the D.O.E.

Housing Needs

Since the end of the last war 8,230,481 permanent houses and flats have been built in Britain. Local authorities built 4,289,545, private builders built 3,693,043, housing associations built 116,897 and government departments built 130,996. Nevertheless, homelessness and overcrowding are scathing indictments of the inadequacy of our housing policy. *Shelter*, the National Campaign for the Homeless, referred to the housing problem as "a national crisis" and called for emergency action for at least one million homeless families and the eradication of the worst overcrowding and squalor. The 1969 report of the Cullingworth Committee into council housing similarly stressed the importance of giving more attention to social need and commented that there was not just one national housing problem but a large number of housing problems of great variety. Unfit dwellings, rundown neighbourhoods, slums, growing housing lists, increasing numbers of applications and admissions to temporary accommodation and of children admitted into care owing to family homelessness or unsatisfactory home conditions, are only some of the problems which make housing the most electorally sensitive of all areas of social provision.

Lord Goodman pleaded in the 1974 Dimbleby lecture for a more passionate and urgent approach to housing, which he described as a "hideous sore that disfigures society". He criticised the total failure of the political process where "Government after government has placed as a top priority the solution of the housing problem . . . yet government after government has failed to deal with the matter". He claimed that land shortages and planning considerations were not responsible and singled out the "system of control and responsibility which gives some responsibilities to local authorities, and overriding surveillance to central authorities. No worse system could be devised unless you are going to give full and total autonomy to one or the other." Local authorities had the power to build, but not to approve contracts, which were subjected to the over-complex control of the yardstick. "If you are going to have people trying to build houses locally, then you must invest the authority with full power." He concluded, however, by suggesting "the establishment of a single authority having total autonomy". Local housing authorities might possibly agree with much of his diagnosis whilst repudiating the suggested remedy, but few students who have attempted to understand the convolutions of housing legislation would disagree with Lord Goodman's plea for a simpler approach: "If you look at the mass, the morass of housing legislation that exists on our legal shelves, you will understand why we have no houses."

3. Town and Country Planning

The towns of industrial revolution Britain were, with few exceptions, unplanned and haphazardly constructed. Some "good" employers attempted to develop planned communities, e.g. Robert Owen at New Lanark, but the majority of entrepreneurs and local authorities were not concerned with land usage. Dwellings were jerry-built and speculators scorned the ideas which were being put into practice at Bourneville in 1879 and Port Sunlight in 1888. The late nineteenth-century town planner, Ebenezer Howard, inspired garden cities at Letchworth (1903) and Welwyn (1920), but such instances are exceptional and most local authorities,

> "still cringing to private enterprise and clinging to the creed of non-interference with business, remained apathetic".[12]

Eventually, in 1909 a Town Planning Act empowered local authorities to prepare schemes for new and undeveloped areas, but despite further legislation the old built-over areas were not cleared and progress, because of heavy compensation costs to landowners, was slow. Moreover, the emphasis was on the control of land use and the prevention of unsuitable development rather than the promotion of beneficial schemes or concern for the wider problems of regional or national planning.

The Barlow Commission (1937) studied "The Location of Industry and the Distribution of the Industrial Population" and reported in 1940. It recommended the redevelopment of congested urban areas and the dispersal of population and industry in order to balance employment throughout the kingdom. The Scott Commission of 1941 reported on "Land utilisation in rural areas" and emphasised the necessity of maintaining good agricultural land, of preserving natural amenities and of reinvigorating certain declining towns by transferring industry to their vacant sites. Also in 1941 the Uthwatt Committee was appointed to make an objective analysis of payment of compensation and recovery of betterment in respect of public control of the use of land. One of its recommendations was the establishment of a co-ordinating body to bring together the work of existing departments dealing with national development. This was achieved in 1943 with the creation of the Ministry of Town and Country Planning, and in 1944 the Town and Country Planning Act permitted the purchase of land by local authorities for planning purposes.

---

[12] H. Hamilton, *History of the Homeland*, Allen & Unwin, 1946, p. 136.

The Town and Country Planning Act 1947, the principal Act for the next fifteen years, reduced the number of local planning authorities from 1,441 to the 145 county and county borough councils. All changes in the use of land had to be approved by the local planning authorities. They were also required to produce development plans every five years and were given wider powers of compulsory acquisition. County local planning authorities were authorised to delegate to county districts any functions relating to the control of development, while a regulation made in 1959 enabled county districts with a population of over 60,000 (or under if authorised by the Minister) to claim delegation of certain planning functions, which included applications for planning permission. The Act also introduced a general development charge, which was abolished in 1952.

Subsequent Acts from 1951 to 1959 did not change the principles of the 1947 Act, but were concerned mainly with drafting changes and financial provisions. The development charge of 1947 was abolished, and in 1959 market value was fully restored as the basis for compensation on compulsory purchases. The Town and Country Planning Act 1962, consolidated previous legislation and is now the principal act for planning.

In order to increase the amount of land available for dwellings and to prevent its development by speculators, the Land Commission Act was passed in February, 1967. Its main features were: the establishment of a Land Commission with wide powers of compulsory purchase; the imposition of a betterment levy on the development value of land at an initial rate of 40 per cent; the introduction of a new "Crownhold" lease system; and improved arrangements for financial assistance to local authorities.

From its inception the Land Commission came under attack from the Conservative opposition and from certain newspapers; for example, *The Financial Times* commented that it "was born by expediency out of muddle" (10 January, 1967), and the *Daily Express* compiled a "Black File of Injustice" which outlined cases of hardship caused by the contentious betterment levy. The pressure upon the government to introduce measures to alleviate some of the worst features of the levy intensified during the early part of 1969 and in April a White Paper *Modifications in Betterment Levy* (Cmnd. 4001) recommended the following changes which were incorporated in the Finance Act, 1969: (i) exemption from levy for chargeable acts or events with market value up to £1,500 subject to conditions; (ii) relief for people who build single houses on plots given or bequeathed to them or sold to them at a low price; (iii) partial relief, by an increase in the base value, on the sale or lease of an owner-occupied house of up to £10,000 in value and a quarter-acre in extent; (iv) allowances of professional fees levy; and (v) waiver of interest on unpaid levy for assessments up to £1,000.

The Commission's second report, published in October 1969, showed that it had increased the total number of assessments from 3,449 in 1967–69 to 15,390 in 1968–69, the gross amount of levy assessed from £1·65 m. to £15·27 m., and the amount of levy collected from £0·46 m. to £8·10 m. On the other hand, its first priority to make key sites available for private development and to make land available for housing associations and for schemes of comprehensive development had progressed slowly, with only 159·6 acres having been sold for development up to 30 September, 1969. Of the 946 acres purchased for development in 1968–69, 274 were bought for resale to builders. In the same year, nine compulsory purchase orders came into force covering 172 acres with an estimated value of £541,000, and twenty-nine draft orders were published relating to 1,140 acres with an estimated value of £6·9 million. There were five public local inquiries, four being concluded in favour of the Commission. On attaining power in June, 1970, the Conservative government quickly abolished both the Land Commission and the betterment levy by the Land Commission (Dissolution) Act 1971.

The Civic Amenities Act 1967 required local planning authorities to designate as conservation areas those parts of their areas which it was desirable, for architectural or historic reasons, to preserve or enhance. Once designated as a conservation area it becomes the duty of the planning authority to pay special attention to the character and appearance of the area, and any application for planning permission for the development of land which would affect the character or appearance of the area must be published in the local press and twenty-one days must be given for the proposal to be inspected by the public. The authority must take into account any representations relating to the application. The penalty for contravening a building preservation order, in summary proceedings before the magistrates, is raised from a fine of £100 to a maximum of £250 or three months' imprisonment or both; if the proceedings are on indictment before a jury, the fine has no limit (and will have regard to the financial benefit which the offender received) and imprisonment may be for as long as twelve months. The Act also gives increased powers and duties to authorities to encourage the planting and preservation of trees (maximum fine for felling increased from £100 to £250); to disposal of abandoned cars and other refuse; to repair an uninhabited building on the Ministry's list of historic buildings; to purchase compulsorily (subject to Ministerial confirmation) any listed building or other building subject to a preservation order if reasonable steps are not being taken for its proper preservation; and to provide off-street parking and playgrounds.

Major changes in planning procedures were effected by the Town and Country Planning Act 1968 which amended the law relating to town and country planning, the compulsory acquisition of land and the disposal of land by public authorities; made provision for grants for research relating to, and education with respect to, the planning and design of the physical environment; extended the purposes for which Exchequer contributions may be made under the Town Development Act 1952; and dealt with connected purposes.

Local planning authorities are to survey their areas and keep under review those matters which might affect development. They are instructed to prepare and submit for the Minister's approval a *structure plan* which will be a written statement with diagrams setting out the broad policy for land use, including proposals for the improvement of the physical environment and the management of traffic. It will also set out in general terms proposals for "action areas" where comprehensive change by development, redevelopment, or improvement is expected to begin within a prescribed period. Local planning authorities are also required to prepare a *local plan* formulating their proposals for the development and other use of land in the light of the structure plan. The proposals must be publicised and public enquiries into objections raised to a structure plan will be conducted by a Ministry inspector, and in the case of a local plan, by an inspector appointed by the Minister.

Part II strengthened the power of enforcement of planning control available to local planning authorities, provided for the grant of established use certificates and gave them power to stop further development pending proceedings on an enforcement notice. Planning appeals (Part III) will be speeded up by empowering inspectors to make decisions on such matters as appeals against a refusal of planning permission to develop land, advertisement control, enforcement notices, or the refusal of planning permission to alter or demolish buildings of architectural or historic interest.

Sections 67 and 69 of the 1962 Act relating to the compulsory acquisition of land were repealed and permitted the minister to authorise a local authority to acquire land compulsorily for development, redevelopment or improvement and other planning purposes. Any minister or local or public authority duly authorised to acquire land by compulsory purchase may vest such land in themselves by a general vesting declaration. The provisions were extended whereby an owner occupier of property whose property becomes virtually unsaleable on account of a development proposed by a public authority (planning blight) may require that authority to buy it.

New powers of control over the demolition or alteration of "listed buildings" of special architectural and historic interest were substituted for those which were exercised by means of building preservation orders. Local authorities may, after giving the owner an opportunity to repair a listed building, acquire any such building compulsorily if it is in need of repair and, if it has been deliberately neglected, compensation need only be paid on site value.

The minister is empowered to set up Planning Inquiry Commissions to look into certain matters, including applications for planning permission, appeals, and development by a government department. Their main concern will be matters of national or regional importance requiring special consideration. Local planning authorities are required to keep a register of planning applications for public inspection, and are empowered to delegate certain planning decisions to a special officer.

These wide-ranging changes were regarded as a major devolution of responsibility and initiative to local planning authorities, and "a charter for citizen participation".[13] This aspect of public participation was given further emphasis by the appointment in March, 1968, of a committee under the chairmanship of Mr. A. Skeffington "to consider and report on the best methods, including publicity, of securing the participation of the public at a formative stage in the making of development plans for their area". Reporting in July, 1969, the committee proposed "guidelines for constructive action" rather than "a deadening book of rules".[14] Among their main recommendations to encourage co-operation between planners and the public were: the establishment of community forums to represent a wide range of local bodies ("the yeast of the community"), which would discuss information from the planning authority and present the views of the constituent organisations during the preparation of structure and local plans; the appointment of community development officers to stimulate the "non-joiners" and to provide them with information, to link with existing groups and to promote new ones, and, particularly at the local plan stage, to put the proposals to the "non-joiners" and act as their advocate both to the forum and to the authority; societies and individuals should be brought in more to advise the planners, with people being able to put their names on a "participation register" to ensure they are notified about the preparation of plans; people could apply some parts of a

---

[13] *The Observer*, 5 *January*, 1969.
[14] *People and Planning*, H.M.S.O.

local plan before the main proposals were passed (e.g. tree planting);
and authorities should involve the local press, radio and T.V. in the
formative stages of a plan, in committee and open council, and
facilities should be provided for broadcasting council debates on big
planning decisions. Four points during preparation are defined as the
right moments to secure participation: the initial announcement
that the plan is to be prepared; the report of survey; the identification
of the choices available; and the statement of proposals favoured by
the local planning authority. The Minister, and the Secretaries of
State for Wales and Scotland, accepted the recommendations in
principle.

In 1970 the office of Secretary of State for the Environment was
created and its incumbent is assisted by three ministers who are each
responsible *inter alia* for certain aspects of town and country planning.
The Minister for Local Government and Development is responsible
for land use and planning policy generally, the countryside, conservation of historic towns and buildings, and planning case work
outside Greater London; the Minister for Transport Industries is
concerned with traffic policy generally and all planning and transport case work in the G.L.C. area; and the Minister of Housing
and Construction is concerned with new towns.

The Town and Country Planning Act 1971 was a consolidating
act and is now the principal act. In July, 1972, the Town and
Country Planning (Amendment) Act was passed which supplemented and amended the provisions of the 1971 Act. Local planning authorities were empowered to work jointly in the preparation
of structure plans for combined areas and to withdraw submitted
structure plans. The act also introduced a new mandatory examination in public, conducted by an independent chairman and a panel,
into objections to structure plans (see D.O.E. Circular 36/73).
Provisions relating to development plans in London were amended.
Control of office development was extended for a further period of
five years; provision was made for the control of the demolition of
unlisted buildings in conservation areas, and for making grants
and loans for the preservation or enhancement of the character or
appearance of conservation areas.

By s. 182 of the Local Government Act 1972 the councils of the
counties and the districts became the local planning authorities for
their areas. A joint planning board may be established by the
Secretary of State for the areas or parts of the areas of any two or
more district councils and for the whole or parts of two or more
county councils. The act provides that all functions conferred on
local planning authorities by the 1971 Act shall be exercisable by

both county and district planning authorities, subject to the following exceptions: county planning authorities are responsible for the
preparation of surveys, structure plans and development plan
schemes for their areas and will be the planning authorities in the
areas of National Parks; district planning authorities will be
responsible for local plans, except in National Parks, and generally
responsible for the control of development and the granting of
planning permission, except in the case of certain "county matters".

At the 1974 conference of the Town and Country Planning
Association Professor J. R. James was reported as being critical of
the planning system and said that asking counties to prepare
structure plans and districts to be responsible for local plans was to
divide an indivisible process and would set county against district.
He thought it might be necessary to withdraw planning powers
from counties, possibly at the same time as elective regional planning authorities were established, and then make districts responsible
for their own structure plans.[15] Another opinion on the division of
responsibilities was that "it has had the result of abolishing the
need for delegation from county to district councils, which has been
a most unsatisfactory feature of planning administration from
1948–1974, but it has also had the effect of increasing the number
of planning authorities" (Hart and Garner, *ibid.*, pp. 563–4). In
place of 145 county and county borough planning authorities
there are now some 340 planning authorities outside London and
the metropolitan areas. A commentator in *The Municipal Year Book
1975* (p. 348) referred to the fears that "a substantially greater
number of planning authorities will result in an uneven and very
thin spread of professional competence, unless special training
provision is made." Difficulty in coping with "the growing flood
of planning applications" was also emphasised. The number of
decisions taken by local planning authorities had risen from 463,000
in 1971 to 615,000 in 1972, and the number of appeals from 10,351
to 15,099. Outstanding appeals, however, had risen from 7,881 at
the end of 1971 to 13,487 at the end of 1972, and to 17,964 by
31 July, 1973. The average time taken to dispose of appeals in
England had risen from 47 weeks in 1972 to 60 weeks in 1973, and
from 45 to 61 weeks in Wales, in the case of those decided by the
Secretary of State after an inquiry. For those decided by the
inspectorate after inquiry, the average time in England had risen
from 33 weeks in 1972 to 44 weeks in 1973 and from 37 to 48 weeks
in Wales. The 1974 Report of the Council on Tribunals said that

---

[15] *Local Government Chronicle*, 13 December, 1974, p. 1203.

the increasing time taken to dispose of planning appeals had caused "much disquiet".

The Land Compensation Act 1973 implemented the policy outlined in the White Paper, *Development and Compensation—Putting People First* (Cmnd. 5124). The act introduced a general right to compensation where the value of an interest in land is adversely affected by any public works, including highways and aerodromes. It conferred powers for mitigating the injurious effects of such works on their surroundings, made provisions for payments and disturbance allowances to persons displaced from land, and considerably amended the law relating to compulsory purchase and planning blight. Certain of its provisions were backdated so as to permit the payment of compensation for depreciation arising from public developments which took place before the commencement of the act.

Lastly, reference should be made to the controversial Community Land Act which, after many amendments, was passed in November, 1975. It implemented proposals outlined in the White Paper *Land* (Cmnd. 5730) to enable the community to control the development of land in accordance with its needs and priorities and to restore to the community the increase in value of land arising from its efforts. The White Paper described a permanent scheme and transitional arrangements leading to the scheme. During the transitional period all land transactions will continue to take place at market value, but the effective cost of land to local authorities will be reduced because they will be enabled to buy "net of development land tax", i.e. the cost to them will be only what the vendor would have received after tax had he sold privately. During this transitional period local authorities will assume new powers and duties, and will progressively come to dominate the market in development land. Concurrently the rate of development land tax will be progressively increased from 80 per cent to 100 per cent. When the acquisition scheme is operating fully in all areas, and when virtually all development value is being recouped by means of development land tax, the permanent scheme will come into operation, and the basis of compensation will be changed to current use value. A complementary Development Land Tax Bill was to detail the development land tax provisions and the arrangements under which local authorities, new town development corporations and government departments would be enabled to buy land net of tax.

It is significant that the implementation of the immense programme of land acquisition and management has not been entrusted in England and Scotland to an *ad hoc* body but to the local authorities. In England the authorities are the county and district councils, the G.L.C., the Common Council of the City Corporation, the new town corporations and the National Park Planning Boards. In Wales, however, there is to be set up a special corporation, the Land Authority for Wales, and following representations made by the Local Authority Associations in Wales the government included a clause in the Bill enabling Welsh counties and districts to apply to the Land Authority for Wales for agency functions.

The Association of County Councils and the Association of District Councils were initially cautious in their reception of the Bill but the Association of Metropolitan Authorities welcomed it as "a major step forward in positive planning to ensure that land is available in the right places and at reasonable cost to meet the needs of housing, industry and all other activities". Sir Desmond Heap, former Comptroller and City Solicitor to the Corporation of London, was more critical of the Bill—"a very remarkable and devastating piece of work"—and particularly stressed the role of the Secretary of State "who takes unto himself more remarkable powers over the conduct of local government than he has ever had before". He also suggested that local authorities would require 12,750 new officers and clerks and some 1,400 new revenue staff to deal with the new duties.[16]

Water Reorganisation

The Water Act 1973 reorganised the water resources of England and Wales, replacing the 29 river authorities, 160 water undertakings and 1,300 sewerage authorities with ten Regional Water Authorities. The reorganisation took effect on 1 April, 1974.

The R.W.A.s are (i) North-West, covering 5 counties; (ii) Northumbrian, covering 4 counties; (iii) Severn-Trent, covering the entire West Midlands from the Welsh border to Yorkshire in the north; (iv) Yorkshire; (v) East Anglian, covering 7 counties; (vi) Thames, serving 6 counties, including Greater London; (vii) Southern, covering 5 counties; (viii) Wessex, covering 4 counties; (ix) South-West, covering Devon and Cornwall; and (x) Wales, covering the Principality, where a Welsh National Water Development Authority was set up.

Each of the R.W.A.s consists of a chairman and members appointed by the Secretary of State for the Environment, and in Wales by the Secretary of State for Wales, two or three members appointed by the Minister of Agriculture, Fisheries and Food, and

---

[16] *The Bankers' Magazine*, August, 1975.

the remaining members, who are in the majority, are appointed by local authorities. The Thames authority, for example, has 24 members appointed by local authorities (7 of whom are appointed by the G.L.C. and 7 by the London Boroughs) and 15 appointed by the Secretary of State.

A National Water Council was established as a consultative and advisory body, comprising representatives of the R.W.A.s and other members. The British Waterways Boards, controlling canals and other waterways, was left intact, and the Inland Waterways Amenity Advisory Council retained its existing responsibilities. The 31 private statutory water companies were left in private hands, though the Labour opposition reserved the right to bring them into public ownership.

New Towns

"The creation of new towns has been perhaps the greatest achievement of post-war town and country planning."[17] Towns such as Coventry and Plymouth were devastated by aerial bombardment in the Second World War and were rebuilt as fine modern cities, incorporating advanced planning ideas. Densely populated London, having borne the brunt of the bombing, was the subject of Sir Patrick Abercrombie's Greater London Plan which was published in 1944. It conceived of London as four concentric circles and proposed that a million people would be moved out of Inner London (the London County Council area), that the second circle of pre-war suburbs would remain as it was, but that the communities in the Green Belt circle and the outer circle of existing towns and of new towns which were to be built would receive the overspill from Inner London.

The Reith Committee was appointed to consider the problems of establishing new towns and to suggest guiding principles. Three reports were quickly submitted and the New Towns Act, 1946, was passed embodying many of the Committee's recommendations. The Minister was given the power to designate sites for new towns and to appoint development corporations to develop and administer the estates until their assets and liabilities could be transferred to the local authorities within whose areas they were built.

The twelve new towns which were initially envisaged were built with the assistance of Exchequer loans, and eight were to be satellites of London. All were to be self-contained communities with their own

---

[17] R. H. Best "New Towns in the London Region", in *Greater London* (ed. Coppock & Prince), p. 313.

shops, recreational facilities and industries, so that people would be able to work within the community and avoid travelling long distances to work. Their population growth has been rapid, increasing during the intercensal years from a total of 134,974 in 1951 to 426,150 in 1961.

The twelve new towns originally planned were at Basildon, Bracknell, Crawley, Harlow, Hatfield, Hemel Hempstead, Stevenage and Welwyn Garden City (all within a radius of 30 miles of London), Newton Aycliffe, Peterlee, Corby and Cwmbran, accommodating the manpower requirements for neighbouring industry. By 1965 the number had increased to twenty-one with the addition of Cumbernauld, East Kilbride, Glenrothes and Livingstone, to relieve overcrowding in Glasgow; Skelmersdale and Runcorn, absorbing families from Merseyside; Dawley and Redditch, taking families from Birmingham and the Black Country, and Washington, taking the overspill from the Tyneside-Wearside area.

The New Towns Act 1959, amended the 1946 Act by providing that when the development corporations were wound up, their assets and liabilities would be transferred to a new body, the Commission for New Towns, and not to the local authorities. The Commission of fifteen paid members would be responsible for the properties and welfare of the townspeople, but the local authorities would be responsible for schools, roads, lighting and refuse disposal. The Commission could assist in providing amenities, water supplies and sewerage. The Commission was required to set up local committees, after consulting with the district councils, to manage their rented houses and it was intended that other local committees would be set up to which the Commission might delegate part of its business. The New Towns Act 1965, now consolidates existing legislation. The New Towns Act 1966 increased to £800 million the limit on advances to be made to meet capital expenditure on new towns and also amended the Land Compensation Acts. The New Towns Act 1969 raised the limit on advances to £1,100 million and this was further increased to £1,500 million by the New Towns Act 1971.

In addition to the new towns, further relief for congested towns was attempted by the Town Development Act 1952, which enabled a congested town to negotiate overspill agreements with towns which would provide accommodation for the former's surplus population. Financial inducements were to be offered by the exporting town, the county council and the Exchequer. A 50 per cent grant was available for the provision of major services for town development, and the Housing Act 1961, increased the subsidy payable in England and Wales from £24 to £28 for every house let to relieve urban congestion.

The Buchanan Report *Traffic in Towns* (1963) highlighted another dimension of the urban planning problem—that of the necessity of integrating the needs of the motorist (2½ million cars in 1953 growing to 7½ million in 1963), of industrial traffic and of the pedestrian into future urban development schemes or having to pay the social and economic price which would result from an increasing chaos of congested roadways.

The most recent stage in planning development began in 1963 with its regional orientation in the publication of a government White Paper, *The North East: A Programme for Regional Development and Growth* (Cmd. 2206). Its emphasis was placed on a "growth zone" from Tyneside to Teeside and an increase in public service investment from £55 million in 1963 to £90 million in 1964–65. Similar proposals were made for the development of central Scotland. In March, 1964 the South-East study was published relating to the area from the Wash to Dorset and containing nearly 40 per cent of the United Kingdom population. An increase of 3½ million people in the South-East was anticipated by 1981, and the study proposed that the increase should be accommodated outside the London conurbation. The Green Belt area around London was to be doubled to prevent the continued expansion of the metropolitan area, and three new cities were recommended at Southampton–Portsmouth, Newbury and Bletchley. Other towns would be greatly expanded and others would be listed for expansion.

In 1965 regional studies of the West Midlands and the North-West were issued, the former recommending the redevelopment of the Birmingham conurbation, the completion of new towns at Dawley (to be known as Telford) and Redditch, certain town expansions and development, house-building around the green belt, and a regional road programme. The North-West study analysed basic data and commented on such matters as housing improvement, the adaptation of the economic structure, and provisions for planned overspill. The whole area needed to be planned as a unity, with a balanced employment structure and ease of access to the countryside and coasts. In 1965 also a comprehensive plan for the urban development of mid-Wales was under active consideration, culminating in the formation of the Mid-Wales New Town Development Corporation in 1968.

The "third generation" of new towns had larger target populations. Milton Keynes was designated in 1967 to provide homes and employment for an estimated incoming population of 150,000 Londoners and a planned total population of 250,000. Northampton and Peterborough Development Corporations were formed in 1968 for the purpose of expanding existing large towns under the New Towns Act 1965 to accommodate and provide work for overspill population from London. Irvine was designated in 1966 and Stonehouse in 1973 primarily to relieve overcrowding in Glasgow, and Newtown (1968) in Mid-Wales was intended to halt the decline in population and provide new opportunities for employment in that area. The Central Lancashire New Town, designated in 1970 in the Preston area, will have a population of 430,000 and is intended to act as a focal growth point in Lancashire's economic regeneration and provide for long-term overspill requirements and regional growth. There are now 28 new towns in Great Britain and 3 in Northern Ireland in Antrim, Ballymena and Craigavon. Although not a new town, mention should also be made of the G.L.C. development of Thamesmead on a site of 1,500 acres in the London Boroughs of Bexley and Greenwich. It is intended to rehouse up to 48,000 Londoners by the 1990s.

4. Police

The maintenance of order is one of the primary functions of a state. In eleventh-century Britain the system of frankpledge existed whereby most men over the age of twelve were grouped into tithings (ten) whose members were mutually responsible for the good behaviour of each other and their families. An Ordinance of 1252 decreed that in every township one or two constables were to be appointed to ensure the due execution of the Assize of Arms, which required every man to furnish himself with arms and armour suitable to his station. This was an essentially military duty for the constables, but they were also conservators of the peace and had right of arrest. With the introduction of J.Ps., the constables were put under their control, and later the J.Ps. became responsible for their appointment and removal. By a statute of 1662 the constable became a parochial officer, still under the J.Ps.' control.

By the eighteenth and early nineteenth centuries the growth of industrial towns strained an already inefficient constabulary, while unemployment and bad harvests after 1815 helped to create a revolutionary social ferment. Various law enforcement expedients were tried until, in 1829, a full-time police force for the metropolitan area was established and put in the charge of the Home Office. The City of London followed suit in 1831, the municipal boroughs in 1835, and counties had the optional power in 1839 to establish a full-time force, but were compulsorily required to do so in 1856.

In 1840 county J.Ps. and borough councils were statutorily empowered to consolidate small police establishments and in 1856 legislation stopped the police grant to any borough with a population of under 5,000 where it had not amalgamated its force with that of the county. By the Municipal Corporations Act, 1882, new boroughs with a population of under 20,000 were not to be authorised to establish a separate police force, while the Local Government Act, 1888, transferred the police powers of boroughs with a population of under 10,000 to the counties.

The Police Act 1946, abolished the separate police forces of all non-county boroughs, unless their population (on 30 June, 1939) had been at least half of that of their administrative county, and transferred them to the county. The Home Secretary had possessed powers since the 1939–45 war to amalgamate forces and the 1946 Act provided for their voluntary or compulsory amalgamation. The former required the Home Secretary's approval, while compulsory amalgamation was a matter of expediency decided by the Home Secretary with one limitation only—no county or borough with a population of over 100,000 could be compulsorily amalgamated, without its consent, with any other police area(s) whose population exceeded its own. Examples of compulsory amalgamation include Cheshire and Chester (1949), Leicestershire and Rutland (1951) and Carmarthenshire and Cardiganshire (1958).

At this stage the main types of police authority were:

(a) *County Police*—the Local Government Act, 1888, transferred the powers and duties of J.Ps. relating to police to a standing joint committee comprising equal numbers of representatives of the county council and of quarter sessions. The standing joint committee was an executive body with powers of compulsion over the county council.

(b) *Borough Police*—by the Municipal Corporations Acts of 1835 and 1882, watch committees were to be appointed by the municipal council and were to consist of the mayor and not more than one-third of the council members. The watch committees were not under the control of their councils, except in financial matters and any extra-police functions which may have been delegated piecemeal to them, e.g. fire services, licensing of street hawkers or pawnbrokers, cinema hours, etc.

(c) *Combined Police Forces*—created by amalgamation under the Police Act 1946, are bodies corporate and consist of representatives of their constituent authorities. Where amalgamation involves the combination of county and borough, the authority with the greater population decides whether the county or borough constitution of a standing joint committee or a watch committee will apply.

(d) *Metropolitan Police*—created 1829 and comes directly under the Home Secretary's control. He recommends to the Crown a Commissioner and five Assistant Commissioners.

(e) *City of London Police*—created 1831 and is organised independently by a Commissioner of the City police force who is responsible to the Court of Common Council and the Home Secretary.

In December, 1959, a Royal Commission on the Police was appointed under the chairmanship of Sir Henry Willink, Q.C. Its Interim Report (Cmd. 1222) was produced in November 1960 and recommended substantial pay increases, the biggest for forty years, which were implemented retrospectively to 1 September, 1960. The Royal Commission produced its Final Report (Cmd. 1728) in May, 1962 and its main recommendations were:

1. Police constables should receive pay increases ranging from 18 per cent on joining to 40 per cent after 22 years' service.

2. Separate local police forces should be retained and not brought under the direct control of the Government. (There was one dissentient who advocated the establishment of a centrally-controlled force administered by regional commissioners. The other members rejected the creation of a national force, seeing considerable value in the local associations and in the local knowledge of forces).[18]

3. Certain responsibilities, including those for the efficient policing of each area, should be centralised under the Home Secretary.

4. The number of police forces should be reduced.

5. A Chief Inspector of Constabulary should be appointed for the whole of Great Britain.

A Home Office Circular commending many of the Royal Commission's recommendations was issued in the same month to police authorities and chief officers of police. In 1963 the Home Secretary (Mr. Henry Brooke) introduced a Police Bill which gave effect to the Final Report's recommendations and consolidated a large body of legislation dealing with the control and administration of police forces in England and Wales, outside London.

The Police Act 1964 is based largely on the recommendations of the Royal Commission and is a consolidating and rationalising measure whose main provisions are:

1. The constitution of police authorities was altered. The watch committees and the standing joint committees are to consist of two-thirds council members and one-third magistrates. The standing joint committee is to be renamed "Police Committee".

---

[18] See *Public Law*, Spring 1967, for an appraisal of the advantages and disadvantages of a national force.

2. The powers of a watch committee to appoint, promote and dismiss police officers are to be transferred to the Chief Constable, as is the practice in counties.

3. The police authority will continue to appoint the chief constable and also, in future, the deputy chief constable and any assistant chief constable (in each case subject to the approval of the Home Secretary).

4. The police authority will have power to require the chief constable or any such officer to retire in the interests of efficiency subject to the Home Secretary's approval.

5. The police authority may now call upon the Chief Constable to provide a report on local police matters, but if he is of the opinion that a matter is contrary to public interest he can refer it to the Home Office for adjudication.

6. The Chief Constable becomes vicariously responsible for the torts of the constables under his command (the Royal Commission recommended that the police authority should be made liable) and the police authority is empowered to make payments in respect of damages against, and costs incurred by, police officers who have had legal action taken against them. Complaints against constables are to be investigated immediately and a report sent to the Director of Public Prosecutions unless no criminal offence has been committed.

7. The Home Secretary is given a greater measure of control over provincial police forces. His powers to amalgamate forces in the interests of efficiency are increased and there is to be no prohibition against the compulsory amalgamation of a police area with a population of over 100,000. He has also a new duty to promote police efficiency by requiring an authority to retire its chief constable, to call for reports from chief constables, to set up a local enquiry into the policing of areas, and to lay down minimum standards of equipment.

8. Increased penalties are laid down for assaulting a police officer.

One commentary upon the Act stated:

> "Although these changes leave unaltered the basic structure of local police forces controlled by virtually autonomous chief constables, the beginnings of a movement towards centralisation is clearly discernible."[19]

The parish constable disappeared at long last, but certain anomalies still remained. One of the largest forces in the country, the Transport Police, was untouched by the Act; Bristol still maintained two police forces, one in Bristol itself and a separate force for Avonmouth Docks; and the Manchester Dock Police was maintained by a limited liability company in the Manchester Ship Canal Company.

---

[19] *Modern Law Review*, Vol. 27, p. 682.

The Final Report of the Royal Commission had been critical of keeping relatively small forces, and mergers had reduced the separate forces in England and Wales from 126 to 117 by 1 April, 1966. In May, the Home Secretary (Mr. Roy Jenkins) announced that the 105 forces in England and the twelve in Wales would be further reduced by amalgamation to forty-five and four respectively. Tyneside reorganisation would reduce the English figure to forty-two. The Home Secretary said that amalgamations would produce: (a) a better career structure and promotion prospects; (b) a more effective deployment of men; (c) better, more advanced and more sophisticated equipment, both in communications and in other fields; (d) the avoidance of wasteful duplication of effort; (e) economies of administration; and (f) the opportunity to deal with problems on a wider scale (*C.C.A. Evidence to Royal Commission on Local Government in England*, p. 7). He hoped the local authorities would recognise the need for rationalisation and enter into voluntary schemes.

"If they do not I must use my powers under the Police Act, 1964, to promote compulsory amalgamations."

Both praise and condemnation followed the announcement of such a radical reduction in the numbers of forces. Some forces felt there would be an increase in efficiency, and economies of scale would be achieved in transport and equipment; conversely, many policemen feared that they would be transferred, that promotion would be more difficult in a larger authority, that there would be an increase in administration and that existing good services would be weakened by having to cover wider areas.

Several police authorities (e.g. Blackpool, Reading, Southend, Cardiff, and Coventry) objected to amalgamation but lost their appeals, and by November 1969 there were forty-seven police forces in operation.

The Local Government Act 1972 amended the Police Act 1964 to take account of the new structure of local government, but the position of the police authority was not affected. Under the 1972 Act amalgamation schemes could be made by two or more counties and could be made before 1 April, 1974, though they could not take effect before that date. Outside the area of the Metropolitan Police Force there were, on 1 April, 1974, thirty-three county police forces in England and Wales each based on a single county, with the police authority constituted as a committee of the county council. Additionally, there were ten combined police forces in Avon and Somerset, Devon and Cornwall, Dyfed-Powys, Hampshire (including Isle of Wight), Northumbria (combining Northumberland and Tyne and Wear), North Wales (Clwyd and Gwynedd),' South Wales (Mid, South and West Glamorgan), Sussex (East and West Sussex), Thames Valley (Berkshire, Buckinghamshire and Oxford-shire), and West Mercia (combining Hereford and Worcester and Salop). All police authorities, including those constituted as the committees of single county councils, include a number of magi-strates as members in addition to councillors of the county or counties concerned.

The chairman of the Cheshire Police Authority predicted as "a cast iron certainty" the creation of regional police forces within a decade, and the chief constable of West Yorkshire stated that one day there would have to be a national police force.

5. Health and Welfare Services

The National Health Service Act 1946, created a tripartite structure comprising (i) hospital and specialist services, (ii) general medical, dental, pharmaceutical and ophthalmic services, and (iii) personal health services provided by local health authorities which were to be the county and county borough councils.

Local health authorities were responsible for the provision of the following services under the terms of the National Health Service Acts 1946 to 1966, the National Assistance Act 1946 and the Health Services and Public Health Act 1968: health centres, maternity and child welfare, home nursing, vaccination and immunisation, services for the handicapped, mental health services, ambulances, services for the elderly, nursing homes, home help services, and family planning services.

Total expenditure by local authorities on these services rose from £34·1 million in 1949–50 to £153·5 million in 1964–65 and to £216 million in 1967–68. The first report of the amalgamated Department of Health and Social Security in July 1969 announced that total expenditure was estimated to exceed £238 million in 1969–70. In 1962 all local health authorities were required to review their services and plan developments to 1972–73. The results were published in a White Paper, *Health and Welfare: The Development of Community Care* (Cmnd. 1973) where plans for capital expenditure amounting to nearly £223·5 million and revenue expenditure of £163 million by the 146 local health authorities are detailed. The National Plan (1965) "takes a more expansive view", forecasting an increase of 34 per cent in net revenue expenditure in the first five years as opposed to a 30 per cent growth rate in a decade forecast by local authorities.[20]

In addition to the personal health services, local authorities fulfilled a broader public health function which included the following environmental health services: water supply and sewerage; the control of air pollution; securing the repair, maintenance and sanitary condition of houses; clearance and redevelopment of unhealthy and congested areas; the abatement of overcrowding; the control of infectious diseases; disinfection; health control at seaports and airports; the composition, description, hygiene and fitness of food for sale for human consumption; street cleansing and refuse disposal; the provision of burial grounds, baths, wash-houses, disinfestation and rodent control; the abatement of noise and vibration nuisances; and the regulation of the provision of sanitary conveniences in places of work, and the health and comfort of workers in Offices, Shops and Railway Premises.

In December 1965 a committee under the chairmanship of Mr. Frederick Seebohm had been appointed "to review the organisation and responsibilities of the local authority personal social services in England and Wales, and to consider what changes are desirable to ensure an effective service". Its report on 23 July, 1968, called for fundamental changes in the administration of health and social welfare.[21] At local level all major local authorities should set up a unified social service department with its own principal officer, who would report to a separate social service committee. At national level there would be one central department responsible for the relationship between central government and the new social service department and for the overall national planning of the service's intelligence and social research.

The new local authority would cover the work of the children's department, welfare services under the National Assistance Act 1948, education welfare, child guidance, home help services, mental health social work, adult training centres, other social work services and day nurseries, as well as certain social welfare work undertaken by some housing departments. It should also become the focal point for voluntary workers. The new department should work through area officers with teams of not less than ten to twelve social workers serving populations of 50,000 to 100,000 and its head should not be subordinate to any other departmental head.

Published on the same day as the Seebohm Report was a Green

---

[20] *The Local Health Services*, Office of Health Economics, 1965, p. 39.
[21] *Report of the Committee on Local Authority and Allied Personal Social Services*, H.M.S.O., Cmnd. 3703, July, 1968.

Paper[22] containing the proposals of the Ministry of Health for the restructuring of the National Health Service. The main proposals which had a significance for local authorities were: the unification of the administration of medical and related services in an area by one authority, an Area Board, which would replace the existing Executive Councils, Regional Hospital Boards, Boards of Governors and Management Committees; these authorities would also take over the functions of the present local health authorities and links would be established between medical and environmental services (refusé disposal, sewerage, clean air, housing, etc). About forty to fifty Area Boards were envisaged, comprising "professional members with direct broad experience of practical problems of the service".

The Green Paper stimulated much vigorous discussion, with the B.M.A. expressing particular concern over the allegedly bureaucratic nature of the system and opposing the transfer of the administration and financing of the N.H.S. to local authorities. These and other criticisms prompted the presentation in 1970 of a second Green Paper[23] which proposed that the N.H.S. should be unified and decentralized into 90 or so area authorities whose boundaries would generally coincide with the unitary and metropolitan districts proposed by the Redcliffe–Maud Commission. The increase in the number of areas met the criticism that 50 boards would have been too remote and bureaucratic. Local participation was to be achieved through about 200 district committees, whilst about 14 regional councils would plan services, particularly hospitals. The area health authorities would serve populations from 200,000 to 1,300,000 and would have 20 to 25 members— one-third appointed from the medical profession, one-third by the local authorities, and one-third by the Secretary of State, who would also appoint the chairmen of each area authority. It was intended that the area authority would administer hospital and specialist services and the school health service, and would take over the ambulance services from local government, except perhaps in Greater London, and the general surveillance of the health of the community. Local authorities would retain public health responsibilities.

At the same time the Local Authority Social Services Bill was published incorporating the main proposals of the Seebohm Committee. The Bill proposed that in each local authority nearly all the personal

---

[22] *National Health Service: the administrative structure of medical and related services in England and Wales*, H.M.S.O., July, 1968.

[23] *The Future Structure of the National Health Service*, H.M.S.O., February, 1970.

social services should come under the control of a social services committee. It would replace the existing statutory children's and welfare committees and would also assume responsibility for social services assigned by existing law to the health committee. A principal officer called the Director of Social Services would be responsible for unifying in each local authority the administration of personal social services, and his functions would include those of the present statutory post of children's officer which would be abolished. The Bill received the Royal Assent on 29 May, 1970, and in August two circulars were issued stating that Social Service Committees had to be set up by 1 January, 1971, and Directors of Social Service had to be in post by 1 April, 1971.

Meanwhile, in June, 1970, the Conservatives took office and in May, 1971, issued a brief consultative document outlining plans for an integrated health service. A White Paper followed in August, 1972, which proposed the abolition of all the existing bodies and their replacement by a unified administration responsible for the total health care of the community in each area, with the planning function exercised at three levels:

(i) *The Central Department*—The Secretary of State for the Department of Health and Social Security would remain responsible for the national health service as a whole. The Department would (a) plan the kind, scale and balance of services in association with the regional and area authorities and with the medical profession; (b) work in partnership with the R.H.A.s and provide them with support and guidance; and (c) carry out central N.H.S. personnel functions. The Welsh Office would be responsible for these functions in Wales.

(ii) *Regional Health Authorities* (14)—to be responsible for major planning decisions and co-ordination between areas, for the general supervision and allocation of resources in hospital and community health services, and for the provision of certain services too specialised to be provided by individual areas. They would absorb the family doctor services, previously administered by executive councils, and the community health services, welfare clinics, district nurses and other services previously run by local authorities. In Wales there would be no regional ties, and the Welsh Hospital Board would be wound up in April, 1974, and its most important functions would be carried out by the new Welsh Health Technical Services Organisation.

(iii) *Area Health Authorities*—about ninety in all, responsible for the planning, operational control and development of health services in the area, in consultation with the relevant local authority and with the R.H.A. Each A.H.A. would be required to set up a *Family Practitioner Committee* to take over most of the work of the existing executive councils. In Wales eight A.H.A.s would be responsible to the Welsh Office. Outside Greater London the A.H.A.s would have the same boundaries as the proposed new counties and metropolitan districts. Collaborative machinery was provided by the statutory Joint Consultative Committees of members of A.H.A.s and the matching local authorities. Another contact point would be the community physician in each A.H.A. whose functions represent a development of the role of the former medical officer of health. He was to be for some purposes the proper officer of the local authority, helping to organise and plan the preventive care services and advising the local authority on environmental and personal social services, and advising the local education authority on school health.

Day-to-day running of A.H.A. services would be based on about 150 *health districts*, each having a population of between 200,000 and 500,000, and each containing a district general hospital or a group of hospitals together serving the purpose of such a hospital. The districts would not constitute a formal tier of authority, but would form the natural community for the planning and delivery of comprehensive health care. As the boundaries of health districts would be related to health care needs, they would not necessarily correspond with the boundaries of local government districts.

In each health district a *community health council* of between 20 and 30 members would be established to represent the views of the consumer. Half its members would be appointed by the local government district council(s) and half by the A.H.A. on the nomination of local voluntary bodies. The councils would have the right to secure information, to visit hospitals and other institutions, and to have access to the area authority and in particular to the senior officers.

The White Paper envisaged the appointment of a *Health Service Commissioner* as an Ombudsman to investigage complaints against authorities. This proposal had previously been made in both Green Papers issued by the Labour government. In November, 1972, Sir Keith Joseph announced that Sir Alan Marre, the Parliamentary Commissioner for Administration, would combine his existing duties with those of Health Service Commissioner for England, Wales and Scotland when the new unified N.H.S. came into existence on 1 April, 1974.

The White Paper's proposals were embodied in the National Health Service Reorganisation Bill which was enacted on 5 July, 1973. Its effect was to abolish all the regional hospital boards, hospital management committees, boards of governors of teaching hospitals, executive councils and local health committees, and the Welsh Hospital Board. Employees of the school health services and local authority personal health services became N.H.S. employees on 1 April, 1974, as local government lost the following services: general surveillance of community health; ambulance services; family planning; health centres; health visiting; home nursing and midwifery; maternity and child health care; medical, nursing and supplementary arrangements for the prevention of illness; care and after-care; and vaccination and immunisation.

Local authorities did, however, retain the environmental health services, *viz.* building regulations, clean air, communicable disease control, food safety and hygiene, home safety, litter control, refuse collection and disposal, rodent control, and street cleansing.

Whereas local government accepted the necessity for reforming the N.H.S., local authorities and their representative bodies had long recommended that unification of the N.H.S. should be achieved within local government, particularly as the new local government areas and the N.H.S. areas would coincide and commence operations on the same day. The arguments for bringing health and social services under a single administration had been acknowledged in the White Paper, but Sir Keith Joseph had concluded that this solution was not practical.

The reaction of local government to the arrangements for local authority representation on the health authorities was one of despondency. The editorial of the *Municipal Review* (September, 1972), under the headline "Another blow for local democracy", criticised the inadequate lay representation. There would be no council representation on the health districts; only four of the fifteen or so members of A.H.A.s would be appointed by the corresponding local authorities; similarly, only four of the thirty members of the Family Practitioner Committees would be members of local authorities; and all the chairmen and members of the regional authorities would be appointed directly by the Secretary of State who would consult a number of organisations including the major local authorities in the region. "The concept of local democracy", said the editorial, "has never played a large part in the N.H.S. . . . but a relatively small, but important, part of the service has hitherto been under local democratic control. This will cease and there is no shirking the fact that the arrangements proposed represent a further derogation from the elective principle in British Government."

Some consolation was drawn, however, from the half membership of the community health councils being allocated to members of local authority district councils. Although only consultative bodies, the community health councils would be the "main channel of public opinion" and "a useful means for bringing pressure on the N.H.S. authorities". It added bitterly: "Yet the voice of the people would be better heard if the area and regional authorities were more strongly representative of local government." The Association of Municipal Corporations later sought "substantial membership" and asked Sir Keith Joseph to reconsider the membership composition because an opportunity "to introduce and maintain an effective democratic element in the N.H.S. was being lost" (*Public Service*, May, 1973). The approach was unsuccessful.

During the passage of the Bill the Labour opposition had been critical of the allegedly "bureaucratic, appointive and undemocratic" nature of the new structure. The Labour Party came to power on the very eve of reorganisation and too late to defer the operation of the act. Soon afterwards, in August, 1974, a D.H.S.S. paper *Democracy in the National Health Service* stated that the government felt that the new management system was "undemocratic and out of tune with the needs of local communities", and added that changes would have to be made to ensure that the N.H.S. became "more responsive to the views of the people it serves". Criticism was levelled at the separation of managerial and representative responsibilities, as exemplified by the members of C.H.C.s being debarred from membership of the A.H.A.s and R.H.A.s, and by the C.H.C.s lack of executive authority. The incompatible boundaries between many health districts and local authority districts also created administrative and representative problems and made "any direct democratic representation on Community Health Councils difficult to achieve". In a memorandum to the D.H.S.S. the Association of Metropolitan Authorities pointed out that the problem was not exclusive to the C.H.C.s in that there was "a need for complete identity between the area of the health authority and that of each separate and matching authority".[24] The "principle of co-terminosity" was totally undermined by A.H.A.s covering more than one local authority and by the creation of overlapping districts.

Despite its earlier criticisms, the government's future plans did not include fundamental changes in the reorganised service "though it will keep its working under review and propose whatever changes seem desirable in the light of experience". This, according to the Association, was a "somewhat weak assurance" and difficult to reconcile with the government's objectives of developing for the N.H.S. a structure which would permit "real devolution to those

---

[24] Supplement to the *Municipal Review*, November 1972, pp. 101–2.

operating the service locally without detailed intervention from Whitehall or from the region".

In order to develop each C.H.C. into "a powerful forum where consumer views can influence the N.H.S. and where local participation in the running of the N.H.S. can become a reality", the paper proposed that each C.H.C. should elect two of its members, at least one of whom should be a district councillor, to be adopted by the R.H.A. to serve for two years as a member of the A.H.A. responsible for the C.H.C.s district. C.H.C.s in single-district areas should elect four of their members including at least two district councillors, providing a minimum of four C.H.C. members for each A.H.A. To ensure that one-third of the total membership of the A.H.A. was drawn from local government one or two additional appointments should, where necessary, be made by the local authority or authorities matching the A.H.A. Concurrent membership of C.H.C. and A.H.A. was to be further examined. Each R.H.A. had about one-third of its members drawn from local government. The Association of Metropolitan Authorities urged that at least half of the members of A.H.A.s and R.H.A.s should be drawn from local authorities, and concluded that it could not "regard as democratic a health service in which the membership of health authorities is not wholly accountable to an elected assembly". The only principle the Association could accept in respect of the N.H.S., and for the Regional Water Authorities, was that "all those who administer public services should be answerable to the electorate".

CHAPTER 8

Finance of Local Government

The expenditure of local authorities accounts for about 30 per cent of all public expenditure. In 1974–5 local authorities in England and Wales spent £5,479 million on revenue account and £2,939 million on capital account. In each of the three years from 1971–2 the current expenditure of local authorities increased by 7 per cent to 8 per cent per year in real terms, i.e. excluding inflation, and possibly by more in 1974–5. The factors which have contributed to the increase in expenditure have been: (a) central demands for the development of local services; (b) increasing public demand for higher standards; (c) rising population and its greater mobility; (d) a proportionately higher increase in the dependent age groups of young and old, who make special demands on the social services; and (e) the intensification of these pressures by inflation and rising costs. The Redcliffe–Maud Report (1968) forecast that these factors were "likely to persist" and that "local expenditure will continue to expand both absolutely and as a percentage of the G.N.P." The proportion of the gross national product accounted for by local authorities grew from 5·1 per cent in 1900 to 15 per cent in 1966–7, and in terms of the scale of local government finance the Royal Commission added pessimistically that "local authorities are in sight of a solution to scarcely any of their problems". The report could not have visualised the economic difficulties which were to exacerbate the problems from 1974 nor the consequent repercussions on the level of public expenditure and on local government services in particular. From a condition of rapid growth at the beginning of the 1970s local authorities now face a bleak future with reduced capital expenditure and a diminishing rate of growth on current account.[1]

The revenue income of local authorities is derived from central government grants, local rates, and a variety of miscellaneous sources which include rents, tolls and fees.

---

[1] *Public Expenditure to 1978–79* (Cmnd. 5879), January, 1975.

1. Central Government Grants

The industrial revolution, the population explosion after 1750, the extension of communities with inadequate public utilities and the ever-present threat of unemployment and destitution on a scale which could not be relieved by the Elizabethan poor law, created an urgent need for remedial services. The main source of wealth before industrialisation was land, and its owners could not be expected on their own, to meet the costs of services. It was their complaints about the burden of rates, however, which led to the appointment of a

TABLE 5. LOCAL GOVERNMENT INCOME—REVENUE ACCOUNT
(£ million)

Year	*Total revenue income*	*Rates*		*Grants*		*Miscellaneous sources*		*% of grants to rates*
		Amount	*%*	*Amount*	*%*	*Amount*	*%*	
1923–24	341·3	143·3	42·0	75·2	22·0	122·8	36·0	52
1933–34	446·6	148·6	33·3	121·6	27·2	176·4	39·5	82
1943–44	739·0	204·1	27·6	228·4	30·9	306·5	41·5	112
1947–48	963·2	283·3	29·4	269·7	28·0	410·2	42·6	95
1950–51	899·3	304·9	33·9	304·6	33·9	289·8	32·2	100
1955–56	1352·3	421·0	31·2	500·4	37·0	430·9	31·8	119
1960–61	2091·0	696·7	33·3	756·0	36·2	638·3	30·5	108
1961–62	2268·2	747·4	32·9	830·6	36·7	690·2	30·4	111
1962–63	2491·9	831·3	33·4	907·0	36·4	753·6	30·2	109
1963–64	2772·2	923·1	33·3	1022·4	36·9	826·7	29·8	111
1964–65	2994·3	991·2	33·1	1103·0	36·8	900·1	30·1	111
1965–66	3394·1	1131·5	33·4	1260·0	37·1	1002·6	29·5	111
1966–67	3742·9	1266·1	33·8	1389·1	37·1	1087·7	29·1	110
1967–68	4100·4	1323·3	32·3	1591·0	38·8	1186·1	28·9	120
1970–71	6258·5	1640·4	26·2	2284·2	36·5	2333·9	37·3	139
1972–73	8214·8	2179·6	26·5	3135·0	38·2	2900·2	35·3	144

Royal Commission in 1835 which advocated a re-assessment which would include the new mills and factories. The outcome was the introduction of grants in aid of rates which were first paid to all local authorities on a uniform basis in 1835 to meet half the cost of administering criminal justice. Social reform measures involved local authorities in increased expenditure and in order to maintain a national standard services were subsidised by further grants. The reformed poor law unions of 1845 received 50 per cent of the salaries of their medical officers and all the salaries of teachers and industrial instructors in the workhouses from grants, and with the repeal of the Corn Laws of 1846 the agricultural interests were further protected by grants from the national exchequer.

Between 1870 and 1880 grants were made for elementary education, public health services, police, prison maintenance, registration of births and deaths, and highways. Since that time grants have been extended in proportion and amount, and have become, since 1950–51, the major source of revenue income. Increased financial dependence has meant the diminution of local authorities' independence and the increased subordination of local authorities to central government 'control.

Grants are made to local authorities for a number of reasons:

(a) as local authorities are required by the State to establish new services, the State should meet part of the cost by grants;

(b) the extension in the number of services and their increasing cost have drained rate resources and the State has felt compelled to shoulder some of the burden;

(c) local authorities lose rate income when State legislation derates fully or partially certain classes of hereditament and grants help to make good this loss;

(d) the disparity in income between local authorities and the necessity to maintain national standards require State aid for the poorer local authorities to help equalise the costs.

Various types of grants have been tried since 1835:

A. *Percentage grants*

These were the main type of Exchequer grant until 1887, and they were so called because the amount of grant was based on a percentage of "approved" expenditure by a local authority on a particular service. The expansion of social services in the early twentieth century was accompanied by percentage grants. The process began with a grant for education in 1902, and followed with grants for roads, small-holdings and allotments, sanatoria, dispensaries, police pensions, housing, etc. The amount of the grant varied according to the service, e.g. class I roads, 75 per cent; class II roads, 60 per cent; individual health, police and the protection of children, 50 per cent; fire service, 25 per cent.

Criticisms have been made of percentage grants because the local authority might have been inclined to have undertaken more grandiose and extravagant provisions than it could have done if supporting the service without grant aid. Moreover, the control exercised over spending by the government has been thought by local authorities to be too detailed, but the government has felt it to be inadequate. Additionally, the grant is tied to one service and any surplus cannot be allocated to other needs.

B. *Assigned Revenues*

By the Local Government Act 1888, many of the direct percentage grants were discontinued and the proceeds of licences issued for the sale of liquors, dealing in game, taxes on dealers in beer, wines, spirits, sweets and tobacco, licences on dogs, game and guns and a proportion of probate duties were assigned to local authorities. Goschen's theory of separating national and local finances as much as possible led to much controversy and complaints about the narrow basis of local taxation, and the inadequacy of the state's contribution led to the appointment in 1896 of a Royal Commission on local taxation. The system was ultimately abolished by the Local Government Act 1929, and to-day, only vestiges remain in the revenue from dog licences which is paid to local authorities, while fines and fees in magistrates courts are retained in proportion to their net expenditure on magistrates courts.

C. *General Exchequer or "Block" Grants*

Local authority expenditure more than doubled after the First World War, and government demands for economy, prompted by the nation's economic position, led to the appointment in 1922 of a Treasury committee to investigate the feasibility of an alternative system to the percentage grant. For various reasons its report was never published, but the Government and the Chancellor, Mr. Winston Churchill, was intent upon replacing the percentage grant by a block grant which would be paid over a limited number of years. There was much hostility to the proposed change and the block grant proposal was withdrawn, but in 1926 Mr. Churchill referred in debate to the percentage grant system, stating:

> ". . . the expenditure, apart from legislation to alter the scale of grants, is uncontrollable. The local authorities call the tune, and it only remains to calculate the percentage upon which the Exchequer pays the piper . . . it is a very unsatisfactory field".

He continued by stating the government's intention to convert the percentage grant system to block grants,

> "that is to say, to pay definite sums instead of percentages to the local authorities, to give those authorities increased discretionary powers, to make them responsible for any extravagance or any unduly bold enterprise to which they may commit themselves, and to give them 100 per cent of any economies they may themselves be able to effect".[2]

---

[2] Maureen Schultz, "The Development of the Grant System" in *Essays on Local Government* (ed. C. H. Wilson), Blackwell, 1948, pp. 131–2.

In 1929 agriculture was derated, industry was partially derated and the losses of the local authorities in rate income needed to be compensated. Thus by the Local Government Act, 1929, despite further opposition and only mild enthusiasm from the local authorities, many percentage grants and most of the assigned revenues were discontinued, and block grants were introduced and apportioned to counties and county boroughs on the basis of a formula calculated "on general characteristics, independent of actual expenditure". These characteristics were: (a) the population of the area; (b) the number of children under 5 years of age; (c) the rateable value per head of the population; (d) the proportion of unemployed insured men to the total population; (e) the population per mile of public road.

Capitation grants were made to county districts at a flat rate per head of the population, with rural districts receiving one-fifth of the amount given to urban districts. The transistion to the new system was achieved over three periods of five years when 25 per cent, 50 per cent and 75 per cent of the block grant were allotted. By the 1929 Act the grants which were abolished were agricultural rates grants, health percentage grants for maternity, tuberculosis, venereal disease and certain grants for mental deficiency and blindness, classification grants for Class I and Class II roads in London and county boroughs, and the maintenance grants for scheduled roads in county districts. The percentage grants which remained after 1929 were those for police, education, housing, roads and certain specialised health services.

D. *Exchequer Equalisation Grants*

The General Exchequer Grants of 1929 were replaced by Exchequer Equalisation Grants by the Local Government Act 1948. Post-war legislation effected changes in the relationship between local authorities and the government over the administration of certain services, e.g. education, where the major authorities were required to act as agents of the government; in addition, the 1944 Education Act removed the power of local authorities to charge fees for secondary education. Some services formerly controlled by local authorities, e.g. hospitals and public assistance services, were transferred from local authorities. Such changes relieved them of certain expenditures and necessitated a revision of the financial relationship between central and local government. The Exchequer Equalisation Grant was, like the block grant, a contribution to a local authority's general expenses and not to specific services.

It was based upon weighted population but calculated on the basis of a formula which was constructed to benefit the poorer areas and to equalise the resources of local authorities. The weighted population was calculated by adding to the actual population the number of children who were under 15 years of age, so that they were counted twice, and in county councils an additional weighting was added where the population per road mile was under seventy. The total rateable value of England and Wales was then divided by the weighted population of all the counties and county boroughs and the result was the average rateable value per head of weighted population. If the rateable value per head of weighted population in counties and county boroughs fell below the national average, the local authority was credited by the Exchequer with the deficiency in rateable value and rates were paid by the government to each county and county borough on the credited rateable value. County councils were to make grants on a capitation basis to county districts (with rural districts receiving half payments), calculations being made annually, as opposed to the five-yearly intervals of the previous block grants. Those counties and county boroughs whose rateable value per head of weighted population was above the national average received no equalisation grants, but county councils were still required to pay a capitation grant to their county districts.

Percentage grants still remained for certain specific services, which included police, education, roads, health services, and town and county planning.

E. *General Grants*

Dissatisfaction with the exchequer equalisation grant system and the percentage grants led the Conservative government to reconsider the "radical recasting of the system of grants", stating that the improvement needed was

> "one which secures that a substantially larger part of the grant aid is in the form of general assistance and is not tied . . . to specific services and expressed as a percentage of expenditure upon these services".

The percentage grant was seen as "an indiscriminate incentive to further expenditure and also carried with it an aggravating amount of central checking and control of detail".[3] These alleged disadvantages were eliminated by the controversial Local Government Act

---

[3] *Local Government Finance (England and Wales)*, 1957, Cmd. 209 p. 3.

1958, which substituted general grants for many of the percentage grants, and the rate deficiency grant for the exchequer equalisation grant. A large number of percentage grants were either absorbed in the general grant formula or discontinued. Excluded from the Act, were the specific grants for housing on a unit cost basis, highways and the police.

The "recipient authorities" were the councils of counties and county boroughs and the grants would be assessed in advance for two or three years "grant periods". The amount of the grant payable for any year would be fixed by the Ministry of Housing and Local Government and would be the aggregate[4] of a basic grant and a number of supplementary grants. The aggregate could be reduced by the Minister on the basis of a rate in the pound. The basic grant would be determined by such factors as population and the number of children in that population under 15 years of age. There were seven supplementary grants which would take into account: (1) the number of children under 5 years of age; (2) the number of persons over 65 years of age; (3) a high ratio of pupils at maintained or assisted schools and at occupation centres to population; (4) a high population density per acre of the authority; (5) a low population per road mile; (6) a high percentage population decline over a prescribed period; and (7) whether the authority or part of it lay within the metropolitan police district.

F. *Rate Deficiency Grants*

These were to be paid to county district councils, metropolitan borough councils, the Common Council of the City of London, county and borough councils. The conditions for payment

> "shall be that the product of a rate of one penny in the pound for the area of the authority for that year is less than the standard penny rate product for the area".

Note that there is no reference here to rateable value. Capitation payments by county councils to county districts were abolished. Arrangements were also made for the "pooling" of expenditure on certain training and educational services.

G. *The Rate Support Grant*

Instituted from 1 April, 1967 by the Local Government Act 1966 the rate support grant (R.S.G.) became the principal grant and replaced both the general and the rate deficiency grants, and specific grants for school milk and meals, and Class II and III roads. The

---

[4] Virtually the expenditure on absorbed grants.

R.S.G. was intended to be a short-term solution until the Royal Commission reported and the entire position of local government finance would be re-examined in the context of its conclusions. The R.S.G.s purposes were to help reduce the rate burden and produce a fairer distribution of Exchequer assistance among local authorities.

Part I of the Local Government Act 1974 modified certain aspects of the R.S.G. system but did not materially change the method whereby the aggregate annual total of the R.S.G. is determined or the allocation of the total between its three constituent elements. The aggregate amount is prescribed annually by the Secretary of State after consultation with the local authority associations and any individual local authority, and he takes into account (a) the latest information available on the rate of relevant spending; (b) any probable fluctuation in demand for services over the country as a whole which is not under the control of local authorities; (c) the need for developing those services, having regard to the general economic conditions; and (d) the current level of prices, costs and remuneration, and any future variation in them which is based on decisions which are final.

Whereas the 1966 Act provided for grant periods of two years, the 1974 Act provided for the payment of an amount to local authorities in respect of their relevant expenditure for the particular year. From the amount available for grants the Secretary of State will deduct the following sums to arrive at the estimated aggregate amount of the R.S.G. for the year: (a) the amount which will be allocated in grants for specific services, with certain exclusions; (b) the amount set aside for supplementary grants for transport purposes (from 1975–6 onwards); and (c) the amount of supplementary grants to county councils which have additional expenditure on national parks (from 1974–5 onwards).

The aggregate annual total of the R.S.G. is divided into three elements, viz. needs, domestic and resources elements.

1. *Needs Element:* is the largest part of the R.S.G. and is similar to the former General Grant but wider in scope. Since reorganisation it is payable to the councils of non-metropolitan counties, metropolitan districts, London boroughs, the City of London and the Isles of Scilly. The 1966 Act provided for its distribution on the basis of population, numbers of pupils and students at different stages of education, road mileages and other objective criteria of need. The Local Government Act 1974 changed the formula and introduced the possibility of some flexibility in the distribution arrangement which can now be varied each year by order. The

amount of needs element payable to local authorities for 1975–6 was the aggregate of:

(i) The number of education units in excess of 200 per 1,000 of the population of the area × £168·00.

(ii) Acreage of the area in excess of 1·5 per head of the population × £0·63 (or £1·81 if it exceeded 3).

(iii) The decline in population between 30 June, 1964, and 30 June, 1974 × £22·10.

(iv) The number of persons of pensionable age living alone × £198·75.

(v) The number of persons in wards or parishes with a density in excess of 50 persons per hectare × £4·46.

(vi) Population at 30 June, 1974 × £2·99.

(vii) 71·3 per cent of the authority's 1974–5 needs element entitlement (pre-Increase Order).

(viii) For London Boroughs and the Common Council of the City of London 8 per cent of the total amounts under (i) to (vi) above.

2. *Resources Element:* replaced the Rate Deficiency Grant, but differed only in being fixed in advance. Payable to local authorities which have rate resources per head of population below the national standard rateable value per head of population (£170 R.V. as at 1 April, 1974).

3. *Domestic Element:* paid to rating authorities and introduced to relieve the burden of increasing rate poundages by permitting reductions on the rate levied on domestic and mixed hereditaments (1975–6 distribution: England 18½p, Wales 36p; mixed hereditaments: 9p and 18p respectively).

The annual report of C.I.P.F.A. in 1975 pointed out that the negotiations for the R.S.G. for 1975–6 were overshadowed by the under-provision for growth and inflation in the 1974–5 settlement, the need for drastically reduced growth in 1975–6, and a background of ratepayer militancy. Forecasts of relevant expenditure were prepared on the basis of four options ranging from nil growth over the 1974–5 expenditure as determined in the actual R.S.G. settlement to the traditional forecast of trends on the basis of existing policies. In examining the options the Secretary of State agreed that very careful consideration would have to be given to such identified inescapable commitments as expenditure arising from mandatory statutory obligations, loan charges and the consequences of demographic trends. In his subsequent speech to the Association of County Councils he warned local authorities explicitly that they should prepare budgets on the basis of no growth in real terms.

The Rate Support Grant (No. 2) Order 1974 fixed and prescribed rate support grants for 1975–6 as follows:

£m.

(1)	Estimate relevant expenditure	8,171
(2)	Aggregate Exchequer Grant at 66.5%	5,434
(3)	Total of Specific Revenue and Supplementary Grant	729
(4)	Rate Support Grant—(2) minus (3)	4,705
(5)	Elements—Needs	2,758
	—Resources	1,328
	—Domestic	619

The 1975–6 settlement was intended to enable local authorities to limit the average increases in domestic rates to 25 per cent. Circular 171/74 contained an analysis of the estimated relevant expenditure together with estimated average growth rates and this is reproduced as Appendix 2.

The specific and supplementary grants for 1975–6 were:

Specific grants	£ million at November 1974 prices
Police	312·9
Improvement grants and area improvement grants	61·7
Magistrates courts	28·6
Probation and after care	23·5
Urban programme	14·2
Slum clearance	10·5
Commonwealth immigrants	10·3
Urban redevelopment	7·0
Clean air	3·4
Sheltered employment	2·0
Civil defence	1·9
Smallholdings	0·5
Derelict land	0·2
Town development	0·2
TOTAL SPECIFIC GRANTS	476·9
National Parks Supplementary Grant	2·3
Transport Supplementary Grant	250·0
TOTAL DEDUCTIONS FROM AGGREGATE EXCHEQUER ASSISTANCE	729·2

2. The Rating System

Since 1601 when a poor rate was imposed upon parish inhabitants to relieve local poverty, the practice has developed of financing current expenditure on services from rates levied locally. Originally, in 1601, the rate was assessed on the basis of a parishioner's visible estate, "both real and personal", but difficulties encountered in its true assessment led to rates being based upon real property. Later, a tangled variety of different rates emerged to finance different services, but attempts to create a simplified and consolidated system in a general rate were fruitless until the passing of the Rating and Valuation Act of 1925. This act abolished the overseers of the poor and trånsferred their powers for making and levying rates to rating authorities, i.e. the councils of county boroughs, municipal boroughs, urban and rural districts. County councils were not rating authorities, but issued precepts to those county districts and boroughs over which they had jurisdiction; these, being rating authorities, then levied a general rate which included not only their own financial requirements but also took into account that proportion which was required by the precepting authority. Parishes were not rating authorities either and issued precepts on the rural district councils to defray their expenses.

Rating authorities continued to value their property for rates until the introduction of Exchequer equalisation grants, by the Local Government Act of 1948, which were designed to help those rating authorities with a low rateable value. The danger that rating authorities would undervalue local property in order to increase their equalisation grant was foreseen, and the act consequently transferred the valuation function to the Board of Inland Revenue where it has since remained.

The Board's valuation officers assess the rateable value of all hereditaments (i.e. visible estate in the form of land or buildings) on the basis of their annual gross value, i.e. the amount which a tenant might reasonably be expected to pay in rent to his land-lord, with the latter being assumed to include repairs and insurance costs in his estimate of a rent. The valuation officers make certain deductions[5] to arrive at a "net annual value" which is, in effect, the rateable value. Valuation lists are required to be prepared by valuation officers every five years for each rating authority, showing the rateable value of every rateable hereditament within the authority. Objections to a valuation or the inclusion of a hered-itament on the valuation list will be heard before the local valuation court, or the case may be referred by agreement to arbitration.

Post-war valuation lists had been based on 1934 letting values,

[5] The Valuation (Statutory Deductions) Order 1973 (S.I. 1973 No. 2139) substituted a new scale of statutory deductions in respect of the annual cost of repairs, maintenance, and insurance of houses and non-industrial buildings.

the 1939 revaluation having been postponed by the outbreak of war. By the Valuation for Rating Act 1953, houses were revalued on the basis of 1939 rents, and by the Rating and Valuation Act 1959, the 1961 revaluation was postponed to 1963 when new lists came into force. The 1968 revaluation was postponed to 1973 by the Local Government Act 1966 and the next quinquennial review scheduled for 1978 has been postponed until 1 April, 1980, by the General Rate Act 1975. The 1973 figures below show the rateable values immediately before and after revaluation. The rateable values in brackets refer to figures at 1st April, 1973.

Type of hereditament	Value of assessments (£ million)	
	At 31 March, 1973	At 1 April, 1973
Domestic—total	1,251·1	3,234·1
Houses and flats with rateable values: Not over £30 (£75)	44·4	72·4
Over £30 (£75) but not over £56 (£100)	199·0	108·2
Over £56 (£100)	981·4	2,995·9
Agricultural dwelling-houses, etc.	26·4	57·7
Commercial	566·2	1,626·7
Unlicensed premises	24·9	65·9
Entertainment and recreational	26·4	67·5
Public utility	123·2	319·3
Educational and cultural	101·9	211·5
Miscellaneous	151·8	240·3
Industrial	355·0	817·8
TOTAL—all classes	2,600·4	6,583·0

Source: C.S.O. Annual Abstract of Statistics 1974, H.M.S.O.

A joint circular *Rating: Domestic Rates Relief (England and Wales)* issued by the D.O.E. (24/73) and the Welsh Office (71/73) explained the arrangements whereby domestic ratepayers whose rate bills would increase substantially in 1973–4 as a result of revaluation would be given some relief. The relief payable was to be half the amount of increases over 10 per cent in domestic rate bills as a result of revaluation. Ratepayers were not required to claim the relief due, but local authorities were required to calculate and give it.

Some hereditaments are not required to pay full rates but are "derated" either partially or wholly. By the Local Government Act 1929, total relief from rate payment was granted to all agricultural land and buildings (not, however, farm dwellings) while 75 per cent relief was granted to industrial hereditaments, i.e. mines, mineral railways, factories and workshops, and to freight transport hereditaments i.e. railways, canal transport and docks. Subsequently, the Local Government Act 1958, derated industrial and freight transport hereditaments to the extent of 50 per cent, and by the Rating and Valuation Act 1961, the derating of industrial and freight transport hereditaments was ended completely.

In addition to agriculture, the main exemptions from rate liability are: undeveloped land; sewers and water courses maintained by river-boards and drainage authorities; places of religious worship; almshouses and charities will have 50 per cent relief, but rating authorities may reduce or completely remit their rates, and those of non-profit charitable, educational or recreational organisations; structures for housing invalid chairs or vehicles; and moveable properties (e.g. caravans) providing they are moved at least once a year. Ex-gratia payments are made in lieu of rates by the Crown. By the Local Government Act, 1966, office premises of nationalised boards were rated where they were not situated on operational land and the Minister could change the formulae for distributing the cumulo rateable values of, and payments made in lieu of rates by, the boards.

A. *The General Rate Act 1967*

The General Rate Act 1967 repealed and re-enacted in consolidated form most of the law relating to rating and valuation in England and Wales. Since reorganisation in 1974 the rating authorities are the district councils, the London borough councils and the Common Council of the City of London, and the Sub-Treasurer of the Inner Temple and the Under Treasurer of the Middle Temple. They alone are empowered to make and levy rates in their respective areas. The other local authorities have no rating powers but each issues a precept which is tantamount to a demand note to the appropriate rating authority or authorities specifying the amount in the pound which they require to meet their liabilities. The rating authorities will include the precepts when they make their rates. Thus a county council will issue precepts for the proceeds of, say, 25p in the pound to all the district councils in its area, and parish councils and meetings and community councils will each issue a precept to the district council in whose area they lie. The expenses of a community meeting, where there is no community council, are met directly by the district council. Other precepting authorities may be joint boards, river authorities, drainage boards and combined police authorities. After collecting the rate the rating authorities must pay the precepting authorities the amounts necessary to satisfy their precepts.

The local authority's financial year extends from 1 April to 31 March, and every year, around January, each spending committee of a local authority meets to consider its financial requirements for the next year. Estimates are prepared which are then submitted to the scrutiny of the finance committee who will propose their acceptance or amendment to the council. From the estimates of all the committees the Treasurer is able to calculate the council's expenditure for the year, and after deducting income from grants, trading undertakings, etc., he will be able to determine the required rate in the pound. This is calculated by totalling all the rateable values of hereditaments within the area,[6] to arrive at the authority's rateable value, and by finding what income the authority would receive if a rate of one penny were levied on every pound of the total rateable value. The rate in the pound is then fixed by dividing the amount of money required by the product of the penny rate. Each occupier's payment is then calculated by multiplying the rateable value of the property (broadly equivalent to its annual rental value) by the rate poundage.

A demand note is then issued to the occupier, and in order to encourage early payment, a local authority may allow a small discount, which must not exceed $2\frac{1}{2}$ per cent, for payment before a stipulated date. Should a ratepayer default upon his payment the local authority cannot sue for rates, but a warrant for distress and seizure of his goods may be issued. The local authority may then sell the ratepayer's goods, but if insufficient money is raised in this way, the ratepayer may also be imprisoned. If the rating authority finds that default is caused by poverty the authority may reduce or remit the rate.

B. *The Local Government Act 1974*

Part II of the Local Government Act 1974 made a number of changes in rating law and introduced several provisions in respect of certain types of property.

The principal act, the General Rate Act 1967, had made property owners liable for half rates on property unoccupied for three months, or six months for newly erected dwellings. Several aspects of this provision had been criticised: the minimum period for

---

[6] After making due allowance for void properties, rate rebates, costs of collection, owners' allowances, empty properties, charitable organisations, write-offs, etc.

exercising the power was seven years, there was no ability to discriminate between properties, and the proportion of the rate which could be levied was fixed at 50 per cent. These limitations were removed by s. 15 of the 1974 Act which repealed the conditions relating to a seven year time limit, allowed rating authorities to levy rates selectively on different classes of empty property and to levy rates of up to 100 per cent on empty property.

Concern over office blocks which had been kept vacant for long periods (e.g. Centre Point) motivated the introduction of a wholly new concept in rating in the penalty surcharge on commercial property. If, for a continuous period exceeding six months, a commercial building (not industrial premises) is not used for the purpose for which it was constructed or has been adapted, a surcharge will be levied for the period of non-use. The surcharge will be double the normal rates for the first 12 months of the period of non-use, treble for the second 12 months, quadruple for the third 12 months, and so on progressively while the period of non-use lasts. The measure of use of a building which escapes liability for surcharge is 80 per cent. Rating authorities have no discretion in imposing the penalty surcharge, but have to decide an owner's liability to pay by taking into account several relevant factors (s. 17A (5)). Appeal against the surcharge lies through the Crown Court as for other appeals against the rate, or as a defence to an action for recovery by a rating authority. A penalty surcharge is a charge on the land and is registered as a local land charge.

The Act implemented in s. 18 the recommendations of the *McNairn Committee on the Rating of Plant and Machinery* (December, 1972) by removing by order (S.I. 1974 No. 413) three classes of machinery from valuation for rating. These were items moved or rotated by motive power as part of the manufacturing process, removable linings having a life of less than one year, and certain categories of transferable plant.

By s. 19 the Secretary of State was empowered, after consulting with the local authority associations and representatives of relevant undertakings, to determine the rateable values of public utilities and certain similar bodies, viz.: water, railway, canal, gas, electricity, Post Office, National Coal Board, certain mines and quarries, docks and harbours, and radio and television diffusion. The methods for determining the rateable values were to be specified by orders made by the Secretary of State, who also had wide powers to modify the normal provisions relating to proposals, appeals and the statutory withholding of rates.

Rate relief for structures accommodating invalid carriages and the like was extended by s. 20 to include the land on which such a structure stands or is used for keeping an invalid vehicle.

A source of annoyance for improving householders was alleviated by s. 21 which provided that there would be no increase in the gross rateable value of dwelling houses or mixed hereditaments as a result of structural alterations for the purpose of installing a central heating system serving two or more rooms, or from making any structural alterations if the increase in the valuation which would have resulted does not exceed a prescribed amount. The Rating of Minor Structural Alterations to Dwellings (Specified Amount) Order 1974 prescribed a maximum of £30.

C. *The Impact of Rates on Householders*

The percentage distribution of rateable value between different classes of property, before and after the 1973 revaluation, shows that the greatest rate burden falls on the domestic ratepayer. The distribution, allowing for resources grant, is shown in brackets:

Property	*Pre-revaluation* %	*Post-revaluation* %
Domestic	49·50 (42·76)	49·78 (43·02)
Industry	13·85 (11·96)	12·33 (10·66)
Other commercial	7·89 (6·81)	7·87 (6·80)
Shops	9·18 (7·94)	9·27 (8·01)
Offices	6·45 (5·57)	8·87 (7·67)
Other (inc. Crown property, hospitals, etc.)	13·13 (11·34)	11·87 (10·26)
Resources grant	— (13·61)	— (13·57)

Source: *Rates and Rateable Values 1973–4, D.O.E. 1974.*

In the five years to 1962–3 the average annual increase in total rates levied was 11 per cent and the 1963 revaluation was followed by such widespread concern that a committee of inquiry was appointed under the chairmanship of Professor R. G. D. Allen to assess the impact of rates on householders in different income groups and in different parts of the country, with special regard to any circumstances likely to give rise to hardship. Its report presented a perturbing analysis of the regressiveness of rates and particularly their effect upon retired householders. Yet the rate increases which stimulated the setting up of that committee were modest in comparison with the substantial increases in the early 1970s. Reference has already been made to the background of ratepayers' militancy during the R.S.G. negotiations for 1975–6, and action groups throughout the country campaigned against the rises with many appeals against the 1973 assessment and threats to withhold payment.

The following figures show that the average domestic rate increase in England and Wales in 1975–6 was 22 per cent:

Local authorities	*Full rate* %	*Domestic rate* %
London:		
Inner	41	40
Outer	44	45
Metropolitan districts	21	15
Non-metropolitan districts:		
England	24	18
Wales	26	46
Overall average (weighted by population)	26	22

This was not directly comparable with the government's estimate of 25 per cent because: (a) The 25 per cent took into account the regional water authorities' general services charge which was added to the general rate. The actual average domestic rate increase was 24 per cent if this is included and the full rate becomes 27 per cent. (b) The actual rate increase did not take account of the government's special relief of £150 million paid in 1974–5 to domestic ratepayers with increases in excess of 20 per cent in that year. The rate increases for 1975–6 were high and, according to the CIPFA Annual Report 1975, "They emphasise once again the inability of the system of local government finance to cope with the present high rate of inflation without increasing dependence upon central government grants." Grants in 1975 constituted 66·5 per cent of relevant expenditure.

There were wide variations in the percentage rate increases in different parts of England and Wales (see table on facing page). These variations cannot be attributed to inflation. A significant factor was the distribution of the R.S.G.s. The increase in domestic rate relief was much smaller in Wales (7½ per cent) than in England (42 per cent), and this led to much larger than average rate increases in Wales. Also the resources element increased as a proportion of the total and was paid to all but 7 per cent of the most wealthy authorities measured by rateable value per head, effecting a further redistribution from richer to poorer areas. However, the

Increase %	London Inner	London Outer	Metro- politan districts	Non- metro- politan districts	Wales	Total
0–9	—	—	1	2	—	3
10–19	—	—	9	51	5	65
20–29	—	1	10	126	12	149
30–39	6	5	3	38	6	58
40–49	3	7	—	3	1	14
50–59	2	5	—	—	—	7
60–69	—	1	—	—	—	1
Total notifications	11	19	23	220	24	297
Total authorities	13	20	36	296	37	402

needs element accounted for only 58·6 per cent of the total in 1975–6, and this was the smallest ever proportion. This element has also been subject to some redistribution with the improvement of needs indicators. The higher costs of local authority services in London are still not fully taken into account by the distribution formula. It should also be added that regional water authority rates and charges are generally collected with the local authority rate. Water rates have increased on average by a larger proportion than have local rates, because (a) water authorities do not receive grant aid and the whole of the effects of inflation must be passed on to the consumer; and (b) a continuing capital investment pro-gramme produces increased loan charges, particularly from high interest rates arising from the restricted borrowing policy under the Water Act 1963.

On 31 July, 1974, the Secretary of State for the Environment announced the membership of a Committee of Inquiry into Local Government Finance under the chairmanship of Frank Layfield, Q.C. One body which gave evidence was the National Union of Ratepayers' Associations, a pressure group formed in 1921 to protect and further the interests of ratepayers. Its members include individual ratepayers and 400 affiliated Ratepayers' Federations and Associations which represent half a million electors. NURA believes that there is "no longer any use tinkering with the present system", the time having arrived "to make sweeping alterations". The Association therefore proposed a radical change based upon two principles: (i) that nationally created expenditure should be paid for nationally, and (ii) that everyone entitled to benefit from local services should contribute equitably to their cost.

In respect of the first principle, education was cited as the most expensive of all services, with little effective control exercisable by L.E.A.s over expenditure: "Standards of design, construction and staffing are laid down by the Government; staff salaries are negotiated nationally; and the number, nature, siting and timing of new schools are effectively decided by the Department of Education and Science. Few and, with one exception (i.e. 'type' of secondary education), relatively trivial matters are now really under local control". NURA expressed the opinion that the administration of the education service could remain local with at least as great a degree of autonomy as currently exists but "without local authorities contributing substantially to the cost". The Association recommended that for those services where local authorities had control over policy and could determine the level of expenditure, the bulk of the cost should be raised locally; where, however, central government had over-riding control and the standard of services was not within the competence of the local authority to decide, the whole cost should be borne by the Exchequer. So far as possible, administration should be decentralised and placed in the control of elected bodies at county or district levels.

The second principle, that every beneficiary should contribute equitably to the cost of services, was an expression of the conviction that "the most glaring fault" of the rating system is its "unfairness". Domestic rates are charged only on the sixteen million householders, while nine million local residents who pay no rates "get off scot-free because they are not statutory occupiers". NURA consequently urged the total abolition of the rating system and its replacement by a local income tax on *all* residents based on net disposable incomes above certain limits. The effect claimed by NURA of making some nine million "non-ratepayers" liable to a local tax would be the reduction of the average amount required from each of the sixteen million ratepayers by more than 40 per cent. Moreover, it would include those local electors in the 18–30 age group who are the biggest users of many of the most expensive local services and encourage them to take a greater interest in the way local authorities spend their money.

D. Rate Rebates

The Rating Act 1966 was framed to enable certain domestic ratepayers with low incomes to obtain rate rebates, and also to provide for rates to be payable by monthly instalments. An estimated two million domestic ratepayers in England, Wales and Scotland were eligible for rebates, while ratepayers already in receipt of National Assistance were excluded, except where a wage stop was in operation. The Act entailed a means test, a greater burden on the majority of ratepayers and further central control over the financial affairs of local authorities. It was intended to be a temporary expedient, "a patching-up operation", as Richard Crossman later called it, pending a radical reform of local government finance. However, orders in 1968, 1970 and 1972 progressively raised the income limits affecting rate rebate entitlement, as did the Rate Rebate Act 1973 which also added attendance allowances to the income to be left out of account when calculating reckonable income for assessing eligibility for rate rebates.

By Part II of the Local Government Act 1974 the Secretary of State was empowered to set up a statutory rate rebate scheme for residential occupiers which corresponded substantially to the rent rebate and allowance schemes established by the Housing Finance Act 1972. The scheme, taking effect from 1 April, 1974, replaced the rate rebate system introduced by the General Rate Act 1967 and repealed the Rate Rebate Act 1973. Instead of adopting the statutory scheme a local authority may establish its own distinct scheme for its area or operate a variation of it, but both alternative local schemes must ensure that no person will be entitled to a lower rebate than he would receive under the statutory scheme. Moreover the total of the rebates under such schemes must not exceed 110 per cent of those which would be payable under the statutory scheme.

The main objects of the new schemes were (a) to extend rate relief higher up the income scale, and (b) by following closely the existing statutory schemes for rent rebates and allowances, to encourage the public to apply and at the same time to ease the administrative task of local authorities.

Eligibility is related to occupation of or residence in a dwelling house or private dwelling, and extends to sub-tenancies. The premises occupied by the applicant must have, on a prescribed date, a rateable value not exceeding a specified limit, this being £1,500 in the Greater London area and £750 elsewhere. In addition, the applicant must satisfy conditions regarding his financial and personal circumstances, although the local authority can make its calculations on the higher income of another person living in the applicant's household. Having assessed eligibility, the local authority will make an assessment of the likely income of the residential occupier and his spouse during the rebate period. A residential occupier receiving supplementary benefit, or whose resources are aggregated with someone in receipt of supplementary benefit, will not be eligible to rate rebate except when this entitlement to the benefit is subject to the "wage stop" provisions or during the first eight weeks of a period of benefit for which he applied when already in receipt of a rate or rent rebate.

The amount of rebate is based on needs allowances, income, the amount of reckonable rates of the premises, the minimum weekly rates, minimum and maximum rebates, and weekly amounts to be deducted for non-dependants. The rating authority is entitled to receive a grant of 90 per cent of the cost of rate rebates as from 1974–5.

E. *Appraisal of the Rating System*

The rating system as a form of taxation has many merits:

1. It is a simple tax which is easily understood by the ratepayer. As a national assessment all authorities are treated according to the same standards and it generally works well. Decisions are subject to appeal, so no householder should pay more than the net annual value of the property.

2. It is the only major independent source of a local authority's income, although the local authority's freedom to use this money is greatly limited by the high cost of the services which it is statutorily required to provide. Nevertheless, the rate poundage is a locally-determined matter which, so long as it is lawful, cannot be changed by central government and allows the local authority some discretion in its spending.

3. It is a stable source of income for a local authority. As rates are assessed on visible property which is immovable the ratepayer cannot avoid paying and the local authority knows precisely how much it will collect.

4. It is reasonably convenient to pay, particularly since payment by instalments has been introduced. The collection costs are low, amounting to about 1·2 per cent of rate revenue, in comparison with 1·37 per cent on the gross Inland Revenue receipt.[7]

5. Whereas income tax is minimal for a married couple with four children and a reasonable wage, rates do require such families to contribute to the cost of local services.

6. As rates are based upon property, they encourage people to occupy only accommodation which is needed. Thus, in areas where housing is scarce and accommodation is limited, it may be essential

---

[7] County Councils Association, Local Government Finance Committee: "Report of a Working Party on the Rating System and Local Revenues", 1963, p. 3.

that individuals do not occupy properties which could be better utilised by larger families.

7. There is no intrusion into the home, nor any requirement to disclose domestic income unless applying for rate rebates.

The rating system's various disadvantages have been the subject not only of much popular criticism, but also of parliamentary enquiries since 1836. The disadvantages are:

i. Rates are a regressive tax because assessments are not based upon a person's ability to pay.[8] Thus the lower a ratepayer's income the higher the proportion of his income paid out in rates. This was confirmed by the Allen Committee's findings.

Rates fall particularly heavily on domestic ratepayers[9] who cannot claim any tax-relief, whereas those who pay rates for shops, commercial or industrial properties are able to class their payment as an expense to be charged against income in computing profits chargeable to income tax or corporation tax. This could have the effect of relieving them of about half their rate burden. It has been argued that similar relief could be given to householders by a tax allowance equivalent to the standard rate of income tax on the rate payment through their P.A.Y.E. coding.

ii. Since rate increases have not kept pace with income increases local authorities between quinquennial revaluations have had to put up rate poundages. Comparisons of anomalies both within and between local authorities attract much criticism and bring the entire system into disrepute.

iii. They are unjust in that they bear no relation to a man's use of a local authority's services. Many local income earners pay no rates directly although they make extensive use of local services. Moreover, many industrial and commercial enterprises are ratepayers but receive no local vote—taxation without representation.

iv. It has been said that occupiers have been deterred from improving their property because this would automatically increase the rateable value of the property.

v. Taking rental value as the basis for rateable value is unsatisfactory. The method for determining rental value is unscientific, arbitrary, and based upon spurious subjective criteria. Moreover, free market conditions do not obtain at present, nor is it likely that the supply of accommodation will match demand and allow free choice for many years to come. Capital values would probably be a better basis for assessment.

vi. They are inflexible and do not grow to meet increases in the costs of local authority services. There was no revaluation between

---

[8] Although Rate rebates make it less regressive.
[9] Although eased somewhat by rate rebates and the domestic element provision of the RSG.

1934 and 1956, the 1961 revaluation did not come into effect until 1963 and the 1968 revaluation has been postponed to 1973.

vii. There is a great disparity in the resources of different local authorities owing to size, density and composition of the population. Even with the former rate deficiency grants the basis of their calculation

"is inadequate to measure need, and . . . no account is taken of the differing resources of those local authorities which do not qualify for it" *(New Sources of Local Revenue*, RIPA 1956).

viii. Agricultural land should not be treated exceptionally and should be re-rated. The poorer rural districts would thus receive a financial boost which would minimise their heavy dependence upon the resources element, and a hidden agricultural subsidy could be replaced by an increased direct subsidy.

ix. Other properties excused from paying rates should be rated. This would include Crown property; nurseries on potential building land in urban areas with buildings used for the "factory production" of eggs, livestock, vegetables and flowers. Pig and calf breeders, many societies and charities "whose financial circumstances are such that relief is not justified", and nationalised boards should also make a contribution to the cost of local services.

The Government White Paper, *Local Government Finance England and Wales* (Cmd. 2923) issued in February, 1966, commented on the fact that "rates as at present constituted are ill-adapted to carry the strain now placed on them", and further stated that the Government was "driven to the conclusion that within the present structure of local government there is no prospect of any major reform of local government finance". The Government consequently looked to the Royal Commission's review, "and the new structure which emerges from their deliberations should provide a more promising context for drastic reform of local government finance". For this reason it was felt impracticable to change fundamentally the grants system but that the severity of rates could be moderated in the short term until the Royal Commission reported. This was subsequently attempted by the rebate and instalment provisions of the Rating Act 1966 and by the new rate support grant introduced by the Local Government Act 1966.

Unfortunately, finance was not specifically included in the Royal Commission's terms of reference, an omission which led *The Accountant* (21 June, 1969) to comment that "a discussion of local government reorganisation without a detailed consideration of its financial basis is rather like staging *Hamlet* without the Prince of Denmark". Nevertheless, a brief chapter of nine pages was devoted to local government finance and indicated that the proposed restructuring would require the "financial map of local government" to be "drastically altered". An adequate local taxation system was seen to be essential and the Commission urged "that the opportunity offered by reorganisation be taken to examine fundamentally the short-comings of the present local taxation system and remove them". It commented how grants were expected to reach 57 per cent of expenditure by 1970–71, with some authorities already receiving 70 per cent or more of their revenue from grants. The Commission had few suggestions, however, which could provide local authorities with the desired "reasonable measure of financial independence".

Thus although aware of the need for a new source of income and the need for a "wider tax base, and in particular for a more buoyant and elastic tax which grows with the advance of incomes" (a local income tax?), the Commission believed that the old standby, "the rate, modernised from time to time, will remain the chief local tax". There was no further appraisal of the rating system beyond pointing out that it "is reasonably productive, well established, simple to operate and is, in fact, the principal local government tax in many countries". Reference was made to its drawbacks, but they were not analysed, although "various modifications" which were suggested in evidence were felt to merit "serious consideration". One of these was that capital values might be substituted for rental values, with valuations in bands rather than in precise figures, and the other was the re-rating of agricultural land and buildings.

3. The Reform of Local Finance

The Conservative government in 1970 believed that the re-organisation of local government should be accompanied by the reform of local government finance and accordingly issued in 1971 a Green Paper *The Future Shape of Local Government Finance* (Cmnd. 4741). It stressed that the rate of growth of local government expenditure was greater than that of the economy as a whole and that local authorities were consequently absorbing an increasing share of real national income. It was estimated that local authority expenditure in 1972 would be about £4,000 million, with government grants bearing 58 per cent of total expenditure, and by re-organisation in 1974 grants would be meeting about 60 per cent of relevant expenditure. The purpose of the Green Paper was therefore not to find an alternative to the rating system or to reduce the rate levy and the burden upon domestic ratepayers, but to discuss *additional* sources of local revenue which would raise £400 million and permit a reduction in Exchequer grants from 60 per cent to 50 per cent.

Six possible sources were analysed under three headings: (a) "administration", i.e. the problems and cost of running the tax and the practicability of genuinely local variation in the rates of tax; (b) "suitability", i.e. the potential yield and buoyancy of the tax, and whether its effects would fall on the local electors in such a way as to impose some discipline on local expenditure decisions; and (c) "economic effects", i.e. on the national economy as a whole. The additional sources of local revenue were:

(a) *Local Income Tax.* An additional levy of about 3 per cent on the standard rate would finance a reduction in grant from 60 per cent to below 50 per cent. The difficulties of linking the central assessment arrangements with the individual local authority and its inhabitants were discussed, as well as those of assessing companies operating in a number of places and of allocating profits to the places where they were earned.

A local income tax has been adopted in Scandinavia and in parts of the U.S.A., and advocated by bodies in Britain. The Royal Institute of Public Administration examined the idea in 1968 and on the basis of a maximum rate of 3d. in the £ on personal incomes the estimated yield in 1956 would have been £150 million and in 1964 £240 million. The Redcliffe-Maud Report referred (para. 529) to Swedish authorities which "are relatively rich because of the highly productive local income tax". The Report also referred to the R.I.P.A. inquiry which found that a local income tax had "now become even more feasible because of the introduction of corporation tax, and will become still more so when the transfer of the Inland Revenue records to the computer has been completed".

(b) *Local Sales Tax or Value Added Tax.* A levy of a little over 2 per cent on consumer expenditure would finance a 10 per cent reduction in grants. In the absence of a precedent for combining a national V.A.T. with local sales taxes, and because of other complexities, this form of tax was not regarded by the government as a practical proposition at that time.

(c) *Local Employment or Payroll Tax.* At a level of 2 per cent a payroll tax would yield the amount required. This would add to the labour costs of employers, might discourage employment in the least flourishing areas and would add an estimated £100 million to export costs.

(d) *Motor Fuel Duty.* The rate of duty in 1971 was 22½p per gallon, yielding £1,250 million in 1970–71. A transfer of about one-third of the duty would compensate local authorities for the required reduction in grant. Among the administrative problems which would be produced was that of supervising the 40,000 retail outlets, and the undesirable economic effects of a scheme which would involve different duty rates in adjoining areas.

(e) *Motor Vehicle Duties.* The transfer of private motor vehicle duties would finance a grant reduction from 60 per cent to about 53 per cent. With the centralisation of vehicle duties it was not thought that the proceeds could be distributed to local authorities before 1977, or that power for local authorities to vary rates of duty could be conferred before 1980.

(f) *Lotteries.* The government felt that the yield from local lotteries would be incalculable and was reviewing the wider issues involved as foreign experience did not provide a guide.

(g) *Increasing the Yield of Rates.* Four possibilities were envisaged:

   (i) *Super-rating* i.e. levying a rateable value on non-domestic properties at a higher rate poundage than on domestic properties. It needed to be 50 per cent higher to reduce the grant from 60 per cent to 50 per cent.

  (ii) *Surcharges on the rates for earning non-householders.* It was concluded that the administrative costs would be substantial and disproportionate to the small yield; moreover it was felt that the surcharges would be distasteful and resented.

 (iii) *Site value rating.* The main disadvantages would be that it would tax not the current income and resources of the taxpayer but his prospective and potential resources, and it would tax land values not only before they were realised but often when it would be quite impracticable to realise them.

 (iv) *Rating of Agriculture.* The Redcliffe-Maud Report had described the derating of agriculture as anomalous, and the Green Paper stated that the reimposition of rates on agricultural land and buildings deserved discussion. There would be no technical problem in valuation but "it would impose a substantial task of valuation on scarce professional staff, and could probably not be completed before the 1980s". No change could thus be proposed for the time being.

The Green Paper went on to review the advantages and disadvantages of the rating system, and suggested that many of the disadvantages could be moderated, if not cured, by improvements in the rating system:

   (i) The regressive aspect of rating had already been softened by rate rebates, with 3 million households in 1969–70 on full or partial relief. A more sophisticated scheme was considered which might eradicate the weaknesses of the rebate scheme by basing relief on net income and not on gross income. Rates would thus become more closely associated with ability to pay, particularly at those levels of income at which they caused hardship.

  (ii) Dwellings should be assessed on capital values as there was more evidence of capital values available in respect of the domestic sector. This was seen to be complicated by personal preferences and by anticipated development values. Moreover, such a change could not be implemented before the 1978 revaluation.

(iii) The rating of empty property.

(iv) The Government was to examine the existing assessments by formula of public utilities to see if changes were justified.

Lastly, the Green Paper appraised the future system of central government grants in the context of reorganisation. It was felt 'that the first question to be settled was the relative weight to be given to block grants and specific grants. The former were dominant but the latter comprised 47 grants of which 44 amounted to only $1\frac{1}{4}$ per cent of local government expenditure. Each specific grant involved a specific control by central government and needed to be accounted for in detail, and this was inconsistent with the desire to give local government greater freedom. The Rate Support Grant's contribution was assessed and its fixing in advance for two years at a time was thought to be too inflexible and it was suggested that it might be settled annually, but with a provisional indication of the total for two years beyond.

4. Miscellaneous Sources

Table 5 showed that over 35 per cent of local authority revenue is received from miscellaneous sources. These sources are so diverse that they are virtually impossible to classify, but they would include:

(a) charges for personal services such as the maintenance of old people in homes, where the charge is based on income, or the provision of police at public functions or entertainments;

(b) charges for work done, e.g. making up private streets, cleaning drains on private property; and

(c) charges for facilities provided including council house rents, putting or bowls fees in parks, etc.

Other municipal enterprises include passenger transport services, cemeteries and crematoria, harbours, docks, piers, putting-greens, markets and car-parks. Before nationalisation, gas and electricity undertakings were also run by many local authorities. Local authorities could exercise their initiative and establish profitable trading services, and some of the more unusual which have been operated include: a municipal bank (Birmingham), a bonded warehouse (York), an oyster fishery (Colchester), plant for the recovery of wool grease from fleeces and its conversion into industrial soaps (Bradford), piggeries (Gateshead), an aerodrome (Bristol), the manufacture and sale of ice (Burnley), hiring out plants for floral decoration (Stockport), a cinema (Oundle), and a race-course and hop-market (Worcester). Such enterprises kept separate accounts from those of the rate fund services, but under the Local Government Act, 1933, profits could be transferred to aid rates. Profits may accrue to individual enterprises, but national figures would indicate a net deficit, e.g. in 1953–54 profits of £1·6 million were transferred to rate funds from trading enterprises run by local authorities in England and Wales, but £7·5 million were transferred in the same year from rates to meet trading deficits. For this reason trading enterprises are severely criticised by the ratepayers where they do not show profits, while within the council there may be political groups who will find difficulty in reconciling the profit motive and community interest. Moreover, in the community, the likelihood of competition from a cut-price local authority will not be welcomed by local commercial groups.

5. Borrowing

In discharging statutory duties and powers, the capital costs of tangible and permanent assets in the form of buildings, roads, bridges and land are not met from grants, rates or other local sources but by raising loans which are repaid over a number of years. Schedule 13 of the Local Government Act 1972 changed the law with respect to borrowing, lending and funds, and with certain modifications and changes replaced Part IX of the Local Government Act 1933.

A local authority which is authorised to borrow money may raise it by (a) mortgage, (b) the issue of stock, (c) the issue of debentures or annuity certificates under the Local Loans Act 1875, (d) the issue of bonds, (e) the issue of bills, (f) an agreement with the Public Works Loan Commissioners, and (g) any other means approved by the Secretary of State with the consent of the Treasury, including borrowing outside the United Kingdom or in foreign currency. The Secretary of State may make regulations, with the consent of the Treasury, to prescribe the form of any mortgage deed and to regulate the issue of stocks and bonds and the transfer, dealing with and redeeming of any mortgage created or stocks or bonds issued.

All moneys borrowed, including temporary borrowing, are charged indifferently on all the revenues of the authority. The ability of a local authority to borrow from internal sources, such as reserve funds or superannuation funds, is codified. A principal council may also borrow, without the Secretary of State's approval, for the purposes of lending money to another authority, including a police, river or harbour authority, or a joint board, for any purpose for which that authority is authorised to borrow.

All loans require the sanction of the Secretary of State and he will be advised by the appropriate department concerned with the scheme for which loan sanction is sought. Loan sanction, whether it is for a specific scheme or is a "block sanction" covering a programme of capital expenditure, will specify the maximum amount to be borrowed and the period of repayment of the loan. This period will be based on the functional life of the asset and must not in any event exceed sixty years, except in the case of land for housing and other purposes when a maximum of eighty years is specified. Local authorities may decide to repay the loan over a shorter period or they may, even though the loan sanction may have been given, resort to meeting their capital expenditure, or a proportion of it, out of revenue income or internal funds. These latter include sinking funds, reserve funds, insurance funds, trust and charity funds, superannuation funds and special funds. Where the loan is for "an undertaking of a revenue-producing character" (para. 9) a local authority may for a period of up to five years suspend making provision for repayment and may borrow money for the payment of all or any of the interest due during that period. Local authorities may also establish and operate a loans fund to defray any expenditure which the authority is authorised to meet out of borrowed moneys (para. 15).

The sources available to local authorities for external borrowing are briefly described below and the extent of the loan debt is shown in Appendix 3.

A. *The Public Works Loan Board*

This is an independent statutory body of twelve unpaid Commissioners appointed by the Crown for four years, with three Commissioners retiring each year. Their functions, derived mainly from the Public Works Loans Act 1875 and the Local Authorities Loans Act 1945,

> "are to consider loan applications from local authorities and other prescribed bodies, and where loans are made, to collect the repayments".

The Board is financed by government loans and the rates of interest are fixed by the Treasury. The amounts borrowed by local authorities have varied considerably within the last twenty years from 64 per cent of the total loans raised by local authorities in 1946–47, building up to 85 per cent in 1951–52 and thereafter declining.

The variations have reflected different phases in the Board's lending policy. Up to 1945 local authorities with a rateable value of more than £200,000 were deterred from borrowing, and its loans were available only to the smaller local authorities. The 1945 Act restricted local authorities from borrowing from any other sources and this policy prevailed until 1952 when they were permitted to borrow from the open market or from the Board. After 1956 there was restriction of access to the Board and only £39·9 million was advanced by the Board in 1959–60. The Radcliffe Committee of 1957–59 recommended that full access to the Board should be restored but this was rejected by the Government.

By 1963 local authorities were able to get 20 per cent of their long-term borrowing from the Board, and the White Paper of that year, *Local Authority Borrowing* (Cmd. 2164) commented that the Board would "continue to act as a lender of last resort" and would "make additional loans if it is satisfied that an authority cannot raise the money on the market". To help smaller authorities, each would be allowed to borrow £50,000 a year from the Board and later possibly £100,000. The 7 years' maximum period for loans would be extended to 10 years, with 40 years for maturity loans and 80 years for annuity loans.

The Public Works Loan Board Act 1964 put the new arrangements into operation, placing up to £750 million at the Board's disposal, and the 20 per cent limitation on long-term borrowing was raised to 30 per cent. In his April, 1965 Budget speech, the Chancellor stated that authorities in selected areas would be allowed up to 50 per cent and a further £40 million would be allowed for the purpose. By July, 1965 he commented that drawings on the Public Works Loan Board during the financial year had been "exceptionally heavy" and in the existing economic circumstances a "more regular phasing of issues" was necessary. P.W.L.B. Circular No. 11, dated 12 April, 1967, stated that the percentage limitation could be based upon the net capital expenditure instead of on long term borrowing. The proportion in 1967–8 was 34 per cent and in 1975–6 was 40 per cent. During 1974–5 the net issues made to local authorities from the National Loans Fund through the P.W.L.B. amounted to £1,126 million.

B. *Stock*

A general power to issue stock is contained in the Local Government Act 1972 and some local authorities have obtained powers to issue stock under local acts. Treasury consent is required and an issue is subject to a minimum of £3 million. This has tended to restrict its use to the larger authorities. The largest local authority stock issue to date was made in April, 1975 by the G.L.C. when it advertised a £75 million issue at 12½ per cent repayable on 25 May, 1982. Although it can be an expensive way to raise money and is costly to administer, stock issues are the only practical way in which several of the larger authorities can assure an adequate supply of finance.

C. Mortgages

A mortgage deed can be issued in the same manner as a local bond for the following types of borrowing: (i) maturity loan; (ii) maturity loan with option clause; (iii) escalators; (iv) C.D. (Certificate of Deposit) loans; (v) loans with a stress clause. Both before 1939 and after 1955 mortgage loans have provided local authorities with a major and regular source of capital. They will be repayable either by instalments or in lump sum at the end of a specific period, and the sources, now that inter-authority lending on mortgage has declined, are mainly the mortgage market and individual investors.

D. Bonds

There are two categories of bonds: (a) housing bonds issued under the Housing legislation, and (b) local bonds and local authority negotiable bonds. Bonds are trustee securities and an increasing number of authorities are using them in preference to mortgages, which have a number of disadvantages, and are issuing them when mortgages are redeemed. Negotiable or yearling bonds are a further development of the local bond. They were first introduced by Manchester Corporation in 1964 and have rapidly gained in popularity. Bank of England approval is needed before their issue and the maximum amount that can be issued is related to the size of the authority's outstanding debt. The Bank of England and the Treasury closely control the timing of, and the rates of interest on, bond issues. As with stock, there is a queue of potential borrowers. They are attractive to small investors being issued in multiples of £5, may be issued below par and on housing bonds have a yield which is paid gross up to £100. Housing bonds have a high popularity, they must be issued at par and the proceeds have to be allocated to housing purposes.

E. Temporary Borrowing

Local authorities are empowered to raise temporary loans or bank overdrafts and if such loans can be raised for periods of less than one year the low rate of interest, "the call rate", makes it a cheap source of capital. The Radcliffe Committee was concerned about the increase in large-scale temporary borrowing after the Government's curtailment of access to the Treasury through the P.W.L.B. in 1955, but the proportion of local authority debt met from this source has increased. By the end of the first quarter of 1969 the outstanding temporary debt reached £2,023 million, compared with only £933 million eight years earlier.

F. *Loans Bureau*

The Loans Bureau was developed under the aegis of the Institute of Municipal Treasurers and Accountants to facilitate the movement of funds between local authorities. Local authorities with temporary surpluses of funds would be put in touch with a borrowing authority by a liaison officer or loans dealer of the Bureau and the terms of the loan would be negotiated between the lender and the borrower. In 1971 the Institute (now the Chartered Institute of Public Finance and Accountancy) took over direct control of the six regional bureaux in operation and by March 1975 all the Bureau's dealing operations were centred on its London office.

New sources of funds are constantly being attracted and currently the sources are: local authorities 27·26 per cent; other public sector bodies 34·18 per cent; commercial and industrial 37·6 per cent; and negotiable bonds (stock market) 0·96 per cent. With several hundred borrowing members among local authorities and certain public bodies, the Bureau has a growing demand for funds ranging from £20,000 to millions and from overnight money to long-term loans. The following figures show the increase in the value and number of loans negotiated by the Bureau:

	Value £m	*Number*
1970	275	3,302
1971	488	3,937
1972	963	6,038
1973	1,982	8,481
1974	3,614	9,120
1975 (est.)	5,100	11,700

There are no charges to lenders for using the Bureau which is financed from annual subscriptions from its members together with charges to borrowers for loans transacted. Charges are significantly below those applying generally.

G. Borrowing Abroad

The Finance Act 1969 permitted, subject to Treasury consent, access to foreign borrowing. The facility was limited to local authorities who had local acts to borrow foreign currency and to issue bearer securities. Only about twenty authorities qualified but immediately over fifty authorities determined to seek such powers. Unfortunately the economic advantages to the government had diminished by the time the local bills were about to be enacted and only Derbyshire county council succeeded. In July 1969 it arranged to borrow 50 million marks (over £5 million) for 6 years at 8¼ per cent from a Frankfurt bank. The rate was cheaper than the rate in the British capital market, and ¼ per cent below the rate for such a loan from the P.W.L.B. In 1973 the Chancellor was anxious to build up his foreign reserves and reintroduced facilities for foreign currency borrowing. The scheme was limited to authorities having local act powers whose loan debt at March 1972 was over £100m; borrowing had to be in dollars, for a minimum of 5 years, and the conditions of the Bank of England and the Treasury had to be met. The Local Government Act 1972 widened the powers available so that from 1 April, 1974 all local authorities, subject to Treasury consent, have power to borrow in foreign currency and issue bearer securities. Authorities have not been able to gain full advantage, however, because the guarantee facilities available to nationalised industries are not available to local government.

The extent of local authority debt can be seen in the figures opposite which cover the last year before reorganisation.[10] Fewer authorities than normal were able to complete returns, but the data convey a general impression of the debt outstanding by service at 31 March, 1974, and the sources of borrowing.

Local authorities are permitted to finance capital expenditure from revenue and this freedom is selectively used. In the locally determined sector of capital expenditure the trend has been for local authorities to finance a considerable proportion out of revenue, but this has not been common in the "key sector" programmes. Here the individual authority is strongly influenced by the way in which the responsible central department administers its loan sanction control. This will determine the local authority's ability to transfer resources from one type of expenditure to another and its ability to execute its plans.

The separation between key and locally determined sectors is thus

---

[10] *C.I.P.F.A. Return of Outstanding Debt,* April 1975.

Service	£m	Form of debt	£m
Housing:		Temporary loans	2,015
Sites, buildings, etc.	7,083	Stock	1,367
Housing advances	1,197	P.W.L.B.	5,187
Improvement grants etc.	211	Bonds and loans	3,190
Education	2,230	Internal advances	364
Public health	904	Mortgages	2,088
Highways and bridges	623	Other	115
Trading services	498		
Other	1,546		
		Total gross loan debt	14,326
		Deduct	
		Sinking funds	34
Total net debt	14,292	Total net debt	14,292

basic to the government's approach to controlling local authority capital expenditure. The key sectors are those where central government has determined the broad strategy of public expenditure and exercises direct control over the plans of individual authorities. There is no such control, however, in the locally determined sector where decisions on priorities rest with local authorities.

The Redcliffe-Maud Report 1968 stated that the rigid mechanism of the loan sanction sometimes led to authorities suffering from the lack of co-ordination between central government departments. Central government is organised functionally and it is in the Public Expenditure Survey Committee (P.E.S.C.) exercise that the expenditure plans of the social spending departments are brought together. The P.E.S.C. approach with the theoretical concentration of decisions on the third year of the five year cycle has been increasingly upset by the need for short-term adjustments in expenditure in the current or following year. The problem is "how, within the constraints of national overall demand management, to bring local government resource planning within the national scheme while preserving local choice".[11] The Department of the Environment does exercise a co-ordinating function between departments on issues of local government expenditure, but there is no one department responsible for the totality of that expenditure.

[11] T. H. Caulcott, "Central and Local Government Resource Planning", C.I.P.F.A. Conference 1975.

In May 1965 a new approach to deciding social policies and spending, the Joint Approach to Social Policy (J.A.S.P.), was agreed between the Prime Minister, the Treasury, and the ministers responsible for education, health and social security, the environment, employment and the Home Office. The approach was designed to improve the way social policy decisions were taken and to investigate specific policy areas which overlap departmental boundaries. The Central Policy Review Staff's programme upon which this joint approach was based was published in August under the changed title of *A Joint Framework for Social Policies*. The *Times Educational Supplement* (22 August, 1975) was critical stating that the change of title denoted the scepticism of some departments "who felt that there was no such thing as social policy and that it was unhelpful to talk as though there was". Another innovation in May was the convening of a consultative council, chaired by the Secretary of State and including senior ministers and leaders of the local authority associations. Its establishment had been announced in the 1975 Budget speech when the Chancellor had said that the government "has been working towards closer liaison between ministers and local authorities on financial issues". The consultative council is to discuss all matters of policy affecting local authorities which have major financial implications. It is remarkable that formal consultations between local and central government on anything except a departmental basis have in the past been confined to talks over the rate support grant. An institution which can bring central and local government together to discuss policy and expenditure on a longer term basis can only be welcomed.

CHAPTER 9

Central Control over Local Authorities

The control exercised by central government departments over the functions of local authorities is extensive. It is deemed necessary to ensure a high national standard of service which otherwise might vary greatly from one authority to another. Any restraint must to some extent limit local autonomy, but the degree of control and its many forms perturb those who feel that local democratic participation in decisions which determine the conduct of local services is being, and in some cases has been, superseded by the remote dictates of a Whitehall juggernaut. Whether the choice is as simple as that between local but democratic inefficiency and centralised competence, as is sometimes suggested, is highly debatable, but we have already seen how local authorities have lost functions to a number of governmental and *ad hoc* bodies and it now remains to see how the services which local authorities retain are subject to central government controls.

1. Legislative Control

Local authorities are administrative and not legislative bodies and require statutory powers to carry out functions which they are required to perform by Parliament. The supremacy of Parliament as the law-making body in the Kingdom implies that it may confer upon or deny to a local authority any powers or services. Moreover, since all county, district, parish and community councils, the Greater London Council and the London Boroughs, are statutory corporations they are subject to the doctrine of *ultra vires*. Before 1974 there were common law corporations, created either by royal charter or by prescription, but on 1 April, 1974, all boroughs outside Greater London ceased to exist, and any district council subsequently granted borough status did so under the authority of the Local Government Act 1972. Thus apart from the City of London, which is a common law corporation by prescription, there are now no common law corporations. Statutory corporations "are merely creatures of the statutes creating them . . . they have only the powers which the statutes creating them expressly confer upon them and those which are fairly incidental to the powers expressly given,"[1] This *ultra vires* principle has been given statutory force by s. 111 of the Local Government Act 1972.

Statutory powers are conferred in a number of ways:

A. *Public Acts*

These establish or regulate certain services for all inhabitants in local authorities throughout the country. Such acts may be (i) obligatory—local authorities are compelled to administer the particular service, or (ii) permissive—powers are conferred but the local authorities decide whether or not to exercise them.

B. *Adoptive Acts*

These are also public acts which permit local authorities to exercise certain powers if the local authorities themselves formally adopt the acts. They were first introduced in the early nineteenth century for the provision of lighting, baths, washhouses and public libraries, by enterprising local authorities who wished to take advantage of the enabling provisions before such services were applied nationally. Much of the Public Health legislation of 1890, 1907 and 1925 was adoptive. The Local Government and Public Health Consolidation Committee reported in 1936 that the method had been "overdone" with some "cases of patent absurdity". The Private Places of Entertainment (Licensing) Act 1967 is adoptive.

C. *Private Acts*

Individual local authorities seek powers which are not contained in general legislation by promoting private bills in Parliament. Extensively used during the industrial revolution to create such *ad hoc* bodies as turnpike trusts, gas undertakings and improvement commissioners the procedure is now utilized to obtain powers to operate trading services, to obtain special borrowing powers or to provide additional welfare facilities, etc. The power to promote or oppose such bills is granted to all local authorities, excepting parishes and community councils which are empowered to oppose only (s. 239 of the Local Government Act 1972). By s. 70 no local authority has the power to promote a bill for forming or abolishing any local government area or for altering, or altering the status or electoral arrangements of, any local government area.

---

[1] W. O. Hart and J. F. Garner, *Hart's Introduction to the Law of Local Government and Administration*, Butterworths, ninth edition, 1973, p. 306.

It is a flexible device but the preliminary formalities before a private bill is deposited in Parliament are complicated. The resolution to promote or oppose a private bill must be passed by a majority of the whole council at a meeting summoned after thirty clear days' notice in the case of promotion of a bill and ten clear days' notice in the case of opposition to a bill. The notice convening the meeting and stating its purpose must also be advertised in one or more local newspapers. The bill must then be deposited in Parliament. A second meeting must be held if a bill is being promoted, and after a similar notice has been given the meeting of the authority must be held after the expiration of fourteen days from depositing the bill. If the first resolution is not confirmed at this meeting by a like majority, the bill must be withdrawn. No second meeting is necessary to confirm a decision to oppose a bill. The procedure laid down by the Local Government Act 1933 by which borough councils had to convene a town meeting and, if opposed, hold a local poll, has been abolished by the 1972 Act, as has the requirement to obtain the permission of the Secretary of State to the promotion of a bill.

The private bill procedure is governed by the Standing Orders of each House. It is a complex and costly procedure and local authorities have thus tended to adopt simpler and cheaper methods of obtaining powers.

D. *Provisional Orders*

These are made by the Secretary of State or the appropriate minister, and the procedure to be followed is laid down in s. 240 of the principal act. The intention of the local authority must be advertised in the *London Gazette* and in one or more local newspapers to provide an opportunity for interested parties to object. The minister will investigate the local authority's application for an order and may either reject it or, more usually, will give interested parties an opportunity to object, generally before a Ministry inspector at a local inquiry. The inspector will make a confidential report on the basis of the evidence he has heard, and will submit it to the Minister for his decision. If he decides in favour of the application he will make the necessary order which must then await confirmation by Parliament before it comes into force. Should the provisional order be opposed by Parliament it will be referred to a Select Committee and dealt with as if it were a separate private bill.

This procedure is less costly and far simpler than that for promoting a private bill, and its passage through Parliament in the Provisional Orders Confirmation Bill ensures government support. The passing of the Statutory Orders (Special Procedure) Act 1945, has greatly reduced the need for provisional orders and substituted a simpler procedure, whereby uncontested orders come into effect automatically after the order has been laid before Parliament for a prescribed period.

2. Administrative Control

Central administrative control over local government was conspicuously absent until the nineteenth century and is not observed until the Benthamite concern for centralised control was put into effect with the appointment of Poor Law Commissioners to manage the system established by the 1834 Act. Yet the centralist idea was not adopted when the municipalities were reformed in the following year, and when public health legislation was introduced in 1848, an attempt was made to emulate the central supervision and control of the then unpopular Poor Law Commissioners. The matter became an issue of principle and the General Board of Health was opposed both within and without Parliament. The result was that subsequent control grew unsystematically, varying in extent according to the particular service and generally on the basis of the authorities' dependence on grant aid. As grants have become an increasing proportion of a local authority's revenue the control has become more sure, and ministerial discretion to reduce grant aid for inadequate standards has developed since 1929 to give the central government great powers.

The forms of administrative control exercised by government departments over local authorities may be summarised as follows:

A. *Ministerial Powers of Direction*

Legislation since the 1940s has emphasised the national importance of services administered locally and has charged the appropriate minister with the duty of co-ordinating all local endeavours and bringing them into line with national standards. The Minister of Housing and Local Government was required to secure

> "consistency and continuity in the framing and execution of a national policy with respect to the use and development of land throughout England and Wales".

The Minister of Education had the duty under the Education Act 1944

> "to promote the education of the people of England and Wales and the progressive development of institutions devoted to that purpose, and to secure the operative execution by local authori-

ties, under his control and direction, of the national policy for providing a varied and comprehensive educational service in every area".

Similar phraseology in subsequent statutes emphasised the controlling executive influence of the central department and the subordinate administrative function and limited discretion of the local authorities. This was further reinforced by the requirement of certain acts, e.g. the Education Act 1944 and the National Health Service Act 1946, for local authorities to submit their plans or proposals for approval by the appropriate department and also to submit reports and various returns such as the annual returns of income and expenditure.

B. *The Issue of Orders, Regulations, Directions and Circulars*

Much contemporary legislation is confined to broad principles of policy and confers upon the responsible Minister and his department powers to make orders, regulations, directions, generally referred to as statutory instruments which fill in the detail of such legislation. Thus the Secretary of State for Education will make regulations which prescribe standards to which local education authorities have to conform, regarding school premises, or attach conditions to the receipt of a grant. Similarly, the Secretary of State may issue general or specific directions to local authorities as to the way they are to exercise their statutory powers or duties, and if the local authorities are given discretionary powers and are deemed by the Department to have acted unreasonably the Minister may exercise the powers himself, or in the words of the Education Act 1944,

"give such directions as to the exercise of the power or the performance of the duty as appears to him to be expedient".

In this respect, Sir William Hart has written,

"Powers which thus permit local discretion to be overruled by the Central Departments go a long way to destroy the idea of local self-government and reduce local authorities to little more than agents of the Central Government".

Departmental circulars amplify, explain and give guidance to local authorities on the provisions of various acts and also explain changes in governmental financial policy; they communicate the particular department's attitude towards economic and financial measures and the department's likely response in the light of such measures to local authority proposals.

C. *Central Inspection and Inquiries*

Since assistant commissioners were appointed after 1834 to inspect the manner in which the poor law was administered, subsequent legislation has made provision for the inspection of services by departmental officers to ensure adherence to national standards. Thus Her Majesty's Inspectors of Schools, first appointed in 1839, visit all educational establishments; Inspectors of Constabulary, dating from 1856, inspect and report on the efficiency of police forces; there are also Inspectors of Fire Services, appointed first in 1938; and since 1933 the Secretary of State has been authorised to appoint Inspectors for children's services. The role of schools inspectors is more advisory than regulatory, while the remaining three groups of inspectors tend towards regulation and assessing efficiency. With police and fire inspection, grants are dependent upon a satisfactory certificate of efficiency from the inspectorate.

Under various acts Ministers are empowered to hold inquiries and s. 250 of the Local Government Act 1972, stipulates the powers to direct such inquiries and the procedure to be followed. Any person may be required to attend and may give evidence on oath and produce any documents in his possession. The costs of the inquiry will be paid by the local authority "or party to the inquiry as he (the Minister) may direct", but the practice of awarding costs is not generally adopted. Where permitted by the appropriate act, the simplified procedure of an "informal hearing" may be adopted, and since the Franks Committee recommendations of 1957 the Minister now gives his reasons for a decision and makes available a copy of the inspector's report and findings. Examples of local inquiries would include planning appeals or objections to proposals to acquire land by compulsory purchase order. In 1965 the Ministry of Housing and Local Government alone held 5,490 inquiries.

D. *Financial Control* is exercised in three ways:

1. *Control over Grants.* The receipt of grant aid for specific functions has always been conditional upon the right of central government to supervise the way it is spent. In theory, a local authority does not have to accept a grant in aid but where the cost of a service can be reduced by a proffered grant the council is unlikely to refuse it unless it is prepared to face the aggrieved ratepayers' wrath. The receipt of such specific grants has thus been accompanied by departmental control, for example the Home Secretary exercises considerable control over the police grant. There are few specific grants today, the major source of income being the annual rate support grant (R.S.G.) which is a global sum determined by the

Minister on the basis of expenditure estimates by the local authorities. It is he who fixes the percentage of that expenditure payable as the R.S.G. Moreover, s. 5 of the Local Government Act 1974 empowers the Minister to reduce the amount of any element of the R.S.G. payable to a local authority if he is satisfied that the authority has not maintained reasonable standards and his report is approved by a resolution of the House of Commons. The power to reduce or withhold grants is at once the most direct and powerful sanction possessed by central government over local authority administration and policy. Note too that many capital projects are grant aided and ministerial approval is essential to an authority's development.

2. *The Audit.* A system of compulsory annual audit was first introduced by the Poor Law Reform Act 1834 which gave auditors powers to disallow illegal poor law payments and to surcharge them upon the responsible persons. When the local government structure crystallised in the last quarter of the nineteenth century, the Public Health Act 1875, the Municipal Corporations Act 1882 and the Local Government Acts of 1888 and 1894 made provision for the "orderly keeping of accounts", and in 1879 the auditors became officers of the Local Government Board and thus civil servants. The Municipal Corporations Act 1835 had not made provision for the audit of borough accounts by central government and consequently they had their own system of private borough auditors. The Local Government Act 1933, which consolidated the previous legislation, empowered borough councils to adopt the standard district audit or a professional audit, but some boroughs continued to have their accounts audited by three borough auditors, two of them elected annually by local government electors (elective auditors) and one appointed by the mayor (mayor's auditor). None needed to be qualified, nor were they to be members or officers of the council, but they had to be qualified to stand as councillors.

The district auditor was required to surcharge persons responsible for monies not duly accounted for, or for any loss caused by negligence or misconduct, or for an illegal payment, and that person was liable to repay the amount surcharged; if the amount was over £500 he would be disqualified from holding public office for five years. No expenses paid by an authority were to be disallowed by the auditor if they had been sanctioned by the Minister, whether legal or not. Any person aggrieved by a disallowance or surcharge made by the local authority could, where they related to an amount exceeding £500, appeal to the High Court; and in any other case could appeal to the High Court or the Minister. The Court and the Minister were then empowered to confirm, vary or quash the auditor's decision. In the case of surcharge the person surcharged could apply for a declaration that he acted reasonably or in the belief that his action was authorised by law, and if the Court or Minister thought he should be excused from personal liability a declaration to that effect might be made.

Between 1947 and 1972 there were 454 surcharge cases including surcharged frauds involving 531 councillors and 43 senior officers, the number of cases declining in each five year period from 143 in 1947–52 to 34 in 1967–72. Though surcharge has been said to be "often a formality imposed to enable the local authority to claim insurance for a loss of monies", the district auditor's power does appear to act as a deterrent particularly in respect of policy decisions. The Maud Report (1967) regarded the fear of surcharge as an inhibiting influence on the attitudes of members and officers, and consequently recommended (para. 290) its abolition. From one viewpoint the district auditor may be seen as "the ratepayer's watch-dog" whose impartial regulation of a local authority's accounts stimulates a more efficient utilization of its resources, and whose threat of disallowance and surcharge have generally been sufficient correctives to ensure financial probity. Conversely, the system has been criticized for "stifling initiative, innovation, or the reasonable exercise of discretion by local authorities".[2] In the House of Lords debate on the Local Government Bill in March 1971 Lord Fiske, a former L.C.C. councillor, referred to the district audit as "one of the most repressive controls that exists anywhere in the state." Eleven councillors of Clay Cross U.D.C. would agree with that assessment for in January 1973, after an extraordinary audit to inquire whether they were liable to surcharge for negligence and misconduct in not implementing the Housing Finance Act 1972, the auditor surcharged them a total of £6,985 which was the loss from the rate fund caused by not increasing rents by the stipulated amounts.

The Local Government Act 1972 radically changed the provisions of the law relating to the audit of local authority accounts. From 1 April, 1974, the accounts of all principal authorities outside Greater London have been subject to audit by a district auditor, appointed by the Secretary of State with the consent of the Minister for the Civil Service, or by a private auditor appointed by the individual council. The private auditor must be approved by the Secretary of State and belong to a professional body named in s. 164 of the Act. The choice lay with each local authority and the decision

[2] R. Minns, "The Significance of Clay Cross: Another Look at District Audit", *Policy and Politics*, Vol. 2, No. 4, June, 1974.

had to be made by resolution passed before 1 January, 1974. In the case of the accounts of parish and community authorities, the choice was to be made by the appropriate district council before 1 January, 1974. A joint committee may make the choice not later than six weeks after its establishment. Authorities in Greater London continued to be audited by district audit but they could, in respect of any financial year beginning not earlier than 1 April, 1976, choose audit by an approved auditor.

An authority may make different arrangements in respect of different parts of its accounts, and may change from district audit to approved audit or from approved audit to district audit by resolution passed before 1 October, to take effect from 1 April in the following year.

The auditor is required to satisfy himself that the accounts are prepared in accordance with regulations made by the Secretary of State and comply with the requirements of all other enactments and instruments applicable to the accounts, and that proper accounting practices have been observed in the compilation of accounts. He is also under a duty to consider whether, in the public interest, he should make a report on any matters so that they may be considered by the authority or brought to the attention of the public. He has a right of access to all relevant documents and can require of any officer or person any information and explanation which he thinks necessary for audit purposes. Wilful or negligent failure to comply with any requirement is a criminal offence, and on summary conviction a person is liable to a fine not exceeding £100 and an additional fine of up to £20 a day on which the offence continues after conviction. If an approved auditor wrongly discloses any information obtained in the course of audit he is liable on summary conviction to a fine not exceeding £400 or on conviction on indictment to imprisonment for a term not exceeding two years or a fine, or both.

Any local government elector may inspect the accounts to be audited and all relevant documents, and may take copies and question the auditor about the accounts. If the audit is conducted by the district auditor, an elector or his representative may attend before the auditor and object to any of the accounts. The district auditor may then take appropriate action under powers specified in s. 161; if the auditor decides not to seek a declaration from the court the elector may require the auditor to state in writing his reasons for not proceeding, provided he does so not later than six weeks after he has been notified of the decision. The aggrieved person may appeal to the court against that decision. If the audit is conducted by an approved auditor these latter rights are not available, but the elector may achieve the same result by asking the Secretary of State to direct a district auditor to hold an extraordinary audit. Within fourteen days of the conclusion of an audit the auditor must send his report to the local authority and a copy to the Secretary of State.

The powers of the district auditor and the court are specified in s. 161 and are substantially different from those which obtained under the Local Government Act 1933. The powers of disallowance and surcharge have been removed and are replaced by new provisions. Where a district auditor considers that any item of account is contrary to law he may apply to the High Court (or to the County Court where the sums are small) for a declaration, unless the item is sanctioned by the Secretary of State. An item is contrary to law if the body concerned is not able to show legal authority for the expenditure, i.e. it is *ultra vires*. Expenditure which is excessive may be contrary to law (*Roberts v. Hopwood* (1925) A.C. 578), and the improper exercise of a discretion may result in an item being declared contrary to law (*Taylor v. Munrow* (*District Auditor*) (1960) 1 W.L.R. 151).

If the court makes the delcaration it may order the person responsible for incurring or authorising any unlawful expenditure to repay all or part of it; if two or more persons are found to be responsible they are jointly and severally liable to repay. If the expenditure exceeds £2,000 and the person responsible is a member of the local authority he may be disqualified for a specified period. The court will not make an order if it is satisfied that the person responsible acted reasonably or in the belief that the expenditure was authorised by law, and in any case will have regard to all the circumstances, including the person's means and ability to repay the illegal expenditure or any part of it.

Where a person has failed to bring into account any sum which should have been included or that a loss has been incurred or deficiency caused by the wilful misconduct of any person, the district auditor must certify that the sum, or the amount of the loss or deficiency, is due from that person. If the person is a member and the amount due exceeds £2,000 he may be disqualified from membership for five years. Both the auditor and the authority may recover the sum or the amount, subject to the right of the person to appeal to the court.

Where the audit is conducted by an approved auditor and it appears to him that there is reasonable ground for believing that any item of account is contrary to law, or that any person has failed to bring into account any sum which should have been so incurred, or that the loss has been incurred or deficiency caused by the wilful misconduct of any person, he must report the matter to the Secretary of State who may then direct a district auditor to hold an extra-ordinary audit.

The Secretary of State is empowered to order an extraordinary audit on the application of a local government elector or the authority concerned or after receiving an auditor's report. It may be held after three clear days' notice in writing to the body whose accounts are to be audited. The expenditure incurred in holding an extraordinary audit shall be defrayed in the first instance by the Secretary of State, but he may recover all or part of the expenditure from that body.

3. *Control over Borrowing.* This has already been considered in the section on the capital account of local authorities. Their borrowing powers require in almost every case the consent of the Secretary of State for the Environment whose decision will be influenced by many factors, including the local authority's financial situation, the advice of his experts, the results of a local inquiry if one is held and the prevailing national economic policy.

E. *Control over Officers*

Before 1974 local authorities were statutorily obliged to employ certain officers and the appropriate government departments exercised control over their appointment, dismissal and payment. The original justification was to ensure the availability of properly qualified functionaries to administer services where high national standards of efficiency had to be maintained and where a degree of independence from the control of the local authority would ensure that no local pressure should affect the quality of the service or the incumbent's security of tenure. This control was substantially relaxed by the Local Government Act 1972 which merely required that, subject to certain important exceptions, authorities should appoint such officers as they think necessary for the proper discharge of their functions (s. 112). An officer so appointed "shall hold office on such reasonable terms and conditions, including conditions as to remuneration, as the authority appointing him think fit". There are also no statutory conditions about qualifications or central control. The few specific statutory appointments are district surveyors and their deputies in the G.L.C., chief education officers, chief and other fire officers, inspectors of weights and measures, agricultural analysts and their deputies, and directors of social services. The freedom not to appoint prescribed officers does not extend to committees of local authorities of which some members are required to be appointed by a body or person other than a local authority, e.g. chief, deputy chief and assistant chief constables, national park officers and fishery officers.

F. *Power to act in Default*

Government departments are empowered by various statutes to deal with local authorities who fail to discharge their appropriate functions. Under the Public Health Act 1936, the Minister may make an order declaring a particular local authority to be in default and direct it to perform its duty within a specified time; if the local authority refuses to comply with the order, the Minister may enforce it in the courts. In the case of a defaulting county district he may make an order to transfer the function to the county council, and where the defaulting authority is a county or county borough he may make an order transferring the function to himself. The cost of performing the transferred function will in either case remain with the defaulting authority. Under the Education Act 1944, the Minister of Education may make an order declaring a Local Education Authority or the managers or governors of a county or voluntary school who have not discharged a duty, to be in default, and give "such directions for the purpose of enforcing the execution thereof as appear to the Minister to be expedient". Such directions will be enforceable in the courts.

In respect of housing the default powers contained in the Housing Act 1957 were considered inadequate and by the Housing Finance Act 1972 the Secretary of State was given extensive powers where he felt that a local authority had "failed effectively to discharge" any of its functions in relation to council houses. After an inquiry the Secretary of State could make a default order and subsequently appoint a Housing Commissioner "to discharge in the name of the authority and at their expense" specified housing functions. The Housing Commissioner was empowered "to do all such things as appear to him to be necessary or expedient for the performance of the functions he is appointed to discharge".

The authority was required to take all reasonable steps to help the Housing Commissioner to discharge his functions, and in particular to provide information and documents, premises and the assistance of officers. The Housing Commissioner could serve notice on the local authority requiring them to produce any document or supply any information, and any officer concerned with the document or information had the duty of ensuring compliance with the notice, without instructions from the authority, under threat of a fine not exceeding £400. Similarly, any member of a local authority who wilfully obstructed a Housing Commissioner or did any act, even before the appointment of the Housing Commissioner, which was likely to impede, mislead or interfere with a Housing Commissioner, or any person carrying out his orders, would be liable to a fine not exceeding £400.

Additionally, the Secretary of State had the power to reduce, suspend or discontinue payment to any authority against whom a default order had been made of any subsidy in respect of housing.

These were radical and comprehensive powers, and when Housing Commissioners were appointed in Bedwas and Machen U.D., Merthyr Tydfil C.B. and Clay Cross U.D., they became the focus of the frustrations felt by these and other Labour councils who had so violently opposed the combination of controls in the Act.

Default powers are nowadays included in all legislation relating to local government and constitute a last-resort check upon local authorities who fail to exercise their proper duties. Local authorities do not generally ignore their obligations, and the Minister is rarely called upon to exercise his powers. The knowledge that the powers exist is generally an adequate deterrent.

G. *Confirmation of Bye-Laws*

The Local Government Act 1972 simplified the powers and procedure for making and confirming byelaws. The power is residual and is conferred on all district and London borough councils exclusively to make bye-laws for "good rule and government" and for "the prevention and suppression of nuisances". Both sets of bye-laws require confirmation by the Secretary of State. Additionally, almost every other local government act confers specific powers to make bye-laws for particular services on county, district, parish and community councils. The procedure laid down in the 1972 Act for making and confirming bye-laws applies to all bye-laws made by any local authority under any act, unless particular acts specify a special procedure which will remain unaffected.

Bye-laws must be made under the common seal of the authority, or under the hands and seals of two members of a parish or community council not possessing a seal. At least one month before application for confirmation of the bye-law is made, notice of the intention to apply for confirmation must be given in one or more local newspapers, and during that month a copy of the bye-law must be deposited at the office of the authority and made available for free public inspection. A copy may be purchased at a sum not exceeding 10p per 100 words.

The confirming authority may confirm, or refuse to confirm any bye-law, and may fix the date on which it is to come into effect; if no date is fixed, the bye-law comes into effect one month from the date of its confirmation. The confirming authority is the authority or person, if any, specified in the act under which the bye-law is made, or in any enactment applied by it. For bye-laws made under s. 235 of the 1972 Act the confirming authority is the Secretary of State, as he also is if the particular act does not specify anyone; the confirming authority for bye-laws relating, for example, to slaughter-houses and knackers' yards is the Minister of Agriculture, Fisheries and Foods as he is expressly specified in the Food and Drugs Act 1955.

The control exercised by central departments over the confirmation of bye-laws ensures uniformity throughout the country. This is further reinforced by the practice of issuing "model bye-laws" to local authorities for their voluntary adoption. Should a local authority wish to deviate from the model, the appropriate government department will invariably reject the authority's bye-law unless there is some local justification; acceptance of the model, however, ensures departmental confirmation.

H. *Powers of Adjudication*

The Minister will be required to exercise a judicial role in the following cases:

1. Disputes between authorities over responsibility for the provision of a service or the division of expenses payable to a joint committee.

2. Disputes between a local authority and its officers will in certain cases be referred to the appropriate Minister, e.g. a dismissed constable has the right to appeal to the Home Secretary.

3. Disputes between a local authority and private individuals—where public and private interests conflict over such a matter as a compulsory purchase order for private property required by a local authority the Secretary of State will hold a public inquiry or private hearing to decide whether the order is to be confirmed.

3. Judicial Control

Until the nineteenth century the administrative powers to deal with local government matters were vested in the J.Ps. who exercised them in the Courts of Petty and Quarter Sessions. Though dealing with administrative matters, in the eyes of the law these were primarily courts of justice subject to the judicial control of the King's Bench so that J.Ps. could be restrained from exceeding their legal administrative powers and be compelled to do their duty. When the J.Ps. were stripped of their administrative functions this judicial control continued and the Queen's Bench Division of the High Court still exercises supervisory jurisdiction over the activities of the local authorities by means of the Orders of mandamus, certiorari and prohibition.

.1. *Order of Mandamus*

This is a High Court Order which compels any local authority to discharge its statutory, though not discretionary, duties where no other remedy is convenient, e.g. to require the election of a chairman or the levying of a rate. Non-compliance with an order of mandamus may lead to imprisonment for contempt of those members of a local authority refusing to comply with its terms, e.g. *R.* v. *Poplar Borough Council*, [1922] 1 K.B. 72. In *R.* v. *Bedwellty Urban District Council*, [1934] 1 K.B. 333 mandamus was obtained by a ratepayer to compel production of the local authority's accounts, but in those cases where the statute itself provides a remedy when there is non-compliance mandamus will not lie.

B. *Certiorari*

This is an order which removes a case from an inferior court into the Queen's Bench Division of the High Court. So far as local authorities are concerned it extends to those acts which are quasi-judicial e.g. where the local authority can impose a liability or make decisions which determine the rights or property of the parties concerned.

In *R.* v. *Hendon Rural District Council*, [1933] 2 K.B. 696 the order of certiorari was used to quash a decision granting development permission because a council member interested in the use of the land had voted on the resolution.

C. *Prohibition*

This order restrains an inferior court or tribunal from proceeding when it has no jurisdiction. It is frequently sought along with certiorari so that the act complained of may be reviewed to determine its validity and at the same time prevent its operation, e.g. *R.* v. *Paddington and St. Marylebone Rent Tribunal*, [1949] 1 K.B. 666 and *R.* v. *Northumberland Appeal Tribunal*, [1951] 1 K.B. 711.

In a wider sense the term "judicial control" includes all matters concerning local government which may come before the Courts. Local authorities, being incorporated bodies, can be sued in the courts for wrongs deemed to have been committed by them, hence they are vicariously liable for damages in respect of torts committed by their servants in the course of their employment. Since the decision in *Cassidy* v. *Ministry of Health*, [1951] 2 K.B. 343 the term "servant" has been extended to include even professional persons over whom the authority concerned has the ultimate power of dismissal. On the other hand it must be remembered that an official appointed by a local authority who in his official capacity exercises an independent public duty placed on him directly by law is not a servant of the authority, e.g., a police officer.

Apart from the City of London, all local authorities are statutory corporations and therefore subject to all implications of the *ultra vires* doctrine. This means that the ambit and extent of the powers and duties conferred on local authorities are contained in Statutes and that nothing shall be done beyond that ambit. Should the powers and duties laid down be exceeded the action is *ultra vires* and void, e.g. *Prescott* v. *Birmingham Corporation*, [1955] Ch 210. A resolution of the Birmingham City Council to allow old age pensioners to travel free on its trains and buses was *ultra vires* as the private acts of Parliament under which the City of Birmingham operated a transport system required it to charge such fares as it thought fit.

Before 1974 borough councils were *prima facie* not subject to the *ultra vires* rule as common law corporations, yet they were not permitted to infringe statutory limitations imposed on them and, in this respect, like other local authorities were subject to the *ultra vires* doctrine.

Any aggrieved person wishing to question the validity of a decision of a local authority alleged to be *ultra vires* may appeal to the court for an injunction or a declaration.

D. *Injunction and Declaration*

An injunction is an order of the High Court which prevents a specific act from being carried out, whilst a declaration is simply a statement made by the court concerning the rights of the plaintiff but of itself provides no method of enforcing them. For example, a ratepayer who wishes to contest his liability to pay rates may bring an action for a declaration against the rating authority—*Waterson* v. *Hendon Borough Council*, [1959] 2 All E.R. 760.

Apart from the two exceptional cases[3] laid down in *Boyce* v. *Paddington Borough Council*, [1906] A.C. 1; 75, an action for an injunction or declaration in respect of public rights or interests has to be brought at the suit of the Attorney General to avoid unnecessary litigation, e.g. where a local authority is accused of failing to prevent

---

[3] W. O. Hart and J. F. Garner, *Hart's Introduction to the Law of Local Government and Administration* (9th Ed.), Butterworths, p. 385.

its sewers from polluting rivers as laid down in Public Health legislation.

A private individual may sue either when the interference with the
public right also amounts to an interference with a private right of the
plaintiff or, though no private right is infringed, the plaintiff suffers
some special damage peculiar to himself. For example, where an
obstruction of the highway is also an interference with a private right
of access to the highway or where as a result of a public nuisance a
person's premises have been made unfit for habitation.

E. Statutory Appeals

The statutory powers conferred on local authorities sometimes
conflict with the interests of private persons. In order that individuals
may avoid the necessity of having to resort to an injunction or any of
the Orders specified above, he is allowed right of appeal. This may
take the following forms:

1. Appeals to Magistrates. The J.Ps. sitting in local courts of summary jurisdiction or in Quarter Sessions may hear appeals under the
provisions of various statutes against local authority decisions e.g.
the refusal to grant a licence to carry on a particular business.

2. Appeals to the County Court. Housing legislation since 1930
allows appeals to the County Court by a person whose local authority
has issued an order in respect of insanitary housing requiring its
repair, its demolition or the closure of part of the house.

3. Appeals to the High Court. An aggrieved party may have
right of statutory appeal against, for example, a clearance or compulsory purchase order where these are made by the local authority
supported by the Department of the Environment. The High
Court can quash the order only if it were made *ultra vires* or if
there were a failure to comply with a statutory requirement.

The controls established during the war and the transfer of gas,
electricity and hospitals from local authorities led to the appointment
of the Local Government Manpower Committee, and one of its
terms of reference was

> "to examine in particular the distribution of functions between
> central and local government and the possibility of relaxing
> departmental supervision of local authority activities and
> delegating more responsibility to local authorities". [4]

The Memorandum of Guidance to its five sub-committees outlined
its "General Approach" as follows:

---

[4] "First Report of the Local Government Manpower Committee", 1950, (Cmd.
7870).

"To recognise that the local authorities are responsible bodies competent to discharge their own functions and that, though they may be the statutory bodies through which Government policy is given effect and operate to a large extent with Government money, they exercise their responsibilities in their own right, not ordinarily as agents of Government Departments. It follows that the objective should be to leave as much as possible of the detailed management of a scheme or service to the local authority and to concentrate the Department's control at the key points where it can most effectively discharge its responsibilities for Government policy and financial administration".

This was the desired working relationship, and the sub-committees, appointed to examine the services supervised by the Home Office, Ministry of Health, Ministry of Education, Ministry of Town and Country Planning and Ministry of Transport, presented their reports containing revised procedures and arrangements. However, as Sir Francis Hill has observed, "not much came of it at last".[5] The controls remained and their application depends very much upon the differing attitude of the various central departments and their civil servants.[6] The formal controls outlined were reinforced by such developing practices as ministries dealing directly with chief officers and by-passing the council or its clerk, or the appointment of informal advisory groups which were made up of members of local authorities who did not specifically represent them nor the associations.

In *Central Departments and Local Authorities* J. A. G. Griffith underlines four major defects in the central-local relationship: policy is insufficiently defined to give local authorities the freedom to make their own decisions within that policy; there are too many small authorities both for present and future tasks; local authorities are financially too dependent on the central departments; and the departments are failing to collect and disseminate necessary information.

The fears of local authorities, grasping at their straws of autonomy, are made articulate at various annual conferences and by individuals who perceive the eclipse of local self-government and condemn the state's centralising tendencies. Professor Robson writes of "Local Government in Crisis" and diagnoses its malaise, while others criticise individual controls particularly the financial dependence of local authorities and the restrictive influence of the doctrine of *ultra vires*.

"It is one of those unfortunate historical anomalies—one of the archaic bits of machinery which we must sweep away",

---

[5] "The Partnership in Theory and Practice", *The Political Quarterly* Vol. 37, No. 2, April–June, 1966, p. 175. See also *Redcliffe–Maud Report*, Vol. 1, p. 30.

[6] J. A. G. Griffith, *Central Departments and Local Authorities*, Allen & Unwin, 1966.

said Sir John Maud to the Society of Town Clerks,[7] and his opinion re-echoes that of many who sense the underlying frustration of enterprising local authorities against the more pettifogging restrictions of *ultra vires*.[8] The Maud Report on Management in 1967 condemned the "deleterious effect" of *ultra vires* "because of the narrowness of the legislation governing local authorities' activities. The specific nature of legislation discourages enterprise, handicaps development, robs the community of services which the local authority might render, and encourages too rigorous oversight by the central government. It contributes to the excessive concern over legalities and fosters the idea that the Clerk should be a lawyer.... The evidence clearly points to the desirability of softening the rigours of the *ulta vires* doctrine".

The Report commented on the relative freedom enjoyed by local authorities abroad from statutory restrictions, and recommended not so much the abolition of *ultra vires* but the granting of a "general competence" to enable local authorities "to do (in addition to what legislation already requires or permits them to do) whatever in their opinion is in the interests of their areas or their inhabitants subject to their not encroaching on the duties of other governmental bodies and to appropriate safeguards for the protection of public and private interests". Additionally, it was recommended that the government should consult with the associations to examine what provisions might be repealed in order to provide authorities with maximum freedom to carry out their work. The application of the doctrine of *ultra vires* was in no way modified by the Local Government Act 1972, and the nearest the act went in conferring a general competence on local authorities was the provision in s. 137 which allowed councils to spend a limited sum of money (at present a 2p rate product) on purposes not specifically authorised.

Any unsatisfactory dependency relationship, particularly one between major and powerful bodies like government departments and local authorities, will contain frustrating elements which could create in the subordinate partner hostility and the desire for independence and autonomy. The defects which have been mentioned go beyond hostility, however, and relate to matters which appear to be seriously undermining local self-government. It is obviously essential for Government departments to ensure that services are uniformly provided, and a measure of supervision and

---

[7] *The Local Government Chronicle*, 9 July, 1966.

[8] See "The Too-Narrow Powers of Council", by Brian Keith-Lucas in *Local Government To-day and Tomorrow* (ed. D. Lofts), Municipal Journal Ltd., pp. 27–32, and the *Maud Report*, Vol. 1, paras. 266–269, 283–286.

inspection will naturally follow. Does this necessitate, however, the almost complete negation of local discretion and the extension of central control well beyond the "key points" and into the detailed day-to-day management of services?

The question is not easily answered for, as O. A. Hartley has pointed out, a fundamental confusion persists as to what the correct relationship should be.[9] Traditionally there exist two separate and incompatible relationships. One perceives local government as an administrative device for the provision of national services within a given area, where the relationship is that between principal (the government department) and agent (the providing local authority). The other perceives local government as a system of local independent bodies, each having its own rights and duties, in which the relationship between central departments and local authorities is a partnership. Edwin Chadwick argued forcefully in favour of the first model for strong central control over all local activities, while Joshua Toulmin Smith argued for equality with Parliament for local government. According to Hartley, it has never been settled which model is the preferred one, as both have been employed and both continue to be used. The law provides no guidance and there is no agreement between local and national governments, the former naturally preferring the partnership model, while central departments incline to the view that local authorities are agents requiring supervision.

Professor J. A. G. Griffith sees a conflict in central–local interests and dismisses the notion of partnership, arguing that the departments are stronger and more important, and concludes that the relationship is determined by what the departments decide are their necessary functions. He describes three types of departmental attitude towards local authorities: (a) laissez-faire—typifying the D.H.S.S., (b) regulatory—the Home Office, and (c) promotional—the D.E.S. From this it would appear that the D.H.S.S. conforms to the partnership model, while the Home Office and the D.E.S. conform to the principal–agent relationship.

The Maud Report was obscure on the issue, placing local authorities firmly under the supremacy of Parliament (para. 252), but later (para. 273) complaining about local government's status as "a subsidiary instrument of public administration". The Redcliffe-Maud Report referred (para 1) to the need for a "valid partnership", and later said "We do not believe that the right relationship exists today" (para. 100). On central control it said

---

[9] O. A. Hartley, "The Relationship between Central and Local Authorities", *Public Administration*, Winter 1971, Vol. 49,

that "central government tries itself to do some of the things that properly belong to local government. . . . In addition, they [local authorities] are subject to a number of minor controls and requirements which detract from their ability to manage their own affairs and to make their own decisions" (para. 100). The Redcliffe-Maud Report argued that control should be at "key points", but that its achievement "will require both a change of heart on the part of Ministers and departments and considerable amendment of the law" (para. 102). Overall, the Report sought to obtain a partnership, but settled in fact for the status of agent. It condemned the existing state of affairs only to accept the cause which led to it, namely the need of government departments to ensure that national policies are carried through.

Perhaps, as Hartley suggested, the confusion may to some extent be deliberately perpetuated by local authorities and government departments for ulterior reasons. The latter may prefer the principal–agent relationship, but do not want to be held responsible for the provision of the services; equally, local authorities may prefer independence, but do not want to be cut off from the major source of their income, nor would they relish independence without powers. Moreover, the lack of specific definition enables senior civil servants to resist uncongenial policies imposed by their political masters by reminding them of the need to preserve the independence of local authorities; while local authorities can blame their own shortcomings on the dictates of Whitehall. Both parties may thus have an interest in preserving the lack of clarity in the relationship. Nevertheless, as long as there is no precise definition, the problem of the relationship and of the location of power will remain.

The 1971 White Paper *Local Government Reform in England* (Cmnd. 4584), which expressed the Government's determination "to return power to those people who should exercise decisions locally" and to create "a genuine local democracy", contained also the following brave statement of intent: "The accumulated legislation since 1888 contains over a thousand statutory controls by central government over local government. It is the Government's intention to reduce these to a minimum." It referred also, however, to the continuing need for government controls, albeit not "excessive", and nicely balanced the hope for a partnership with the role of agent in respect of policies: "It is the Government's intention to allow authorities the maximum discretion to take their own decisions within national policies."

The Local Government Act 1972 did give local authorities wider discretion in, for example, the appointment of staff (s. 112), the general power to "delegate" decision-making to officers and to discharge functions through a number of internal and external arrangements (s. 101), and to pay allowances to members attending conferences (s. 175). Nevertheless, in the summer of 1972, the government, despite its declared aim to reduce central controls, suspended the work of the D.O.E. working group on ministerial controls over local authorities, and demonstrated once more the gulf which separates governmental words from deeds. Moreover, the government's control over the purse strings has been highlighted by the economic situation and the counter inflationary measures which have led to cuts in public expenditure, to rate monitoring, to the requirement for stringent restraint over staffing levels, salaries and spending on services, and to the Prime Minister's accusations in February 1974 of the "gross irresponsibility" of local authorities who were condemned of "spending money like water". Add to these the trauma which followed the enforcement of the Education (Milk) Act 1971 and the Housing Finance Act 1972, and local authorities are themselves under no illusion as to their status in the relationship.

APPENDIX 1

Population of English and Welsh Counties at 30 June 1973

Metropolitan Counties

Greater Manchester	2,729,900	Tyne and Wear	1,198,390
Merseyside	1,620,780	West Midlands	2,785,460
South Yorkshire	1,319,180	West Yorkshire	2,079,530

Non-metropolitan Counties

Avon	914,180	Humberside	847,230
Bedfordshire	481,050	Isle of Wight	109,680
Berkshire	644,650	Kent	1,443,960
Buckinghamshire	496,470	Lancashire	1,362,800
Cambridgeshire	533,480	Leicestershire	824,360
Cheshire	895,770	Lincolnshire	512,880
Cleveland	566,740	Norfolk	643,940
Cornwall	393,480	North Yorkshire	644,830
Cumbria	474,080	Northamptonshire	487,930
Derbyshire	888,340	Northumberland	283,310
Devon	920,550	Nottinghamshire	982,460
Dorset	566,360	Oxfordshire	529,640
Durham	609,840	Salop	347,770
East Sussex	657,720	Somerset	398,900
Essex	1,397,840	Staffordshire	984,620
Gloucestershire	481,700	Suffolk	561,540
Hampshire	1,422,060	Surrey	993,820
Hereford and		Warwickshire	468,270
Worcester	577,140	West Sussex	629,890
Hertfordshire	939,520	Wiltshire	501,200

Welsh Counties

Clwyd	368,880	Mid Glamorgan	536,080
Dyfed	316,960	Powys	99,370
Gwent	441,090	South Glamorgan	392,250
Gwynedd	222,090	West Glamorgan	372,560

APPENDIX 2

Local Authority Relevant Expenditure at November 1974

PRICES IN £M

	Service	Estimated 1974–75 outturn	% Growth to year following[1]	1975–76 Government Proposals
D.E.S.	Education	3,793·1	4·1	3,947·2
	Libraries, museums, art galleries	130·8	2·5	134·1
D.H.S.S.	Port health	1·4	14·3	1·6
	Personal social services	621·7	6·7	663·3
	Concessionary fares	35·1	1·4	35·5
HOME OFFICE	Police	619·7	1·3	628·0
	Fire	170·7	3·6	176·8
	Magistrates' courts	33·9	5·3	35·7
	Other courts	4·7	4·3	4·9
	Probation and aftercare	27·0	8·9	29·4
	Probation homes and hostels	0·6	Nil	0·6
	School crossing patrols	6·8	Nil	6·8
	Registration of electors	7·0	Nil	7·0
	Civil defence	2·4	Nil	2·4
	Urban programmes	16·2	17·3	19·0
D.O.E. L.T.	London Transport finance	729·2	5·5*	973·4
D.O.E. Environmental Services	Refuse collection and disposal	213·8	4·0	222·3
	Recreation, parks and baths	221·8	5·6	234·2
	General administration	214·8	4·2	223·8
	Environmental health	94·4	0·9	95·2
	Town and country planning	137·9	1·0	139·3
	Agriculture and Fisheries	33·1	11·0	36·7
	Trading services G.R.F. contribution	23·9	Nil	23·9
	Miscellaneous	112·2	5·1	117·9
D.O.E. Housing	Housing	324·0	20·9	392·3
D.E.	Careers	14·2	6·0	14·7
	Sheltered employment	5·0	—	5·0
	TOTAL	7,595·4	4·8*	8,171·0

* Estimated growth rates using figures on a comparable basis.
[1] Individual local authority growth rates should not normally be as large as indicated in this column.

Source: Rate Fund Expenditure and Rate Calls in 1975–76, D.O.E. Circular 171/74, December 1974.

Local Authority Loan Debt

Type of Debt at 31 March in each year   £ million

Year	Total	Quoted securities	Negotiable bonds	P.W.L.B. mortgage	Advances from own super-annuation fund	Advances from other internal funds	Other longer-term debt	Revenue balances temporarily used for capital purposes	Other temporary debt
1964	8,966	1,046	—	3,065	270	173	2,672	231	1,509
1965	9,916	1,127	55	3,302	274	191	2,825	317	1,825
1966	10,913	1,252	150	3,837	256	206	3,227	329	1,656
1967	12,044	1,360	208	4,380	246	218	3,594	391	1,647
1968	13,281	1,472	260	4,801	259	212	3,817	473	1,987
1969	14,487	1,569	322	5,277	233	221	4,414	497	1,934
1970	15,706	1,641	320	5,814	249	228	4,916	615	1,923
1971	17,151	1,727	360	6,502	256	205	5,403	769	1,929
1972	18,657	1,818	570	7,331	233	206	5,621	853	2,027
1973	20,604	1,764	667	8,255	229	237	5,677	1,128	2,647

Source: *Annual Abstract of Statistics 1974*, H.M.S.O., Table 362.

Devolution and Local Government

The White Paper *Democracy and Devolution: Proposals for Scotland and Wales* (Cmnd. 5732), issued in September 1975, pointed out that public response to the invitation to comment on the schemes outlined in the consultative document of August 1974 had been disappointing, with no clear majority for any one solution. Over sixty organisations submitted views, however, and there was considerable support for Scheme A or variations of it, very few favoured Schemes B or C, and there was some support for Scheme E (see pages 25–30).

Subsequent discussions reinforced the opinions expressed in written submissions, but it was apparent that opinion in Scotland was still divided and no consensus of opinion had emerged in Wales. Nevertheless, the Government felt there had been sufficient debate in Scotland and Wales to enable it to propose the creation of directly elected assemblies for both countries. The assemblies would not be expected to assume existing powers from local government, since this would undermine rather than improve democracy, but a new relationship would need to be established between the assemblies and local government.

Detailed proposals were set out in the White Paper *Our Changing Democracy: Devolution to Scotland and Wales* (Cmnd. 6348), presented in November 1975, which envisaged "a massive handover to the new elected Assemblies of responsibility for the domestic affairs of Scotland and Wales, within the firm continuing framework of the United Kingdom". It was proposed that both Assemblies would control policies and spending priorities over a very wide field of devolved functions which would include:

1. *Local Government*—general supervision of most aspects of local government, including in Scotland the power to change the structure; financial arrangements including the amount and distribution of the rate support grant, the approval of capital investment in the devolved fields and the detailed application of the local tax system.
2. *Health*—the structure and operation of the N.H.S.; policy on private practice and private hospital facilities; and general health matters.

3. *Personal Social Services*—care and support of children, the handicapped, the elderly and others in need of special care, supervision of private provisions in these fields, and grants to voluntary bodies.

4. *Education and the Arts*—schools, their organisation, attendance requirements and curricula; further and higher education, except universities; certain student awards; adult education; youth and community services; national and local museums and libraries; the arts.

5. *Housing*—provision, upkeep and improvement of housing accommodation by private owners and public authorities; public sector housing finance, subsidies to local authorities and housing associations, the control of rents in public and private sectors.

6. *Physical Planning and the Environment*—land use and development; environmental improvement and rehabilitation of derelict land; water, river management, drainage, sewerage and sewage disposal, water recreation and amenity planning; new towns; most executive functions of the community land scheme; and a wide area of other environmental functions e.g. refuse collection and disposal, sport and recreation, allotments, etc.

7. *Roads and Transport*—planning, construction and standards of roads including motorways, local application of rules for the management of road traffic; road safety publicity; road service licensing; local transport planning; subsidising 'bus and railway passenger services; local authority airports; inland waterways.

8. *Development and Industry*—factory building by the Scottish and Welsh Development Agencies, new town corporations and local authorities.

9. *Natural Resources*—forestry functions; freshwater fisheries; smallholdings, etc.

10. *Scottish Law Functions*.

11. *Tourism*.

12. *Other Matters*—including fire services; licensing of taxis, liquor and places of entertainment; shop hours; betting, gaming and lotteries; byelaws; registration of births, marriages and deaths, etc.

In these devolved functions the Scottish Assembly will be responsible for primary legislation and will be free to amend or repeal existing laws. The Government will have reserve powers, however, to halt the progress of Assembly bills and final legislative sovereignty will remain with Parliament. The Welsh Assembly will have substantial policy-making and executive powers but will not have legislative powers and "will therefore work within the limits of Westminster Acts". In controlling the devolved services the Welsh Assembly will take over whatever powers those acts confer on central government, including the power to make delegated legislation. In subjects not devolved, Parliament will make and control legislation for the whole of the United Kindgom.

The Devolution Act will not change the structure of local government in Scotland or Wales, nor will either Assembly be responsible for any functions which Scottish or Welsh local authorities continue to carry out in matters not devolved, and the responsibilities of central and local government in these matters will not be changed by the Act. The administration of each Assembly will, however, oversee the work of local authorities in devolved matters. Each Assembly will have a block grant from the Exchequer and will decide how much should be distributed to local government and how to allocate it among individual authorities. The Assemblies will also have an optional power to make a surcharge on local authority taxation.

Local authorities were fearful of the possible implications of the proposals. In Wales many authorities demanded a referendum on the confident assumption that the proposals would be rejected, and at C.I.P.F.A. conferences in Cardiff and Glasgow members and officers were reported to be "clearly worried lest their own activities should be cramped by the creation of Scottish and Welsh assemblies" (*The Times*, 20 January, 1976.) The relative remoteness of Westminster and the resultant lack of detailed interference were seen as advantages which would be lost when Assembly members, anxious to fulfil their supervisory role, exerted a more direct and pervasive control over local authorities.

The Council for the Principality, the Welsh arm of the Association of District Councils, felt that local authority discretion would be eroded if the Welsh Assembly or its committees or sub-committees chose to interfere in day-to-day decisions. The White Paper's assurance that the proposals did "not entail any removal of current tasks or powers from local government", appeared to imply that new functions and extensions to existing functions would not be allocated to local authorities but would be taken over by the Assembly.

The allocation of the block grant was viewed with misgiving. The Assemblies were free to spend it or allocate it as they wished, with no obligation on either Assembly to pass on a given amount to authorities. Moreover, if the costs of staffing and running the Assemblies were higher than forecast, local government's share of the grant could be reduced. The assumption that Scottish and Welsh authorities would receive in relation to their needs and resources "provision comparable with that for local authorities in England", could be interpreted to mean a reduced allocation. The Council for the Principality pointed out that expenditure per head on local authority services in Wales was greater than in England (£218 in Wales compared with £194 in England in 1975–6). Also the average domestic ratepayer in Wales paid 69% of the amount payable by his counterpart in an English non-metropolitan district, because the rate support grant per head was £156 in Wales and £113 in England. A comparable provision could thus mean a reduction in the subsidy from the block grant when it is determined in Wales and Scotland, and clarification of this proposal was required.

The Assemblies' optional power to make a surcharge on local authority rates, for which there was no prescribed maximum, could also sour relationships. In Wales the districts are already burdened by having to raise rates and charges to meet the expenditure of counties, communities and the water authority. The districts as collecting authorities would attract the antagonism of ratepayers but not themselves benefit from the full amounts collected, whilst the Assembly could, if it wished, distribute less of the block grant and leave the authorities in a position of having to make up the deficiency by levying even higher rates.

In view of such considerations and the expense of establishing and running the Assembly, the Council for the Principality considered that "in the present difficult economic climate it might be prudent to delay, even for some years, the introduction of this far reaching constitutional change" and allow local authorities a period of stability after reorganisation.

Index

PRINTED IN GREAT BRITAIN BY OFFSET LITHOGRAPHY BY
BILLING & SONS LTD, GUILDFORD, LONDON AND WORCESTER